WRITING

A PRACTICAL GUIDE

WRITING
A PRACTICAL GUIDE

JOSEPH P. DAGHER

Schoolcraft College

HOUGHTON MIFFLIN COMPANY • Boston

Atlanta · Dallas · Geneva, Illinois · Hopewell, New Jersey · Palo Alto · London

To the memory of my father
whose language was universal and
my daughters Jeanice and Lauri

Library of Congress Card Number: 74–11784

ISBN: 0–395–18621–8

CONTENTS

v

PREFACE

IN TWENTY-FIVE years of teaching English composition, I have become more and more sensitive to the demands of students who need individual help of teachers who must, unfortunately, devote most of their time to a steady flow of required papers. *Writing: A Practical Guide* attempts to relieve some of the problems which perplex and burden both the student and the instructor. It includes a number of special features which have been worked out and tested in my own classes and have proved to be effective. The chief of these features are as follows:

1. Systematic instruction on every step of the composition process, from preplanning to revision and evaluation, stresses thinking throughout.
2. Performance objectives at the beginning of each chapter, and a set of exercises or "Applications," specifically state the goals of each work unit.
3. "Applications" cover the work of every chapter, all of them on tearout sheets; and each set ends with "You Be the Judge," which helps teach students to write by training them to evaluate the writing of their peers under the instructor's guidance.
4. Examples of student writing set realistic standards and encourage those who use the text to do as well.
5. Extensive instruction and practice in structure and types of organization give students a method for developing and organizing materials.
6. Patterns given for successful introductions, internal divisions, transitions, and conclusions are easy to follow and increase student confidence.
7. Flexibility: since each part and each chapter is a self-contained unit, the material can be taught in independent study programs or in any order the instructor prefers.
8. A separate chapter on the research paper teaches how to gather material for special projects and reports and how to write them up.
9. A "Handbook of Correct and Effective Usage" groups material on grammar, usage, spelling, punctuation, diction, and mechanics for ready reference.

It is a common complaint that students don't know how to go through a thinking process systematically, especially in preparation for a class paper. Hence this book stresses every aspect of thinking as it relates to writing. It begins with two chapters on logical and illogical thinking, devotes the next four to the kind of thinking a writer should do before he or she begins to write, shows how directed thought is reflected in the structure of writing, and discusses the kinds of thinking and organizing used in special kinds of writing: e.g., definition, classification, causation, comparison, and contrast.

The book also stresses the point that writing is a generative activity. It shows how a writer frequently begins with a vague idea or a loose collection of feelings, suspicions, and opinions, and by successive stages limits, fleshes out, and organizes these into the expression of a single clear idea which is developed with a particular reader response in mind. The book, then, teaches the student to follow through a thinking process systematically.

Writing: A Practical Guide is student-centered in several unusual ways. I mentioned in point 4 that most of the specimen writing is by students. Fewer than a dozen examples are by professionals. It is hard for students to escape the implication that if others can write this well, so can they. Moreover, the "You Be the Judge" application at the end of each chapter provides student participation at the very heart of the course activity: the evaluation and grading of student papers. Some students appear to be more receptive to criticism and correction by their peers than by their instructors, from whom they may feel separated by an inevitable distance. And many learn a great deal by evaluating somebody else's work and writing a careful analysis of it in terms of the skill covered in the chapter being studied. Every instructor knows how much a person learns by teaching. Writing a paper of one's own, and evaluating someone else's on the same assignment, provides the student a kind of total involvement in a well-rounded learning situation.

Because many students are helped by a clear preview of what lies ahead, particularly when it helps to sort out main points from lesser ones, every chapter begins with a numbered set of "Objectives" which enumerates the points the chapter is to cover and puts them in order of importance. For similar reasons (and to reemphasize the cumulative, interrelated nature of the exercises) a list of objectives precedes each set of Applications. Between the two there is little opportunity for the ordinarily attentive student to lose sight of where he or she is at any point in the book or in the writing process.

I gratefully acknowledge my debt to all those who assisted, tolerated, and cared for me during the years I devoted to the completion of this textbook. I am especially grateful to my colleague David Perkins, and also to Mary Toomey and Lawrence Ordowski, and to members of my family, Ann Metzger, Victoria Shiekh, Helen Kirk, and Fred, my brother. It would be an injustice if I did not express my gratitude to the hundreds of students who have served in my classes, testing the principles and applications in this text. And I wish particularly to acknowledge the generosity of those who have granted me their permission to reprint their compositions in whole or in part. Their names are given with their writing, and my thanks are implicit on every page on which their work appears.

J. P. D.

PART 1

THINKING AND WRITING

CHAPTER 1

WRITING: THINKING ON PAPER

After studying this chapter and completing the applications that follow it, you should be able to do the following:
1. To differentiate: *facts, inferences,* and *opinions*.
2. To write correctly: *terms* and *qualifiers*.
3. To write as you intend them to be understood: *facts, inferences,* and *opinions*.
4. To identify and apply: *reliable sources* and *reliable evidence*.
5. To apply these principles in writing a full-length composition.

WRITING is thinking on paper. Thinking is mind at work, finding facts, seeing relationships, testing the truth of them, reaching conclusions, forming opinions. In these ways our minds produce a huge variety of ideas, and the facts that support them are the material which goes into any piece of writing.

FACTS, INFERENCES, AND OPINIONS

We can divide all written expressions into three classes: facts, inferences, and opinions. By knowing what these are, how they differ, and how to use them, you will be able to select those needed for a particular composition and to avoid those not needed. You will also be able to express yourself so that your readers will clearly see whether each statement is meant as a fact, an inference, or an opinion. It is, after all, what readers understand and how they respond to it that determines the effectiveness of most written communications.

To see whether or not you can already tell the difference between a fact, an inference, and an opinion, do the following exercise carefully. Examine the illustration, read the statements beneath it, and place an X in the proper column opposite each statement: (F = fact, I = inference, or O = opinion.) Be prepared to explain each answer. Later we will try this exercise again.

What Is a Fact?

Before asking you to read the next section, your instructor may wish to analyze your answers to the questions on the following page. An analysis may increase your appreciation and grasp of the discussion.

3

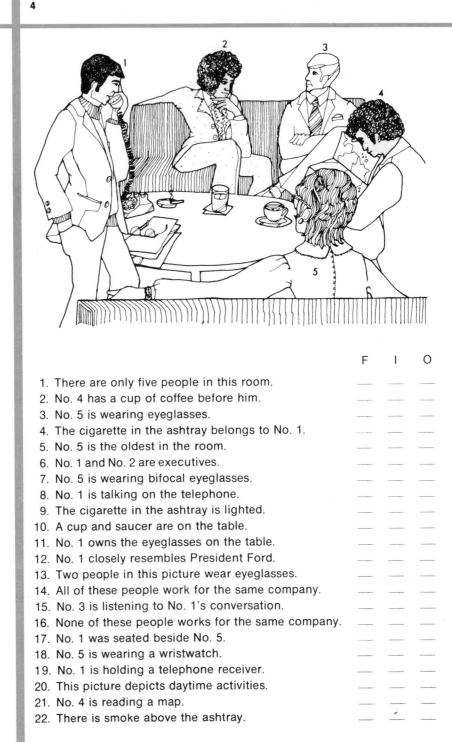

	F	I	O
1. There are only five people in this room.	—	—	—
2. No. 4 has a cup of coffee before him.	—	—	—
3. No. 5 is wearing eyeglasses.	—	—	—
4. The cigarette in the ashtray belongs to No. 1.	—	—	—
5. No. 5 is the oldest in the room.	—	—	—
6. No. 1 and No. 2 are executives.	—	—	—
7. No. 5 is wearing bifocal eyeglasses.	—	—	—
8. No. 1 is talking on the telephone.	—	—	—
9. The cigarette in the ashtray is lighted.	—	—	—
10. A cup and saucer are on the table.	—	—	—
11. No. 1 owns the eyeglasses on the table.	—	—	—
12. No. 1 closely resembles President Ford.	—	—	—
13. Two people in this picture wear eyeglasses.	—	—	—
14. All of these people work for the same company.	—	—	—
15. No. 3 is listening to No. 1's conversation.	—	—	—
16. None of these people works for the same company.	—	—	—
17. No. 1 was seated beside No. 5.	—	—	—
18. No. 5 is wearing a wristwatch.	—	—	—
19. No. 1 is holding a telephone receiver.	—	—	—
20. This picture depicts daytime activities.	—	—	—
21. No. 4 is reading a map.	—	—	—
22. There is smoke above the ashtray.	—	—	—

How do we recognize facts, inferences, and opinions? *A fact is something which is known with certainty to be true. True* means capable of being verified (tested by somebody else and found to be true) by reliable witnesses as actually existing or happening at a certain time or place, because it has been seen, heard, smelled, felt, or tasted. *Reliable witnesses* usually means more than one. Our senses play tricks on us, and it is not unusual for people, including scholars and scientists, to think they saw something when they really didn't. During the famous East Coast power blackout on November 9, 1965, a number of people reported seeing unidentified flying objects because a radio announcer suggested that they might have; what they actually saw was the full moon. Even scientists miscalculate formulas and equations now and again and feel sure they have a fact only to be disappointed later.

Reliable evidence is derived from a qualified source, one recognized as having adequate skill, experience, or education to verify something as a fact—a blind person would not be qualified to verify the architectural design of a building. Also remember that often readers will not accept verification unless the source is qualified. Your readers don't care whether the source is your Uncle Ben, your Aunt Martha, or someone on the far side of the earth: the question is not who the witness is, but how well the witness is qualified.

When you are the writer, it is your responsibility to tell your readers who or what your sources are in order to help them accept your facts. This is especially true when they are not familiar with the source or have some reason to doubt you. If you are the source, you may have to tell your readers what qualifies you to recognize and report a fact when you see one. Here are a few examples of factual statements.

1. Lyndon B. Johnson was President of the United States.
2. The earth is not the only planet orbiting the sun.
3. In 1974, Chris Evert replaced Billy Jean King as Women's Singles champion at Wimbledon.

These statements will probably be accepted as facts without expressed support, especially if they are stated firmly and your reader has no reason to doubt you. But statements such as the following probably will not be accepted in the same way.

1. Among artists, Martha Graham holds a place of honor for her dancing.
2. The national Capitol is the most beautiful building in the United States.
3. Jim Thorpe was the greatest athlete of all time.

You as a writer should support your statements when you expect that your readers will doubt or disagree with some of your important facts. You may give the name of an authority whom readers will believe, or you may refer to a book, article, or report where readers can check the information for themselves. If it helps to bring out the main idea, you may spell out in some detail the evidence for the truth of your statement. Or, if references and the names of authorities clutter up the discussion, you may put them in footnotes.

Most of the facts cited or referred to in writing are accepted because they have been long known and unquestioned. For example, no reader is likely to doubt "Charles Dickens wrote *A Tale of Two Cities*" or "Emily Brontë wrote *Jane Eyre.*"

It is important to remember that the truth of a fact is often limited in both time and space. In June 1971, the military draft of young men in the United States was a fact; in July 1973, it was not. Facts are also limited to present and past time. The things of the future, even an hour in the future, cannot be facts now. So you must always be alert to the time limitations on your facts.

Facts are also limited in space. What is true in the United States may not be true in Iceland. When you say "People eat raw blubber as part of their regular diet," you must add "in Arctic regions" if you want to be believed.

Facts exist independent of people. The same sun will probably exist 100 years from today whether or not we are here to observe it. When we discuss opinion, we will learn that opinions begin and end with an individual. But facts and inferences exist as long as the evidence for them exists, and as long as the same logical deductions can be made from them.

From what we have seen of facts you may think that you won't be able to write many facts because your skills, training, and experience do not qualify you to be sure of them. That is not really true. Unless you prove untrustworthy, a reader will accept your factual statements about things on which you are qualified. Every hour of the day you make firsthand observations of a multitude of facts which a reader will accept without question. The weather, automobiles, people, buildings, events, the cities and country you see have many characteristics about which you can say something factual. All of the things you see, hear, smell, feel, and taste may be factually stated. You must, however, express these statements as facts which the reader will be able to accept. Many facts which your readers might challenge can be easily proved by the thousands of books on the library shelves. There is no end to the number of facts you can use in your writing. But your reliability will be affected most of all by how carefully you distinguish between facts and other kinds of statements. Your reader's trust is your most valuable asset. Treat it well.

What Is an Inference?

An inference is a conclusion logically derived from reliable evidence, but for which there is not enough evidence to prove it to be a fact. Although there may not be enough evidence to prove an inference, the factual evidence from which it is derived may give it a high degree of probability. Degree of probability plays an important role in causing people to act with confidence on their inferences. Many students attend college to earn a degree which they believe will some day assure them a good position. Corporations invest huge sums of money in new plants for future expansion, inferring that they will need the space for an increased volume of business. Neither of these conclusions may prove to be a fact.

Our everyday thinking is loaded with inferential statements, many of which we almost automatically accepted as facts. Here are a few typical ones.

1. The driver must have been drunk because the car zigzagged down the road.
2. Alaska and Russia were once connected by land.
3. Statistics show that death will come to 5,000 people on our highways within the next 24 hours.
4. The barometer indicates that it will rain tonight.

None of these statements can be proved true at the present moment, even though there is good evidence that some of them may later become facts. An inference is a logical conclusion derived from more or less reliable evidence. Because we can reach such conclusions, we are not limited to actions based on facts alone.

Many important scientific developments started out as inferences. Until only a few years ago, we had to be content with many inferences about the moon. Since recent trips to the moon, some of those inferences have been established as fact, and others have been proved incorrect. This has produced new conclusions based on new information, which provide another basis for inferences until *they* are proved either fact or fiction.

All of us rely heavily on our ability to draw logical inferences from reliable evidence. From the expression on someone's face we infer happiness, sadness, or worry, though in fact it may only express doubt about what to have for lunch. When we see deer tracks in fresh snow, we conclude rightly that a deer has recently gone by that way. When we see broken glass and black tire tracks on a highway, we conclude that one of the cars involved turned in a certain way, was probably going too fast, and may have been the cause of an accident. We work hard to save money because we believe we will need it when we retire. But we may never retire; we may not live that long, or we may work on past the usual retirement age. We are reasonably sure when we infer what time the sun will rise, the moon will set, and the tide will be high — but we have very reliable experience on which to make these predictions. With much less certainty we predict tomorrow's weather, but we plan our activities on both safe and unsafe predictions because we must; it is the best we can do.

An inference is usually not restricted in time and space. Facts can exist only in the past or the present. Inferences also deal with the future.

What Is an Opinion?

An opinion is a conclusion or belief based on personal experience or preference more than on objective, reliable evidence. Inferences try to establish truth, sometimes when facts are not available. Opinions express personal judgments, likes, dislikes, beliefs, and disbeliefs on matters which cannot be actually proved or disproved. Our opinions include our value judgments and other conclusions which arise out of our attitudes, our background, and our emotional reactions to people, events, things, and ideas. As a writer you are not accountable for your opinions in the same way that you are for your facts and inferences. Opinions cannot be verified by checking against the objective world. But we all react strongly to opinions, and we often judge others by their opinions more sharply than we do by their grasp of facts and their ability to draw logical inferences. Here are a few opinions. What do they make you think of the people who express them?

1. Summer is the most enjoyable time of the year.
2. Sign at a ski resort: "Help stamp out summer."
3. Astrology can foretell a person's future.
4. My cousins are fools. All they think about is stars and horoscopes.
5. The majority rules.
6. "Your people, sir, your people is a great beast."
7. Everything works out for the best.
8. In this world, sooner or later, you get what you pay for.

Opinions come from many causes, may be reached in haste or after long and careful thought, and range from the trivial to the profound. Which is the prettier color, red or blue? Do redheaded people have hot tempers? Are drugs harmful? Is Chinese music beautiful or ugly?

Although many opinions are based on slight evidence or none at all, this does not mean that no opinion is reliable. When you phone your doctor to say you don't feel well, he may give you the opinion that you should come in for a check-up. Because you know he is qualified to express a reliable opinion about your health, you take the advice. Your lawyer may tell you to plead guilty to a charge of speeding, thinking from knowledge of judges, courts, and law that you may receive better treatment if you do. Again, you respect informed opinion. Experience, knowledge, and a good record give many such opinions a good deal of weight. They should be listened to.

On the other hand, many opinions are intended only to show our feelings about something, not to express an important belief or recommend a course of action. When we say, "She's terrific," "That car's a dream," or "I could die eating pizza," we are intentionally exaggerating to express an emotion, not a logical judgment. In such statements there is little danger of being misunderstood.

But other opinions, including some of those in the list above, look as if they were meant as statements of fact, or at least of serious belief. Whenever there is any danger that such a statement may be misunderstood, it should be clearly labeled an opinion by the use of such a phrase as "I think," "I feel," "in my opinion."

**WRITING FACTS,
INFERENCES, AND
OPINIONS**

It is not only what you the writer says that counts, but what your readers think you have said. For this reason you should be very careful to label opinions and distinguish judgments from facts. The best way to tell your readers whether a composition is to deal mainly with fact, inference, opinion, or some mixture of the three is for you to state or imply your purpose near the beginning. If you plan to inform, you will deal mainly with fact. If you want to persuade or to move to action, you will also be expressing inferences and perhaps opinions based on facts. If you mean merely to entertain, then it matters little whether you are dealing with fact or something else, and readers need not bother to separate one from the other.

Whether a statement is accepted in the way the writer meant it depends on how it is phrased. The flat statement that "there is moisture on Mars" looks like a fact, and since most informed readers know that many scientists are doubtful on this point, they may quickly lose confidence in the credibility of the writer. It would be much better to put this statement as an inference, indicating the source and including necessary qualifiers, perhaps like this: "Recent photographs of Mars show some change in the size and shape of its ice caps, leading some scientists to believe that there is moisture on the planet." If the writer does not know the source or the necessary qualifiers or the evidence for the statement, it will be wise to make the statement merely as an opinion: "It seems probable that there is moisture on Mars," or, "What I have heard about the planet makes me think that there is moisture on Mars."

As we implied earlier, you do not have to state the support, proof, or source of every statement you expect your readers to accept. As long as you seem reliable and are making reasonable statements, most readers will give you considerable benefit of doubt. But once it is lost, a reader's confidence is very hard to get back. To be believed, you must pay careful attention to the way you word and label your statements as provable facts, logical inferences, or reliable opinions. To do this well, you must pay close attention to the following things.

Terms

By terms we mean main words, usually nouns (names) and verbs which are the main parts of defining sentences. In informative writing, the accurate use of the right terms is essential if a reader is to understand the intended meaning of any statement. There are three common types of errors in the use of terms.

1. The use of the wrong term:
   (wrong term)   In ancient Rome, *Aphrodite* was the goddess of love.
   (right term)   In ancient Rome, *Venus* was the goddess of love.
   (wrong term)   In 1941, the Japanese *destroyed* the U.S. fleet.
   (right term)   In 1941, the Japanese *crippled* the U.S. fleet.
   (wrong term)   A ship *will* sink if it hits an iceberg.
   (right term)   A ship *may* sink if it hits an iceberg.
2. The omission of a necessary term:
   (needed term omitted)   Water freezes at zero degree.
   (needed term added)   Water freezes at zero degree *centigrade.*
   (needed term omitted)   A lemon is yellow.

(needed term added)	A *ripe* lemon is yellow.
(needed term omitted)	In 1956, a soldier photographed a UFO.
(needed term added)	In 1956, a soldier photographed *what he thought was* a UFO.

3. The use of a general term when a specific term is needed:

(term is not specific enough)	Animals are carnivorous.
(more specific term)	*Lions, wolves, tigers, jackals* are carnivorous.
(term is not specific enough)	Birds do not have wings, and therefore, can't fly.
(more specific term)	*Penguins* and *Kiwi* birds do not have wings and therefore can't fly.

Qualifiers

In addition to naming the main parts of things and ideas with the right terms, almost any mature statement also needs qualifiers. Qualifiers are words or groups of words that identify or describe and that limit the meaning of the terms in the statement to make them more meaningful or more precise. If you tell *when* or *where* a thing is or an event took place, *what* something looks, tastes, sounds, or feels like, *how* it was done, or *under what conditions,* you are adding a qualifier to the term. By doing this you are adding to or changing its meaning in one way or another. The principal types of qualifiers follow.

Descriptive Qualifiers

Adjectives and adverbs that tell how something looks, sounds, feels, smells, or tastes are descriptive qualifiers. You may use them to express your judgments and feelings, but such words as *gorgeous, miracle, wonderful,* and *terrific* convey nothing but feeling and give no real information about what a thing or person is like. Good descriptive informative qualifiers are not vague and empty.

Not: This *marvelous* plastic will enable you to manufacture *wonderful* new products.
But: This *styrofoam* will enable you to manufacture *floatable surfboards, toy boats,* and *animals that will not sink.*
Or: This plastic known as *Melmac* is used in the manufacture of *nonbreakable and attractively colored dishes ideal for use in summer cottages and vacation homes.*
Not: This is the *best* car in the world.
But: The *Slugger* is the *most economical* and *fastest* American sports car *in the middle-priced range this year.*

The first sentence in the pair above says that the writer has actually tested every car in the world and soberly concluded that this one rates number one in more ways than any other. Of course no reader would swallow such a statement. Most would merely judge the writer as emotional, uncritical, and probably not interested in presenting facts.

Time Qualifiers

Qualifiers that limit an idea in time by telling when it is or was probable or true are time qualifiers. They often provide an important part of the setting in which facts are to be understood.

Inexact: Most of the earth's crust consists of basaltic rock.
More exact: *During the first half billion years of the earth's existence,* most of its crust probably consisted of basaltic rock.
Inexact: The United States had a population of only 100,000,000.
More exact: *As late as 1930,* the United States had a population of only 100,000,000.
Inexact: Our ancestors believed in ghosts and goblins, witches and warlocks, and debated how many angels could stand on the head of a pin.
More exact: *As recently as 300 years ago,* some of our ancestors believed . . .

Space Qualifiers

Space qualifiers also help readers to understand and accept the truth of your facts and the reasonableness of your inferences. As we have said before, what is true and reasonable in one place may not be true or probable in another. When necessary, be sure the space limitations are indicated to make facts and inferences more acceptable.

Inexact: Bicycles are more numerous than automobiles.
More exact: *In small Korean villages,* bicycles are more numerous than automobiles.
Inexact: The rate of magnetic change on the ocean floor last year was one inch.
More Exact: The rate of magnetic change on the ocean floor *off the coast of Iceland* was one inch last year.

Quantity Qualifiers

Qualifiers that tell how many or how much of something is true or probable are quantity qualifiers; they are one of the most common causes of incorrect or inexact statements in written expression. Such words as *all, every, some, few, any* can cause misstatement and misunderstanding in either of two ways: when they are incorrectly implied, and when they are incorrectly stated.

When the writer states a point in a way that implies one of the quantity qualifiers such as *all* or *every*, a misstatement results.

Not correct: Fish fly. (Not correct because it implies that all fish fly.)
More correct: A *few kinds* of fish fly.
Not correct: Politicians are crooked.
More correct: *Some* politicians are crooked.

Conditional Qualifiers

Qualifiers that tell under what circumstances something is true or reliable are conditional qualifiers; they are often necessary to establish the truth or reliability of facts or inferences. Often, when these conditions are not expressed, statements intended as facts or inferences become worthless. To say you will get wet if you go outside is foolish if it isn't raining.

Inexact:	The value of the dollar will decrease next year.
More exact:	*If inflation increases*, the value of the dollar will decrease next year.
Inexact:	There is moisture on Mars.
More exact:	*If there are seasonal changes in the shape of its icecaps*, there is evidence of moisture on Mars.
Inexact:	It is not illegal to kill an enemy.
More exact:	*In battle*, it is not illegal to kill an enemy.

Reliable Sources

Citing your sources often induces a reader to accept your points. When it does help, be sure you use sources your reader will approve of as being qualified authorities. To establish the dependability of your sources, you may have to give your reader some background information about them. Notice how the weight of the evidence can vary with the source.

Not qualified:	The police officer on the corner said that there is moisture on Mars.
Better qualified:	The Harvard astronomer said that there is moisture on Mars.
Not qualified:	The hotel manager said that twenty-one U.S. airplanes were hijacked to Cuba in 1973.
Better qualified:	The U.S. Aeronautics Commission reported that twenty-one U.S. airplanes were hijacked to Cuba in 1973.

Every human being is an authority about some things, but there are many more things about which he or she is not an authority. It is good to remember this when you are trying to convince a reader. Whenever you think your reader may challenge or doubt you, it is a great help to refer to your sources for support.

Reliable Evidence

Evidence must be adequate to support whatever the writer intends the reader to accept as fact or reasonable inference. When you believe or even suspect your readers may challenge or disagree with you, you should produce the evidence in proof of your statements.

No evidence:	The leaders of the Flying Saucer club contended that the UFOs came from a planet, Clarion, which exists, but which we cannot see because it is on the other side of the moon.
Reasonable evidence:	The astronomer, Dr. Ellsworth Dean, said that if Clarion existed, its gravity would affect the orbit of Venus, and after careful observation of Venus, he could detect no such disturbance. Therefore, he concluded a UFO could not have come from such a source.

Having read through this chapter, go back to page 4, restudy the picture and try answering the questions again. Now that you know more about facts, inferences, and opinions as we define them, you should be better able to understand why some of your answers may have been incorrect the first time.

PRACTICE in Achieving This Chapter's Objectives

Practice with facts, inferences, and opinions.

	Applications
1. Identifying facts, inferences, and opinions.	1, 2, 3
2. Making and writing facts, inferences, and opinions.	4, 5
3. Identifying reliable sources.	6
4. Identifying and using terms and qualifiers.	7
5. Writing a composition of several paragraphs applying the topics in this chapter.	8
6. You Be the Judge	

APPLICATION 1-1

In the blank at the left of each statement, print F if it is intended as a fact, I if it is intended as an inference, O if it is intended as an opinion:

_____ 1. It is assumed that like today's reptiles, some dinosaurs were egg-laying.

_____ 2. Judging from their dull teeth, most dinosaurs were herbivorous.

_____ 3. Some dinosaurs were at least sixty feet in length, judging from their skeletons.

_____ 4. Toads cause warts.

_____ 5. All looters during a riot should be shot.

_____ 6. The earth is between four and one-half billion and five billion years old, university geologists reported.

_____ 7. NASA says that by the year 2000, the U.S. spaceships will have landed on Mars.

_____ 8. Rutabagas taste good when boiled.

_____ 9. On the average, we may expect every year one gigantic earthquake, ten major earthquakes, and 100 destructive shocks taking place on the earth, according to Harvard scientists.

_____ 10. Milk from milkweeds will cause a wart to disappear.

_____ 11. Rosa Stack is jinxed.

_____ 12. The ancient Romans worshipped Diana.

_____ 13. Driving in rush-hour traffic is an endurance contest for me.

_____ 14. In leap year, February has twenty-nine days.

_____ 15. *Oliver Twist* was written by Charles Dickens.

_____ 16. "Casablanca" is a classic film.

_____ 17. Men and women should both be drafted into the armed forces.

_____ 18. Having a rabbit's foot brings good luck.

_____ 19. Recent moon photographs reveal that the earth is not a sphere.

_____ 20. A whale is a mammal.

APPLICATION 1-2

Each of the sentences in the following paragraph is intended by the writer as a fact, an inference, or an opinion. In the blank before each sentence, write F, I, or O.

_____ 1. (1) The substances expelled by volcanoes today include carbon dioxide, nitro-
_____ 2. gen, hydrogen, and water. (2) On primitive earth, where the atmosphere contained no oxygen, carbon monoxide must have been expelled from the incom-

15

_____ 3. plete combustion of materials within the earth. (3) Ultimately, water vapor from volcanoes must have saturated the atmosphere and fallen as rain, creating

_____ 4. rivers. (4) Most of the earth's crust probably consisted of basalt rock brought to

_____ 5. the surface by volcanoes. (5) When brought into contact with water, basalt liberates calcium and sodium ions and produces an alkaline solution having a

_____ 6. pH of about 9.6. (6) Thus, the rains and rivers dissolving the materials in basalt

_____ 7. would have created oceans of pH 9.6. (7) But atmospheric carbon dioxide, dissolving in the raindrops as they fell, would have produced a slightly acidic solution which neutralized some of the basic rock salts and lowered the pH of the

_____ 8. seas to between 8 and 9. (8) Thus, carbon monoxide, nitrogen, and hydrogen probably were left to constitute the primitive atmosphere.[1]

Eugenia Keller, "The Origin of Life," *Chemistry*, December 1968, p. 10.

APPLICATION 1-3

Study carefully the picture and answer each question beneath it by placing an X in the appropriate column. Be prepared to explain your answers.

	F	I	O
1. Two people are playing chess.	—	—	—
2. The cup contains hot chocolate.	—	—	—
3. Two of the women are sisters.	—	—	—
4. It is the young man's move.	—	—	—
5. The game is taking place in a ski lodge.	—	—	—
6. Two of the men are talking to each other.	—	—	—
7. This scene is taking place during the winter.	—	—	—
8. There is a log burning in the fireplace.	—	—	—
9. The couple sitting on the fireplace is engaged.	—	—	—
10. One of the men is wearing a ring.	—	—	—
11. Everyone in this picture is happy.	—	—	—
12. It is dark outside.	—	—	—
13. The woman in the white sweater is playing chess.	—	—	—

	F	I	O
14. There is a fire in the fireplace.	—	—	—
15. The three couples are "going steady."	—	—	—
16. None are members of the same family.	—	—	—
17. The woman with dark hair knit her sweater.	—	—	—
18. There are no other people in the room.	—	—	—
19. These people are in their twenties.	—	—	—
20. Everyone is wearing shoes.	—	—	—

APPLICATION 1-4

Using the illustration on page 17 as a guide, prepare a similar application. You may use a drawing or photograph of your own or you may cut one out of a newspaper or a magazine. Paste the picture on a piece of white paper, draw in the columns headed F, I, and O, and write at least fifteen statements telling what you detect or infer from details in the picture. Finally, insert an X in the proper column to indicate that each statement is a fact, an inference, or an opinion. Be prepared to explain your answers. Be sure to have at least three of each kind of statement in your list.

APPLICATION 1-5

On a separate sheet of paper, write five sentences which express thoughts clearly intended as facts, five which express thoughts clearly intended as inferences, and five which express thoughts clearly intended as opinions.

APPLICATION 1-6

On the lines beneath each of the following passages, identify the sources and tell why each source is or is not qualified. Also, explain why the evidence supporting the claim of each source is or is not reliable.

1. Two shipyard workers in Pascagoula, Mississippi, claimed they were forced aboard a UFO and examined carefully by silver-skinned creatures with big eyes and pointed ears. They said they were fishing from an old pier on the west bank of Pascagoula River about 7 P.M., Thursday, October 4, 1973, when they noticed a strange craft about two miles away emitting a bluish haze. One of the men said, "It hovered about three feet off the ground and three whatever-they-were came out either floating or walking and carried us into the ship. The things had big eyes. They kept us about twenty minutes, photographed us and then took us back to the pier. The only sound they made was a buzzing-humming. They left in a flash." The other man said the "Martians" were about five feet tall and had two big eyes. They were pale in color, wore skin-type coverings and there was some type of opening below their eyes. A captain from the sheriff's department who questioned both men reported, "We did everything we knew to break their stories," but both men were not lying to him, he thought.

   Several top space scientists from the University of Michigan who interviewed the two men concluded that the men probably were startled by natural phenomena and were so affected that the sequence of happenings they experienced were imagined.

   _____

   _____

   _____

   _____

   _____

   _____

2. The nation's most respected surveyors of consumer attitudes warned Monday that a "recession by early next year must be regarded as quite possible, perhaps even probable." The prediction by two University of Michigan economists came after their survey of consumer sentiment uncovered more pessimism in August and September than at any time in the twenty-five year history of their periodic study.

   _____

   _____

   _____

   _____

   _____

   _____

APPLICATION 1-7

Each of the following is intended to reliably express an accurate statement. In the blank at the left of each, place the letter from the list below that identifies the element essential for its reliability and accuracy.

A. precise term(s)   E. quantity qualifier
B. descriptive qualifier   F. conditional qualifier
C. time qualifier   G. source
D. space qualifier

_____ 1. Stock market investors who do not take unreasonable risks are speculators, not gamblers.

_____ 2. The Chairperson of the National Democratic Party reported that the majority of the votes for the leading candidate were from middle-class citizens.

_____ 3. Devices of persuasion, not logical fallacies, are used intentionally.

_____ 4. This year, many firms will scrap 20 percent of what they produce.

_____ 5. In England, petrol is used as automobile fuel.

_____ 6. The Dallas/Fort Worth airport is the largest in the world.

_____ 7. No report can be made of a tree falling in a forest unless someone sees or hears it fall.

_____ 8. Between 1960 and 1972, the average annual rise in United States steel production was 3.1 percent.

_____ 9. If labor produces more, labor will receive increased wages.

_____ 10. To be a Christian, a person must believe in God, the teachings of Christ, and immortality.

_____ 11. Most people with credit cards are honest.

_____ 12. Inflation is very harmful to an economy when it continues for a long time.

_____ 13. Other planets in the universe may be inhabited by creatures like ourselves.

_____ 14. If you don't study enough, you'll fail the course.

_____ 15. Queen Elizabeth II was not a contemporary of William Shakespeare.

APPLICATION 1-8

Write a composition of several paragraphs to change a reader's mind about something. Support your conclusion with factual statements and logical inferences. Include an opinion or two. Be sure you make it clear whether your points are intended to be understood by your reader as facts, inferences, or opinions. Support your important contentions, especially those statements your reader might challenge.

Be careful in writing this composition. Your instructor may decide to have another student evaluate it, using the You Be the Judge evaluation forms on the next two pages and the instructions inside the back cover of this book. Read these carefully before you start writing your composition so that you will know what criteria the evaluator will use in grading it. If your instructor decides to have another student evaluate your composition, you of course will evaluate someone else's: another reason for becoming familiar with the instruction and evaluation form at your earliest opportunity. Below are some topics which you may limit or adapt for your composition, or you may choose a topic of your own.

1. It is time for prohibition again.
2. The human race has not achieved progress in the things that count.
3. Cultural identity is a major factor in every student's life.

If you have questions about grammar, spelling, or other mechanics while writing, refer to Handbook of Correct and Effective Usage in this text.

YOU BE THE JUDGE

Evaluator's
Initials [ ][ ][ ]

Date _____

Section _____

Grade _____

Writer's Name _____

Date _____ Section _____

Title of paper _____

Chapter _____ Application No. _____

General Instructions on the You Be the Judge Applications and specific instructions for Parts I and III are printed inside the back cover of this book. Read those instructions carefully; then do Part I.

In the lines below, and on another sheet of paper, answer the questions in Part II. Then enter a grade for the paper in the space above left, and write your evaluation for Part III. Reread the composition to see how well the writer understands and applies the principles studied in this chapter. As you read the composition write any helpful suggestions that occur to you in the margins.

PART II

1. Does the writer intend to inform readers or to convince them? Explain your answer. _____

   _____

   _____

   _____

   _____

   _____

2. Does the writer incorrectly state any opinions as if they were facts? Explain your answer. _____

   _____

   _____

   _____

   _____

   _____

3. Does the writer incorrectly state any inferences as if they were facts? Explain your answer. _____

   _____

   _____

_____

_____

_____

4. Does the writer cite reliable sources and give evidence for important points? Give examples. _____

_____

_____

_____

_____

_____

_____

5. Indicate whether the author handles the following well or poorly, and cite a good or bad example of each.

   a. Terms. _____

   _____

   b. Qualifiers. _____

   _____

6. Are there significant gaps or omissions in the writer's materials?

_____

_____

_____

_____

_____

_____

PART III   Grade and Explanation:

_____

_____

_____

_____

CHAPTER 2

FALLACIES: ERRORS IN THINKING

After studying this chapter and completing the applications that follow it, you should be able to do the following:
1. To define and identify common logical fallacies: *rationalizing* and *wishful thinking; hidden assumptions; sweeping generalizations; circular reasoning* and *begging the question; black-or-white reasoning; the what's-one-more-or-less fallacy; false cause.*
2. To avoid fallacies.
3. To detect these fallacies in the context of a full-length composition.

A T THE beginning of Chapter 1, we said that writing is thinking on paper, and we devoted that chapter to examining the three main building blocks of thinking: facts, inferences, and opinions. We defined a fact as something known to be true because it can be observed and verified by someone else. We said that an inference is a conclusion carefully and logically drawn from one or more facts. And we defined an opinion as a less systematic belief based on personal experience or preference rather than on verifiable facts. Thinking consists of grouping and examining facts and forming inferences and opinions from them. It is the process of discovering meaning in our experience and the world about us, of reaching conclusions or generalizations — of having ideas.

But the paths of thought are filled with pitfalls. Errors in thinking, commonly called logical fallacies, are mistakes in this process. It has been said that there is no one and only way to catalog fallacies since fallacy is error, and there is no limit to the number of ways in which the human mind can make mistakes. Yet minds make some mistakes more frequently than others, and it is possible to catalog the most usual of these. If there is anything like *a common denominator for fallacies,* it *is going wrong somehow in forming inferences or conclusions.* It is reaching false generalizations, and then using these false generalizations in our further thinking.

RATIONALIZING

The easiest type of logical fallacy to recognize is *rationalizing,* the invention of reasons we hope will look respectable for conduct which actually springs from very different and usually less admirable causes or motives. We rationalize to protect our self-concept. To make ourselves look good to our friends, and more particularly to our acquaintances, we go through an endless assortment of mental gymnastics. We invent stories, explanations, excuses to make ourselves appear intelligent, logical, courageous, unselfish. As the philosopher James Harvey Robinson once expressed it, we invent all kinds of "good" reasons to conceal our "real" reasons, to make ourselves look better than we are. The only problem with rationalizing is that it seldom deceives anyone. For example:

1. I enrolled in the remedial English class because I want to get a mastery of the English language.

  This student is obviously giving a "good" reason for taking remedial English. Because he is ashamed to admit it, he hides the real reason — that the college administration made him take the remedial course because he failed the English admission examination. Although his stated reason helps him to protect his ego, it has no logical relation to his actual reason.

2. I don't ski because it doesn't make sense. It wastes time, driving to the slopes and waiting for the chairlifts, usually the whole weekend.

  The student who wrote this was keeping her real reason hidden. She neglected to say that she has a fear of high places. She saves face by giving a reason unrelated to the truth in order to deceive her friends and comfort herself.

We all rationalize. And we should realize that often we do it unconsciously, so that we can begin to recognize the symptoms and learn to avoid this pattern of behavior.

A special form of rationalizing is sometimes called *wishful thinking*. This is trying to make ourselves and others believe something is true because we want it to be or can't face the consequences if it isn't. "I can't stay up and study any later tonight because it isn't good for my health—I catch cold too easily as it is." "A little more gas and I'll make that light before it changes." "Why study now? I'm so far behind I'll never catch up anyway." "The only way I work well is under pressure. I've never been able to learn anything by studying gradually. The best way for me is to stay up all night before an exam."

Rationalizing is finding reasons or excuses which look good for doing or believing something rather than admitting the real reasons even if it hurts. Wishful thinking is a special form of rationalizing which relates to the future in that it tries to justify things we want to do or hope will happen. We discuss them first among logical fallacies because they are easy to recognize (especially in other people!) and have many things in common with other types of fallacious thinking that reach faulty generalizations from twisted evidence or none at all.

HIDDEN ASSUMPTIONS

The commonest type of faulty reasoning by far is *hidden assumptions* —beliefs or opinions which we assume to be true and never question. Many of these come to us from early experiences. A curious child climbs on a stool to investigate the medicine cabinet. The child slips, falls, is severely punished by mother, and from then on is influenced by the unconscious belief that it is better to be safe than curious. Another youngster, seeing an older sister get a licking after confessing to breaking father's favorite fishing rod, quickly decides that honesty is not the best policy. Many of our religious convictions, political beliefs, moral standards, and social inclinations come to us in this way. We reach conclusions unconsciously on the basis of experience or teaching, and they may stay with us in the form of hidden assumptions all our lives.

Our thinking, and thus our speech and writing, is riddled with such assumptions. The cultural atmosphere in which we live and the institutions to which we belong give us great complexes of assumptions we accept unthinkingly.

Since hidden assumptions are of many kinds, and may concern any subject, there is no simple rule for unmasking them. But practice helps. The best way to become sensitive to them is to examine a few. Here are some on a variety of topics. Some of them look completely innocent.

1. Buy the blue suede jacket. It's imported.

What is the hidden assumption lurking beneath this simple piece of advice? When somebody says that the blue jacket is better because it's imported, the implication is that imported goods are better than domestic ones. This is the assumption. Is it true? Sometimes yes and sometimes no. The assumption is too broad, too sweeping, and is all the more dangerous because until recently most foreign goods were more expensive, and for that reason many people thought they were better, whether or not they actually were. This is the hidden assumption.

2. That's the third dumb soldier I've met. From now on it's civilians for me.

What's the "reasoning" in this case? Soldier No. 1 was dumb. No. 2 was dumb. No. 3 was dumb. So guess what: all soldiers are dumb. Does this follow? Not at all. Then why believe it? For two reasons. The first is that it's dangerously easy to generalize from a very few cases that all cases are the same. The second is that a stereotype or rubber-stamp opinion to this effect already exists—a hidden assumption—and makes belief without sufficient evidence all the easier.

3. Take it easy, kid. You've had four narrow escapes. This time your number may be up.

Do you detect any similarity between the reasoning in Example No. 3 and Example No. 2? In both, the conclusion is based on a very limited number of cases, but in both there is another element, a hidden assumption that makes the faulty thinking easy to accept. There is a widespread belief in something loosely and mistakenly called "the law of averages." The real law of averages says that in truly chance events, such as tossing a coin, 1,000 tosses will give equal alternative results, 500 heads and 500 tails. The false law of averages, the hidden assumption in this example, says that luck tempted too often will turn the other way. Thousands of people who take risks firmly hold this belief, feeling that with each exposure to danger their chances are poorer than before, that luck is running out. The fact is that extent of danger has nothing to do with frequency, but with other factors; and that other things being equal, one's chances are the same on the tenth exposure as on the first.

4. To cure warts, you cut them out with a horn-handled pen knife in the dark of the moon. My cousin did it, and it worked.

Here is a remarkable tangle of causation and proof. The "proof" is that it worked. But why did it work? We are told it worked because it was done with a certain kind of knife at a certain time. The real evidence is that it worked because the warts were cut out. The dark of the moon and the kind of knife had nothing to do with it. The type of hidden assumption illustrated in this case is less common today than those in the first three examples, but that is only because the kind of superstitions involved are no longer so widely held.

5. Joe and Marie Jackson got so deep in debt that they had to borrow $500 from a finance company to consolidate their bills. When they got the loan, they went out for a $40 dinner to celebrate.

As this and the preceding examples show, not all the hidden assumptions we have to contend with occur in our writing. Just as many occur in our daily lives. What was Joe and Marie's error? Short-sightedness. Their temporary relief at getting their creditors off their backs was so great that they lost sight of the real reason for borrowing money: it was not to give them cash for future follies but to help pay for those already committed.

SWEEPING GENERALIZATIONS

This is a picturesque name for a kind of generalization which frequently has no more support than an unexamined opinion but is offered with all the solemn assurance of a well-researched generalization or even an easily verifiable fact. Most people who make such statements like to believe that they are expressing some deep truth to which they have given careful thought, but usually they have merely accepted a conclusion from someone else without bothering to find or examine the evidence that went to support the original assertion. We have a right to hold whatever reasonable opinions we choose, but not to present unsupported ones as if they were facts.

Following are a few typical sweeping generalizations. It would take years to discover — and volumes to record — the evidence that would be required to make these statements with full knowledge of the facts behind them.

1. Adolph Hitler was the most horrible of all the tyrants who ever lived.

To establish this statement as a reliable inference, the writer would not only have to make an exhaustive study of Hitler, but learn enough about all the other tyrants who ever existed to make dependable comparisons among them. The probability is that there is no more support for this sweeping assertion than a few bits of hearsay, some vague recollections of things read and heard, and the desire to make a dramatic statement. The writer is only expressing personal feelings about Hitler.

2. Doberman Pinschers are more vicious than any other kind of dog.

This is also a generalization requiring a large amount of investigation by many people to dig up reliable evidence in support of the broad statement. All breeds of dogs would have to be examined in detail and judged objectively for viciousness.

3. Walking on the moon is the greatest accomplishment of human beings.

This statement involves a number of unprovable value judgments. Is walking on the moon greater than the invention of the wheel, the alphabet, the printing press, or the discovery of cures for many illnesses?

Before a reader could accept this as a reliable inference, the assumptions upon which it is based would have to be supported with much more evidence. The solution is easy, insert a qualification which limits the assertion: "Walking on the moon is *one* of the greatest accomplishments of human beings."

4. Watching television has a harmful effect on children.

This generalization is based on the many charges in newspapers and magazines, and perhaps on radio and television, that programs which depict dramatic action and violence have a harmful effect on young viewers. On this point there has been much controversy but not enough proof.

5. Italians never get drunk because they are brought up on wine; they become immune to intoxication from it. I was in Italy two weeks last year, and I didn't see even one intoxicated Italian.

Is the writer assuming that no Italians get drunk? Would two weeks be enough time for him to find evidence for such a sweeping statement?

6. The people at that university are snobs. I went to one of their parties last week, and they didn't even talk to me.

This experience is likely to tell us more about the writer than about the people at this particular university. Not only is the evidence limited to a single observation, but a reader can't help wondering whether even that is grossly misinterpreted.

**CIRCULAR
REASONING**

The fallacy of *circular reasoning* occurs when a writer makes a show of supporting a conclusion when he is actually only restating it. The fallacy takes several forms, more or less easy to detect depending on whether the restatement uses words similar to the original assertion or finds others which seem to say something different.

The simplest form is the circular definition in which the writer actually uses the same term twice:

1. A *bad* dog is a dog that has *bad* qualities.

2. A *hero* or *heroine* is someone who has performed *heroic deeds* or has the *characteristics* of a *heroic character*.

In the first of these definitions, the second part of the statement makes absolutely no advance on the first part. We could diagram it like this:

In the second definition there is some slight advance: the words ''deeds'' and ''character'' give us at least the faint clues that a hero can do things and be somebody. We can diagram this one like this:

A subtler kind of circular reasoning uses different words in the second part, and can go undetected by readers who aren't very much on their toes:

3. A high rate of employment will bring economic prosperity because both labor and capital prosper when people have enough money to buy all that industry can produce.

In slightly simpler language this says:

4. High employment brings prosperity because prosperous labor makes prosperous industry.

In still simpler language this means:

5. High employment brings prosperity because prosperity is prosperous.

This brings us out just at the point where we went in. It may surprise you, but if we diagram this one it comes out like the first one as above, not the second.

There is yet a third form of circular reasoning, which is perhaps more accurately described as spiral.

6. We need more enrollment in this college in order to get more tuition with which to build more classrooms to accommodate more students.

Perhaps this type of spiral is best illustrated in a statement like this one:

7. I am glad I have a job because that enables me to buy a car so I can drive to work.

Here it is easy to detect the fallacy: without a job the person would not need to drive there and so would not need a car.

Another variety of circular reasoning is *begging the question,* which is assuming the truth of the proposition you wish to prove. In a sense it is using loaded words, a kind of "name-calling" to avoid unconsciously the real issue. For example, "Classical music is finer music than rock because *people of good taste and musical knowledge* prefer classical music." Or, "The student hated roast beef because it *tasted unpleasant."* In such circular reasoning, the same statement is made twice, but in slightly different terms. If the terms were exactly or nearly the same there would be no danger of being misled: "I hate red because it is a disturbing color." But sometimes the two formulations are different enough so that it is hard to recognize that they actually do say the same thing: "Sexual freedom is a great advance over our previously *hidebound moral stand-ards,* for it is better to be free than to be *slaves."* What this says really is that it is better to be free because it is better to be free, which may be true but is not proof.

BLACK-OR-WHITE REASONING

The cliché "There are two sides to every question" doesn't mean what it says. It means that there are *at least* two sides to every question. A person arguing that "you are either with me or against me" is guilty of the *black-or-white fallacy.* Most conclusions have many shades of rightness or wrongness between the two extremes. Acts that are not crimes are not necessarily angelic behavior. A watermelon which is not sweet may not be sour, but simply not as sweet as you expected.

1. We must not deny the newspapers freedom or we will have abuse of the doctrine of freedom of the press.

Should newspapers be allowed slander, pornography, subversive material, highly restricted information? This generalization expects the reader to assume that the slightest regulation will cause total forfeit of freedom of the press. It would be very difficult to provide enough evidence in support of either extreme. But there are many alternatives between these two extremes which will provide freedom of the press without abuse of that freedom.

2. We must control all prices and wages or rampant inflation will result.

This writer is asserting another either-or, black-or-white solution, with no reasonable area between.

3. We must destroy Cuba now or else give up trying to live in peace with other South American countries.

Is there no solution short of destroying Cuba? Does the writer provide enough evidence to support this drastic assumption? Can't we develop peaceful relationships with most of the South American countries without destroying Cuba? This harsh alternative is obviously a result of faulty black-or-white reasoning, an assumption impossible to support adequately.

**THE WHAT'S-ONE-
MORE-OR-LESS
FALLACY**

This type of fallacious reasoning results when a person wants to justify a thought or an act which is questionable, illegal, immoral, or unethical. It often results from not knowing the full consequences of a proposed action, in other words, from ignorance. Sometimes it is called the "argument of the beard" because of the difficulty of deciding just how many hairs are required to make a beard — one thousand, one hundred, ten, or one?

1. My Volkswagen can hold six people easily, and when it has to, it can hold a couple more; so I don't see why in an emergency it can't take twenty.

Obviously, there is something wrong with this reasoning; there has to be a cut-off point somewhere.

The following examples illustrate how this type of faulty reasoning can lead to serious problems. A 250-pound patient with heart trouble is placed on a strict diet, but gets hungry and uses the following argument:

2. What harm can one more piece of mince pie do when I have already had two?

Sometimes this fallacy is used to justify crime. The shoplifter argues:

3. What's one fur coat more or less for that huge department store; there's a whole rack of them just like this one.

Or a pheasant hunter explains to a game warden:

4. Sure, I shot more than my limit of two, but there are so many pheasants here that shooting one or two more won't do any harm.

One can guard against this fallacy by the reminder that small differences can accumulate to tremendous amounts even though each increment is insignificant by itself. The adage about "the straw that broke the camel's back" has some truth to it when there are enough straws.

FALSE CAUSE

This fallacy results when a person automatically and unintentionally assumes incorrectly that because one thing exists or occurs shortly after or before another, one causes the other. It is obviously foolish to say, "Since I stopped eating popcorn, I haven't had any more dandruff." This is illogically linking two unrelated events simply because one occurred after the other. Here is another: "Since they started dropping atomic bombs, we've had a lot of freakish weather." There is no evidence that dropping atomic bombs is related to the weather in any way. The only link is the hasty conclusion that because one came shortly before the other it was the cause of the other.

Many superstitions have grown out of this kind of fallacious reasoning. We accept handed-down conclusions out of habit, even though they are based upon unrelated events. A common false cause fallacy says that if you see a shooting star, someone you know will die, although there is no known relationship between a falling star and a human life.

Two hunters explain that they won't go bear hunting without a certain bone-handled knife because the last time they took it on a hunting trip, they shot a bear. A neighbor always carries an umbrella even when the sun is shining and says, "Whenever I carry my umbrella, it doesn't rain."

1. I've been drinking all my life, I have twenty-three grandchildren, and I'm over ninety. So, if you want to live a long fruitful life, you ought to drink like me.

This nonagenarian doesn't know it, but it is more than likely that work and healthful diet were responsible, not alcohol.

CONCLUSION

Many other habits of thought besides those listed in this chapter have been called fallacies. Here we have discussed those which occur most often in thinking — in developing ideas and deciding what to say. These are the errors most likely to happen when planning one's message, whether it is a paper, a letter of application, or a report to one's boss. Later we shall examine other pitfalls in thinking, such as faulty comparisons and analogies (Chapter 13). Still later we shall look again at some of the fallacies discussed in this chapter, but in a wholly different context, for we shall re-examine them as devices which a writer may use quite intentionally to persuade someone else (Chapter 17). At that time we shall consider many other devices used for that purpose, mostly through the careful choice of words that arouse strong feeling for or against a course of action or a point of view (Chapters 5 and 15).

PRACTICE in Achieving This Chapter's Objectives

Practice in detecting and avoiding fallacies

	Applications
1. Recognizing common types of fallacies	1, 2
2. Explaining common types of fallacies	2
3. Discovering fallacies in published writing	3
4. Detecting fallacies in your own writing	4, 5, 6
5. You Be the Judge	

APPLICATION 2-1

On the first line beneath each of the following, place the letter from the list immediately below that best identifies the kind of fallacy represented. In the remaining space explain your choice.

A. rationalization   E. black-or-white reasoning
B. sweeping generalization F. false cause
C. hidden assumption   G. what's-one-more-or-less fallacy
D. circular reasoning

1. The New York Mets will lose the baseball game today because the team's manager is wearing his black derby hat. _____

   _____

   _____

   _____

   _____

   _____

   _____

2. If you want to succeed in life, get a college degree. _____

   _____

   _____

   _____

   _____

   _____

   _____

3. Some people dislike going to tennis matches because tennis is something they don't enjoy. _____

   _____

   _____

   _____

   _____

   _____

   _____

4. Anyone opposed to the free enterprise system is an enemy of the United States. _____

_____

_____

_____

_____

_____

_____

5. College professors are absent-minded. _____

_____

_____

_____

_____

_____

6. Some people who lose a friend say they don't care because they have too many friends anyway. _____

_____

_____

_____

_____

_____

7. Debra has already missed six classes in algebra; missing one more won't hurt her grade. _____

_____

_____

_____

_____

_____

8. My uncle would be alive today if he hadn't broken the bathroom mirror three days before he was killed in an automobile accident. _____

_____

_____

_____

_____

_____

_____

9. You have to be rich to be happy. _____

_____

_____

_____

_____

_____

_____

10. Artists are all temperamental. _____

_____

_____

_____

_____

_____

_____

APPLICATION 2-2

In the blank opposite each of the following, insert the letter from the list below which best identifies the kind of fallacy or faulty reasoning the statement contains.

A. sweeping generalization
B. circular reasoning
C. black-or-white reasoning
D. rationalizing

E. hidden assumption
F. false cause
G. what's-one-more-or-less fallacy

_____ 1. This cheese has to be good; it's imported from Switzerland.

_____ 2. Virginia Woolf is a great novelist because her novels have all the things great novels should have.

_____ 3. Mexico has doubled the size of its military forces during the past two years; therefore, the United States will be invaded by Mexico soon.

_____ 4. I know you are diabetic, but one more teaspoon of sugar won't hurt you. You've already had two.

_____ 5. If you accept even one principle of Marx, you are a traitor to the United States.

_____ 6. An applicant for a very high-paying job says she didn't get the job, but she doesn't care because at that company only the friends of the bosses get jobs.

_____ 7. Little pitchers have big ears.

_____ 8. Politicians are all crooks.

_____ 9. Illinois drivers are the best drivers.

_____ 10. It is good to study a foreign language because a foreign language is good to know.

_____ 11. I stopped having sore feet as soon as I stopped eating sauerkraut.

_____ 12. A student who is failing a course reasons that it would be better to drop the course than work a little harder because the instructor doesn't like him.

_____ 13. They can say all they want about loyalty to a friend; to my way of thinking a person is either for me or against me.

_____ 14. Movie stars buy their clothing in Italy; Italian fashion designers must be good.

_____ 15. A student wanting to enroll in an overloaded class because his girl friend is in it argues, "The class is already filled, so what harm can one more student do."

APPLICATION 2-3

From the editorial or the "Letters to the Editor" section of a magazine or newspaper, bring to class two arguments expressing two different points of view about the same issue. In each, underline any logical fallacies. Be ready to explain the fallacies.

On the lines opposite the italicized statements, in Applications 2-4, 2-5, and 2-6, place the letter from the following list best identifying the kind of fallacious reasoning represented.

A. sweeping generalization   E. hidden assumption
B. circular reasoning   F. false cause
C. black-or-white reasoning   G. what's-one-more-or-less fallacy
D. rationalizing

APPLICATION 2-4

_____ 1. A husband and wife should be required to secure a permit from the state before they are allowed to have a child. (1) *By doing this, the couple can be sure of the*
_____ 2. *kind of children they will have.* (2) *If they don't get permits, they will have retarded or deformed offspring.*
Before granting a couple a permit to have a child, the state should require that the couple have their financial standing checked by a counselor much like
_____ 3. a tax consultant. (3) *Some families with too many children feel that one more child won't make much of a dent in their budgets because another infant doesn't eat much.*
The solution to both these problems is simple. Married couples must be required to secure permits from the state before having a child.

APPLICATION 2-5

One of the major issues of our time is whether the government should grant
_____ 1. amnesty to draft dodgers. (1) *If one really stops to think about it, really stops to do some serious soul searching, he can only come up with one answer to this question: a draft dodger is not worthy of being an American.*
_____ 2. (2) *When a person is so willing to leave his country just to dodge the draft, he is in effect saying, "I'm through with America; I neither want nor need to be an*
_____ 3. *American."* (3) *In either thinking or saying this he is knowingly relinquishing all of his American rights.*
_____ 4. (4) *When a man goes to war to defend his country, he reinforces his belief in the principles for which it stands; consequently, he becomes a better citizen*
_____ 5. *when he returns to civilian life.* (5) *If a man, on the other hand, dodges one war, he will refuse to fight in all subsequent wars, even if his country is attacked: therefore, how can he be a good American?*

APPLICATION 2-6

_____ 1. (1) *When a student graduates from high school, he or she isn't ready for college.*

_____ 2. (2) *I don't say this because only I feel this way, but because most freshmen*

_____ 3. *throughout the United States feel the same way.* (3) *I learned this from discuss-ing the problem with my many freshman friends, and they agree with me.*

Many students enroll in college before they should mainly because their

_____ 4. counselors urge them to. (4) *All their counselors really care about is telling the student what they are supposed to, not what is best specifically for him or her.*

In my own particular case, for example, being enrolled in college happened too fast. One day I was a happy high school student, and not more than two

_____ 5. months later, I was enrolled in college. (5) *Now that I'm here, however, I'm will-ing to tolerate it because I know that if I don't get a college degree, I will be*

_____ 6. *digging ditches the rest of my life.* (6) *I also know that with a college degree I will get into the high income brackets.*

APPLICATION 2-7

Evaluate the composition below, using the You Be the Judge pages that follow. Refer to the Handbook of Correct and Effective Usage if you have questions about the correctness of grammar or other mechanics. See how many grammar and spelling errors you can find along with the fallacies.

The Constitution of the United States guarantees everyone the right to practice any religion as they understands it. A constitutional right is a privilege established by the united states constitution, and a persons religion are the moral principles in which he believes. Therefore, to deny the members of a sect in Tennesee the right to use rattlesnakes in their religious worship is to forbid them one of their constitutional rights given them by the founders of our country.

There should be no restrictions upon the practice of religion in the United States. If a parent wants his child to pick up a rattlesnake and let it crawl all over him to prove his religious faith the parent should be allowed to let him do it. After all, the child is his: Like the great American Patriots who wrote our Constitution, a parent must always be on guard to protect his rights. If he is denied religious freedom in any way then our Constitution is dead.

Some will argue that religious freedom should be limited. They say, for example, that a person shouldn't be allowed to take his own life, to comit suacide — handling rattlesnakes is suacide. This, of course, is far from true. Take Kalab Dribbs, for example, a devout member of this Tennesee religious group. One day during a religious service, he reached for a rattler and its fangs suddenly pierced his arm. He prayed loudly as the blood oozed out of the holes in his arm. He was taken home, and several weeks later, he was completely recovered. This proves that if your faith is strong no rattlesnake can harm you.

Yes, if taking a part in a religion involving snakes is suacide, then it should be declared illegal, but the religion of Tennesee sect is not suacidal. Suacide is the act of a mentally disturbed person, but a person who practices whatever religion he believes in faithfully can't be considered out of their head. Furthermore, suacide is comitted by people who want to die, but people who risk their lives to prove their faith do not want to die. They simply believe that their faith is much stronger than one snake bite more or less.

If these Tennesee worshippers are not allowed to practice what they believe, our Constitution is of no value. Refusing them the right to use rattlesnakes in practicing their religion would establish a precedent. Consequently, anyone who disagreed with the "establishment" would be arrested and imprisoned on religious grounds. Therefore, people who believe in women's lib, abortion, and racial equality could be imprisoned for the same reason, and the Constitution of the United States would be worthless.

YOU BE THE JUDGE

Evaluator's Initials ☐☐☐

Date _____

Section _____

Grade _____

Writer's Name _____

Date _____ Section _____

Title of paper _____

Chapter _____ Application No. _____

General instructions on the You Be the Judge Applications and specific instructions for Parts I and III are printed inside the back cover of this book. Read those instructions carefully; then do Part I.

In the lines below, and on another sheet of paper, answer the questions in Part II. Then enter a grade for the paper in the space above left, and write your evaluation for Part III. Reread the composition to see how well the writer understands and applies the principles studied in this chapter. As you read the composition write any helpful suggestions that occur to you in the margins.

PART II

1. Put an X in the appropriate blank to identify any types of faulty reasoning which the composition contains.

_____ sweeping generalizations   _____ hidden assumptions

_____ circular reasoning   _____ false cause

_____ black-or-white reasoning   _____ one-more-or-less fallacy

_____ rationalizing

2. Did the writer, in your opinion, use fallacious reasoning unknowingly? Explain. _____

_____

_____

_____

_____

_____

_____

_____

_____

_____

3. If the answer to Question No. 2 was yes, indicate which of the following you think was the cause, or name some other cause. Explain your answer with examples.

a. Personal emotions, biases, prejudices. _____

_____

_____

b. The influence of others. _____

_____

_____

c. The influence of the person the writer thinks he or she is or wants to be. _____

_____

_____

d. The influence of the writer's culture or environment. _____

_____

_____

4. Does the writer convince you by logical reasoning? _____

_____

_____

PART III   Grade and Explanation:

_____

_____

_____

_____

PART 2

PRETHINKING AND PREWRITING

CHAPTER 3

THE SPECIFIC SUBJECT

After studying this chapter and completing the applications that follow it, you should be able to do the following:
1. To prethink the *specific subject* for your own use.
2. To identify its parts: *general topic, specific topic,* and *main idea.*
3. To differentiate the *specific subject* from the *general* and *specific topic.*
4. To define the scope of the *specific subject* for your own use by means of: *specific nouns, descriptive and modifying words, time limitations,* and *space limitations.*
5. To use the *specific subject* in your thinking and while doing your research in preparing to write.
6. To apply these principles in a full-length composition.

S O FAR we have talked about the general importance of thinking in writing. We now sharpen our focus, and look more closely at the particular kinds of thinking which the writer must do in the planning of any particular communication, from a report or a business letter to a term paper or a full-length book. This thinking concerns three necessary decisions on three important matters which we may call the *predetermined elements,* since they should be completely clear before putting a sheet of paper in the typewriter or picking up a pen to begin the actual writing. These are: the *specific subject,* the *dominant general purpose,* and the *writer-reader relationship.*

In the next three chapters we shall discuss these three elements in the order in which they are listed above, although our diagram shows them in a different order. The three affect and influence each other in many different ways. Sometimes you know your reader like the palm of your hand, and so can easily decide just what to say to get the reaction you want. Sometimes you start by knowing just what you want to say, and then have to think whom to address and how best to say it to that reader. And sometimes you know just what kind of influence or rapport you want to develop, and then think up the message that will do it. But since we can't discuss these three predetermined elements all at once, we shall take them up one at a time in this chapter and the next two, beginning with the *specific subject.*

It must be emphasized again that the predetermined elements are identified at this point to help the writer, not the reader. They are identified long before starting to write and often even before starting to think specifically about a topic.

THE MAIN PARTS OF THE SPECIFIC SUBJECT

Regardless of which of the predetermined elements occurs to the writer first, obviously not very much can be written unless there is something to

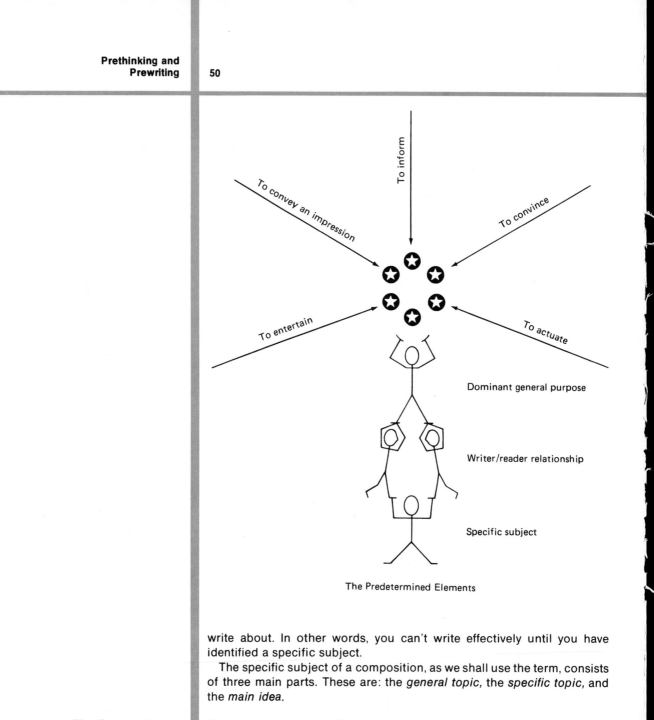

To inform

To convey an impression

To convince

To entertain

To actuate

Dominant general purpose

Writer/reader relationship

Specific subject

The Predetermined Elements

write about. In other words, you can't write effectively until you have identified a specific subject.

The specific subject of a composition, as we shall use the term, consists of three main parts. These are: the *general topic,* the *specific topic,* and the *main idea.*

The General Topic   The *general topic,* as the name implies, is merely a broad area within which the writer intends to work. But because it is general, it isn't a great deal of help in writing specifically. If, for example, you select elephants as a general topic and go to the library to do research, you will find dozens of books and articles on this massive pachyderm; you could read and write indefinitely about such a broad topic. If you do not limit the topic, you will more than likely take many notes about elephants which will never find a place in the final paper because you can't find a way to use them; they will be irrelevant. It is true that everything in such a paper could be in some way related to elephants, but many of the items might not be very closely related to each other.

A writer is often limited in available space. Magazine editors often stipulate the number of words to which an article must be limited. Busy executives demand that technical reports be as brief as possible. Writing assignments in college courses often indicate length. Even essay examinations are limited by time—the end of the examination period. Therefore the writer must whittle down a general topic so that it is appropriate to the purpose and space. It is true that a writer can say many things about a general topic. If you do, however, you must realize that you are in grave danger of merely skimming the surface much like a waterspider.

The Specific Topic

The *specific topic* is the general topic narrowed down and limited so that it is appropriate to the length as well as to the dominant general purpose and writer-reader relationship of the intended paper. The general topic may suggest a dominant general purpose to which it lends itself naturally. For example, if the topic is circuses, you may decide to entertain your reader with it; therefore, you would probably limit it in one kind of way. But if you had a special reason to inform your reader about circuses, you would be more likely to limit the topic in a very different way. Of course, you must always limit your general topic by making it appropriate to the intended length. If you are writing a 10,000 word paper, you can carve out a much bigger segment of the general topic than if you intend to write a 1,000 word paper. In either case you must be careful to establish the scope of your treatment somewhere near the beginning. In this way, you identify the specific topic first for yourself and later for your reader.

Limiting the Specific Topic

Limiting or establishing the scope of the specific topic is the way you identify for yourself—and later for the reader—the degree of detail in which you intend to work. You limit, narrow, and whittle the topic down so that it becomes first a specific topic; then you add a main idea which says something about this topic and so formulate a specific subject sentence. Here are the ways by which these things are done.

1. By using more specific nouns (telling what).
2. By using descriptive and/or modifying words (telling what more exactly).
3. By using time limitations (telling when).
4. By using space limitations (telling where).
5. By adding a main idea (telling exactly what you want to say and how to say it).

All of these need not be used at any one time, though they may be. But there must always be a specific noun and a main idea.

You narrow or limit the range of the general topic by using specific nouns or names. Instead of treating the arts in general, you may discuss music. Later you may limit this topic with a modifier to classical music. When you do so, you make it clear that you are not now concerned with rock music or country music or music in general.

Next, by using a time limitation, you can confine the topic to a narrow chronological range. For example, "Classical Music in the Second Half of the Seventeenth Century." When you do this to adapt the topic either to your purpose or to your readers, you are further limiting the scope of your preliminary thinking or the area in which you should do research in the library.

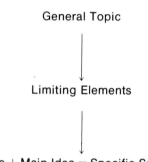

General Topic

Limiting Elements

Specific Topic + Main Idea = Specific Subject Sentence
(Particular)

By means of space limitation, you may further limit the topic to one geographical area. To adapt the general topic to your purpose and to the needed writer–reader relationship, you might limit it as follows: "Classical Music in the Second Half of the Seventeenth Century in Germany." Now the general subject is further limited in scope; it is even more appropriate to a given dominant general purpose and writer-reader relationship.

The Main Idea

The final and most important step in transforming a specific topic into a specific subject sentence is the addition of a main idea, the thing you want to say about the topic. This sentence expresses the actual specific subject of a piece of writing. Phrasing it before actually writing enables you to focus more precisely upon the idea which will guide you in selecting material. It will also help you to decide how to express it so that it will be appropriate to your purpose and to the desired writer-reader relationship. This specific subject sentence will let you identify for yourself the kinds of ideas and information you will need to develop the paper.

Now to continue with an example. To "Classical Music in the Second Half of the Seventeenth Century in Germany," let's add the main idea, "introduced new instrumental forms." All your prethinking from this point on should be concerned directly or indirectly with what is in this sentence. Everything in the composition will be related to elements in it: "Classical Music," "Second Half of the Seventeenth Century," and "in Germany"; but the main effort will be directed to thinking about and gathering information which will develop the main idea, "new instrumental forms." Actually, the whole composition will be focused on developing the key word "new" within that main idea.

The following illustration will help you to see the importance of formulating your specific subject and phrasing it in a specific subject sentence. Notice that the real target is the main idea: "is superior to foreign makes." *Be sure to notice the key word "superior," which is the heart of the main idea.*

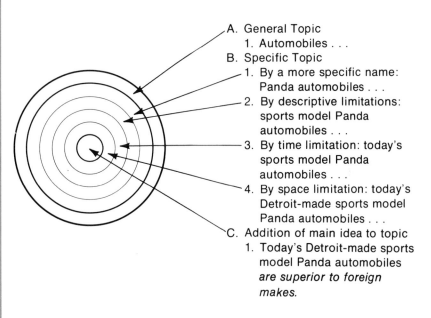

A. General Topic
  1. Automobiles . . .
B. Specific Topic
  1. By a more specific name: Panda automobiles . . .
  2. By descriptive limitations: sports model Panda automobiles . . .
  3. By time limitation: today's sports model Panda automobiles . . .
  4. By space limitation: today's Detroit-made sports model Panda automobiles . . .
C. Addition of main idea to topic
  1. Today's Detroit-made sports model Panda automobiles *are superior to foreign makes.*

You will probably not have much trouble selecting a general topic. It can be anything you want to write about, from photography to religion. But this is only the beginning of your responsibility. You must narrow its scope so that you can treat it in the space you have. To do this, you must pay special attention to limiting the specific topic and identifying the main idea. It is the main idea that will be the real beacon, enabling you to identify and gather the facts, inferences, and supporting ideas that you need to convey your message clearly — to accomplish a specific purpose with a specific type of reader. *The main idea is the essential subject of the composition.*

The chart on the facing page illustrates how the intended length of a written communication is predetermined by the manner in which the writer limits the topic.

"ONENESS" OF THE SPECIFIC SUBJECT

You know how irritating it is when your television set begins to roll or drift horizontally or vertically, introducing pictures related vaguely or not at all to the program you are watching. This is similar to the irritation a reader experiences with a composition for which the writer did not prethink and phrase his specific subject.

Drifting from the Specific Topic

A writer's ideas and the way they are expressed do not usually swerve away from the subject abruptly. They usually drift away a little at a time, and their growing irrelevance is hardly ever detected immediately by the writer, if it is detected at all. When a writer does not prethink the subject, there is no beacon or guide, and consequently the drift: one thought slightly off target suggests another a bit further off, and this suggests another still further off, and so on, until the gap in the relationship between the beginning and the end of the resulting composition is considerable.

Everything stated or implied in a piece of writing should be directly related to its specific subject. Here is an example of a composition in which the writer drifts from one topic to another and finally concludes by saying something which is scarcely related at all to the original topic.

A horn is a wind instrument which when blown gives off a musical note. To learn to play a horn, a person must spend many hours at practice. If he isn't determined to learn, he will more than likely give up after a few painful lessons. There are many different types of wind instruments; the trumpet, trombone, french horn, cornet, and the flute are just a few. The horn is popular in jazz. Harry James and Louis Armstrong played horns. I prefer wind instruments to the strings. The guitar, however, is a very popular string instrument today.

This paragraph is about horns, and the first sentence tells what a horn is. The second and third sentences are about learning how to play a horn. The fourth names different kinds of horns, and the fifth tells about the kind of music for which the horn is popular. The first part of the sixth talks about well-known band leaders who played horns, but the second part introduces the writer's preference for strings. By the last sentence, the writer has drifted away from horns altogether and is talking about the guitar, a different kind of instrument entirely. Did you notice how this drifting away from the topic took place gradually rather than abruptly?

Another example of drifting away from the topic follows. Even though all the ideas in this composition are related to the main idea, "were quite

Limiting the Topic

General topic, too broad	Specific topic for a long paper, limited by description or a more specific name (tells what)	More specific topic for shorter paper, by using space limitations (tells where)	More specific topic for still shorter paper, by using time limitation (tells when)	Main idea phrased in specific subject sentence
Dyes	Synthetic dyes	Synthetic dyes in the United States	Synthetic dyes in modern fabric manufacturing in the United States	In modern fabric manufacturing in the United States, synthetic dyes have replaced natural dyes.
Tornado	The violently destructive tornado Beulah	The violently destructive tornado Beulah severely damaged Chesterfield, Montana	The violently destructive tornado Beulah severely damaged Chesterfield, Montana, during the Civil War	The violently destructive tornado Beulah severely damaged Chesterfield, Montana, during the Civil War, causing a delay in a battle.
Pretzels	Baking crisp knotted pretzels	Baking crisp knotted pretzels in Germany	Baking crisp knotted pretzels in Germany during WW II	Baking crisp knotted pretzels in Germany during WW II was illegal.
Crime	Armed robbery	Armed robbery in Detroit	Armed robbery in Detroit during 1968	Armed robbery in Detroit during 1968 skyrocketed.

old-fashioned," they are not all related to the topic of the specific subject sentence, "fire stations." Notice how the ideas stray away from "fire stations." The second, third, and fourth sentences deal with "fire trucks." The fifth and sixth deal with the source of water with which to fight a fire, and the last is concerned with changes in the amount of knowledge about preventing fires.

Fire stations at the turn of the century were quite old-fashioned compared to those of today. Most often a fire would completely destroy a house before the fire truck could get there (it was pulled by horses). Today, it is only a matter of minutes before the fire truck arrives, usually saving the major part of the building. In the old days, the supply of water was limited to what could be carried on the fire truck. Now we have fire hydrants within feet of the fire truck, with a large supply of water. Also more has been learned about how to prevent fires.

Probably the easiest way to correct a composition which lacks unity or oneness because the supporting sentences do not all relate to the specific subject sentence is to separate it into more than one paragraph, perhaps with more material in it. If the ideas expressed in the sentences that are not related to the specific subject are important enough, they can be developed in separate paragraphs of their own. For example, the preceding passage could have been written as follows:

Fire stations at the turn of the century were primitive compared to those of modern times. The fire station and the equipment which it housed had not changed for at least fifty years even though the number of houses had multiplied to accommodate the thousands of immigrants.

Most often a fire would completely destroy a house before the fire wagon could get to the fire. The wagon was pulled by horses over unpaved streets, and after a heavy rain, it often did not arrive until long after the house had disappeared in flames. Today, it is only a matter of minutes before the fire truck arrives, usually in time to save a major part of the building.

In the old days, the supply of water was limited to what could be carried on the fire truck. Now, we have fire hydrants often within feet of the fire truck, with a large supply of water.

In addition to learning how to improve the equipment needed to fight fires, more has been learned about how to prevent fires.

Jim Smith

Remember, though, that too many short paragraphs can seem choppy and disjointed and in more formal kinds of writing can appear out of place.

**Maintaining the
Relationship to
the Main Idea**

It is important to remember that unity means a singleness of relationship to the whole specific subject sentence, that is not only to the specific topic but also to the main idea. A detail which is related to the topic but not to the main idea disrupts unity. In the following example, notice how most of the supporting sentences are hardly related to the main idea, "the best activity." The second, third, and fourth sentences explain the arrangements that were made for the trip. Sentence five summarizes the activities that took place. And sentence six refers to future vacations.

My trip to the beach this year was the best activity I did all year. I drove to the beach with some friends during our Spring vacation. We shared the cost of a cabin on the Pacific Ocean. And a friend of ours loaned us a boat for the occasion. We relaxed and played. I look forward to my next vacation.

Following is another paragraph which loses some of its impact because it does not maintain unity. Again the disruption is caused by the obscure connection between the ideas expressed in some of its supporting sentences and the main idea of the specific subject sentence.

My trip to Canada this year was great fun. My friends and I took my car, because it's the most comfortable. I'm the best driver. And my car has an 8-cylinder engine with some real pick-up. We were able to seat six in the car, and we even slept in the car some nights. Canada has some beautiful scenery.

There are two different ways of correcting the fragmented relationships in this paragraph. One way is to rewrite its beginning sentence so that it identifies all the main ideas which the paragraph is intended to develop: "fun in Canada" and "the size of my car." For example, the subject sentence might be written as follows: "This year some friends and I went to Canada in my car." Another way to correct it is to write two separate paragraphs, each with its own controlling sentence to identify and deal with these two main ideas separately. In that case, the present specific subject sentence might come at the beginning of the first paragraph or might be "understood" and not expressed at all.

This year some friends and I went to Canada in my car. The landscape was breathtaking as we traveled through the lush north with its forests and unspoiled greenery. We had a good time together and even got to play in some of the waterfalls along the way. At our own pace we were able to spend the month of August touring the beautiful country of Canada.

Unity will be discussed again in Chapter 15 with reference to sharpening vividness. At this point it is important to remember that the main aim of your prethinking is to clarify the predetermined elements—specific subject, writer-reader relationship, and dominant general purpose. On the first, you limit a general topic to a specific one, add a main idea, and express these elements in a specific subject sentence, which is your guiding beacon from this stage onward.

PRACTICE in Achieving This Chapter's Objectives

Practice in prethinking, and identifying the parts of the specific subject.

		Applications
1.	Limiting a general topic for length.	1, 3, 4
2.	Identifying the parts of a specific subject.	2
3.	Limiting a topic in time and place.	5
4.	Limiting a topic, and writing a composition.	6
5.	You Be the Judge	

APPLICATION 3-1

The following general topics are too broad for a 500-word composition. Narrow the scope of each so that you have a specific subject that is appropriate for a composition of that length. Be sure to limit the topic adequately and to add a worthwhile main idea.

1. children _____

_____

2. music _____

_____

3. careers _____

_____

4. hunger _____

_____

5. responsibility _____

_____

6. presents _____

_____

7. parents _____

_____

8. hobbies _____

_____

9. social reform _____

_____

10. entertainment _____

_____

APPLICATION 3-2

In the following list, print GT before each item that is a general topic, ST before each specific topic, SS before each specific subject. For specific subjects underline the main idea.

_____   1. Present St. Louis traffic laws should be strictly enforced.

_____   2. Drugs.

_____   3. Fried oysters.

_____   4. Women.

_____   5. The value of the dollar was high in 1929.

_____   6. Our trip to Mexico last summer.

_____   7. The writer was less than honest.

_____   8. Television programs.

_____   9. Our trip to Mexico last summer was enchanting.

_____   10. Timex watches.

APPLICATION 3-3

A. Narrow the scope of five of the following general topics by limiting each by means of a more specific name (noun) or descriptive word (adjective).

automobiles _____

fish _____

buildings _____

T.V. programs _____

soap _____

astrology _____

friends _____

freight cars _____

B. Now select three of these narrowed topics completed for the preceding exercise and limit each further by means of time or space limitations. _____

_____

_____

C. Make each of the three specific topics into a specific subject by adding a worthwhile main idea. _____

_____

_____

APPLICATION 3-4

Each one of the following sentences contains a specific subject that is either too broad or too narrow in scope for discussion *in depth* in a 500-word composition. There also are others which establish an appropriate scope. Mark B before those that are too broad, N before those that are too narrow, and A before those that are appropriate.

_____ 1. There is a vast variety of computers used for a multitude of purposes throughout the world.

_____ 2. Laser beams are being used in the treatment of cancer.

_____ 3. Over the years, the corporation sent many of its presidents on long trips around the world to visit its many plants and call upon friendly governments.

_____ 4. All but a few of the novels in our library are worth talking about.

_____ 5. Jujitsu is an ancient form of unarmed combat.

_____ 6. Automobile accessories are manufactured by different companies in many countries.

_____ 7. Food prices have been high from time to time throughout the world.

_____ 8. A ping-pong ball is circular.

_____ 9. Spain, France, and England each took different lengths of time in which to develop and establish its legislative and judicial branches of government.

_____ 10. There are many good books on the stacks of our local and national libraries, dealing with a great variety of topics.

APPLICATION 3-5

In the order in which the italicized elements occur in the following sentences, in each blank at the left write one of the letters from the list below that best identifies how each *italicized* element is related to establishing the scope of the subject. Be sure to put only one letter for each group of words. There should be as many answers for each sentence as there are blanks at the left.

A. time limitation
B. space limitation
C. topic (general or specific)
D. main idea

_____ _____ _____ _____ 1. *In the United States, during the past two years, the use of harmful drugs has increased among teen-agers.*

_____ _____ _____ _____ 2. *Dome style Victorian houses of the nineteenth century are challenging subjects for American artists.*

_____ _____ _____ _____ 3. *Rapid transit systems of the 1980's will be vital for Philadelphia commuters.*

_____ _____ _____ _____ 4. *Today's breeder and his dog must live up to certain standards to be allowed a showing in Madison Square Garden.*

_____ _____ _____ _____ 5. *Contemporary paper currency of the United States has seriously affected the world economy.*

APPLICATION 3-6

Following are several suggested general topics which you might use to write a composition. (You are not limited in your choice to these.) Establish the scope of one of them and write a 300 word composition of several paragraphs about it.

1. Comedians
2. Airplanes
3. Nightmares
4. Amusement parks
5. Skin diving
6. Pollution

Your instructor may decide to have your composition evaluated by another student, using the You Be the Judge evaluation form at the end of this chapter and the instructions inside the back cover of this book. Read these before you start writing, so that you will know what criteria the evaluator will use in grading your composition. If you have questions about grammar or mechanics while writing, refer to the Handbook of Correct and Effective Usage.

YOU BE THE JUDGE

Writer's Name _____

Date _____ Section _____

Title of paper _____

Chapter _____ Application No. _____

General Instructions on the You Be the Judge Applications, and specific instructions for Parts I and III, are printed inside the back cover of this book. Read those instructions carefully; then do Part I.

In the lines below, and on another sheet of paper, answer the questions in Part II, then enter a grade for the paper in the space above left, and write your evaluation for Part III. Reread the composition to see how well the writer understands and applies the principles studied in this chapter. As you read the composition write any helpful suggestions that occur to you in the margins.

PART II

1. Did the writer narrow the scope of the subject so that it is appropriate to the length of the composition? If it is too broad, how could it have been narrowed? _____

_____

_____

_____

_____

_____

_____

2. If it is too narrow, how could it have been made broader? _____

_____

_____

_____

_____

_____

3. Did the writer use limitations which weren't needed? Which? _____

_____

_____

_____

_____

_____

_____

4. Is the specific subject's main idea worth developing? Explain. _____

_____

_____

_____

_____

_____

_____

5. Did the writer develop the specific subject adequately? If not, explain.

_____

_____

_____

_____

_____

_____

6. Number each of the sentences in the student's composition. Under the headings below, place the numbers of the sentences which express ideas vaguely related to the specific topic or the specific subject and those which express ideas not related at all.

Vaguely related   Not related

_____   _____

_____   _____

_____   _____

7. Does the composition drift away from the specific topic or the specific subject? Explain _____

_____

_____

_____

_____

_____

_____

PART III   Grade and Explanation:

_____

_____

_____

_____

_____

CHAPTER 4

THE DOMINANT GENERAL PURPOSE

After studying this chapter and completing the applications that follow it, you should be able to do the following:
1. To prethink the appropriate dominant general purpose to achieve the intended reader response: *to entertain*, *to convey an impression*, *to inform*, *to persuade*, or *to actuate*.
2. To select and write details appropriate to the purpose (the reader response) intended: *sense*, *emotion*, *action*, *causes*, *reasons*, and *information*.
3. To maintain the purpose in a composition consistently.
4. To apply these principles in a full-length composition.

BEYOND limiting and stating the subject sentence, you have other responsibilities. You must also predetermine the manner in which you will write about the subject, in other words, the way you address your readers to achieve your objectives. The way or manner in which you will express your ideas is determined by the kind of response or reaction you want to arouse in the reader or type of reader being addressed. Therefore the second predetermined element is your *dominant general purpose*.

IDENTIFYING THE DOMINANT GENERAL PURPOSE

Every writer must identify and define the purpose before writing. Knowing your intended purpose and having it clearly in mind enables you to use it as a guide in thinking about the subject and in doing any library research required to gather needed information.

Everything we say, every sentence, implies a predetermined purpose. Even so simple a statement as "Have you got a match?" or "Please erase the blackboard" indicates that before making the request, the speaker decided what kind of response was wanted and worded the statement in a manner calculated to get the reaction sought. In both these statements, an action response is asked for. When one makes a statement such as "Democracy is a state of mind," a more subtle and complex response is elicited from a reader or listener, one which calls for intellectual or emotional agreement.

In every piece of writing the dominant general purpose is to arouse a specific response in the intended reader. There are five dominant general purposes, each of which arouses a different kind of response or reaction.

It is seldom that a writer has only one purpose in mind completely divorced from all others; hence the qualifying word *dominant*. Sometimes there are two or more purposes in combination, though one will stand out above the others.

**Dominant General
Purpose**

Dominant General Purposes	Reader Response
To entertain	To experience amusement, pleasure, satisfaction, excitement, fascination, and so forth.
To convey an impression	To experience imaginatively the writer's sense and emotional details so vividly and so intimately as to live the writer's experience vicariously.
To inform	To understand and accept information which is new or different, and to add it to his or her store of knowledge.
To persuade	To agree by abandoning conclusions or convictions and to replace them with those of the writer.
To actuate	To act physically or be willing to act as soon as possible.

Dominance is especially evident when the purpose is to persuade or to actuate. You cannot convince your readers without first informing them. You must show new relationships of information in order to change your readers' thinking. So you will be persuading and informing, and the relationship between these two purposes will be your most important guideline.

Also, when your dominant purpose is to actuate your readers, you must first inform them so that they can be convinced to take a certain action. When this is the purpose, the ideas and their arrangement are selected to induce readers to act as you recommend. The action you want your readers to take will be clearly stated or implied.

To Entertain

Writing need not be explicitly humorous in order to entertain. Accounts of mysterious crimes and gruesome murders entertain many people. Much of the content of the daily papers is intended to entertain. Gossip columns about famous people, profiles or character sketches, sports news, stories about crimes and sensational events of all kinds, along with amusing happenings, are gobbled up avidly by readers of newspapers and magazines. *To entertain, the writer tells about something which arouses the reader's senses and emotions in a way to please, amuse, or excite.*

The title and opening section of many compositions are designed to capture the interest of the reader (see Chapter 8). Often this is done by amusing or entertaining; the reader is induced to read because the writer promises enjoyment.

When your purpose is to entertain, you must be careful not to forget yourself and introduce complex issues; you must avoid technical terms; you must keep your desire to teach a moral lesson under control if it in any way defeats your purpose. In some kinds of writing, however, the real meaning of what the writer is saying is hidden. This is true in satire, which ridicules the frailties of human nature.

Below is a composition intended to entertain by satire. It uses irony, saying one thing but meaning the opposite, to ridicule human nature in a sarcastic tone.

"ABSOLUTE PARDON" GIVEN FACULTY ON OVERDUE BOOKS; NO CONDITIONS SET

Library Director Patrick Butler last night told a shocked campus that he was granting "full, free and absolute pardon" to all Schoolcraft faculty and staff for any overdue library books they have borrowed or may have borrowed since September 1, 1964. The historic pardon was granted, Butler said, because it was "merciful" and "good for business."

Butler is known to have consulted earlier in the day with God and other top advisors but the decision, he emphasized, was entirely his own.

"As head of the library I have learned," he said, "that the book stops here."

Over the years several hundred books have stopped permanently in staff members' homes and offices. It is these books that Butler hopes will be returned. "Books are the glue which holds the library together," he said, flying into metaphor, "and we are coming unglued."

Immediately following the startling announcement one instructor returned a book he had taken in 1969. "I can see now that I was mistaken," the instructor said. "I should have acted more decisively in returning this book. Many honest people may interpret my delay as selfishness. That is what hurts. I shall live with this knowledge all of my life. Or at least until I get a good dinner and a couple of drinks."

Following this statement the instructor borrowed the book again. "I never did get it finished," he explained.

The pardon, so sweeping and unexpected, was met with disapproval by students. Was there one law for the staff and another for the students? Would the Director's mercy extend to them as well? Butler reacted sharply to this question. "Are you trying to tell me," he asked, "that students have suffered enough?"

In the immortal words of Eliza Doolittle, not bloody likely!

J. F. terButler

The following is comedy, an easier kind of humor to write. It uses a mock-serious incident to entertain.

Mobile home living is a barrel of laughs if your family has a lot of friends who like to visit. Here is a typical Saturday night in our little mobile palace. John and Sandy arrived at about 8 P.M. Shortly after, while we were all vituperating about the abuses of landlords, Louise and Tom knocked at the door and came in. They were able to squeeze into our small, but cosy, living room. Not five minutes later, my brother, his wife, and their three children came, and we started to have a bit of a problem. Should we put the kids on the rafters or in the shower room, because my parakeet and pet dog occupied the little kitchen. My parakeet became excited at our trying to force one of the little ones into the kitchen, and it began screaming at us. This started the basset hound howling, making us all laugh for something better to do. At 10 P.M. our neighbor came over to see if we were having some kind of trouble. He quickly decided that we were and stayed to help us have more of it.

Ann Metzger

When writing to entertain, you don't worry about factual accuracy, reliable inferences, or dependable opinions. You are not accountable for the reliability of your information. You and your readers silently agree to accept what you express without holding you accountable. You can be as fantastic or preposterous as you choose as long as you entertain, for that's all you promise to do.

I really believe my husband thinks the two computers he works with are human. I suspect he is in love with one of them, Bertha, the big one. The other one, Sigmund, is much smaller than Bertha, and is the one that refuses to work properly, perhaps because he is jealous of my husband's attentions to Bertha. When my husband comes home late at night, he tells me he has had to take care of Sigmund. He mutters that this cantankerous little fellow has pouted by "zapping his flip-flops." Sometimes he wrings his hands and whimpers about Sigmund's drunken behavior after he has saturated his coils and thrown up his programs. When my husband works all night, he explains to me the next day that he was making sure that Sigmund felt right. But I often suspect he has been paying more attention to Bertha. The input I get from my neighbor Hortense about all this is to put my husband out. What do you think?

Victoria Shiekh

**To Convey
an Impression**

To convey an impression is to recreate a sense or emotional experience so vividly that readers will feel that they are actually experiencing it themselves. The most important thing to remember is to describe the sense and emotional details of the experience amply and vividly, so that readers

can see, hear, smell, and feel the details of the experience and imaginatively live the emotions that went with it.

From the preceding definition, it is easy to see that the quality of writing
needed to convey impressions comes close to the quality of fiction. The
same kind of vividness is often used in advertising copy, travel brochures,
and other kinds of descriptive nonfiction which enable readers to experience imaginatively whatever it is the writer wants to share with them,
whether it is skindiving in the Bahamas, playing the guitar, writing a poem,
or falling in love. The impression the writer wants to share may be an
intensely emotional one. It may be the experience of affection or devotion
to a friend or relative. It may be the experience of dying or being born
again.

When your purpose is to convey an impression, you will be less concerned with establishing facts than with expressing your own personal
interpretations and opinions. Notice how Louise Dickinson Rich, a professional writer, expresses them in the following passage. Also, notice
how the vividness of her details enables you to feel that you are almost
living the experience with her. To do this, she uses not only visual details
but also those appealing to the senses of sound, smell, taste, and touch.

Whenever I hear the words "summer place" a feeling of felicity flows
over me. I can't say that I think of certain things because what happens can hardly be called thought. It's more a matter of the senses
and the emotions than of the mind. It's rather as though I were riffling
the pages of a catalog of pleasure and catching quick glimpses of a
hundred delightful items. All mixed up together are long sea beaches,
white under a flawless sky, and dark, mirror-still mountain lakes, and
surf crashing on pink granite ledges. There's the scent of bayberry
and sweet fern and the taste of wild strawberries, and the softness of
a dusty country road under bare feet. There's the drumming of rain
on a cabin roof, and northern lights in midnight sky, and the breath-
less hush of high tide at noon in a tiny Down East harbor. Then there
are all the summer faces, brown and merry and friendly; and above
all a sense of tremendous well-being. In fact, my immediate uncon-
sidered definition of "summer place" would be a "sunny, lovely, outdoor place where it rains only at night, where there are no responsibilities and where people are always happy.[1]

Here is a student composition written to achieve the same purpose. Note
how vividly the sensory and emotional details describe the experience of
deep contentment.

Nothing on earth could have filled me with more contentment than
our camping trip last summer. I can still see my husband and myself

[1] *Woman's Day Magazine* and Collins-Knowlton-Wing, Inc. Copyright © 1967 by Fawcett
Publications, Inc.

lazily reclining on the soft, warm grass with the brilliant sun browning our bodies, the children leaping playfully through the grass chasing butterflies, and the baby sleeping peacefully and ever-so-soundly under gently rustling lilac bushes. In the distance, a group of boys, I remember, were excitedly enjoying a nature hike. Not far from the hikers, girls on swings reached for the sky with skirts flowing behind them. Nearby, an elderly couple held hands and dozed on a shaded bench. Emanating from a neighboring campsite, the aroma of fresh coffee and bacon, cooking outdoors, mesmerized us with tranquility, a deeply sensed feeling of contentment.

Andrea Hawker

To Inform

When your purpose as a writer is to inform, you aim at bringing about an intellectual change, enabling your readers to add new information to their store of knowledge, perhaps resulting in new insights and understanding. To do this, you present your information so that they can understand and accept it.

Unlike writing to entertain or to convey an impression, writing to inform implies that the writer will be held accountable for the reliability of the information. Therefore you must rely heavily on what you regard as verifiable facts, reasonable inferences, and reliable opinions. You must continually check the reliability of your information and the qualifications of your sources.

No one will deny that it is easier for a reader to grasp and retain information which is interesting in itself or which is presented in a dramatic, colorful, interesting manner. When writing to doctors about medicine, you can safely presume that the subject matter itself will interest them. But when you write to doctors about internal combustion engines, you may have to write in a more lively way in order to get and hold their interest. Obviously the ability of the writer to judge how much the readers already know about the specific subject will help determine the kinds of ideas which will interest those readers.

To keep your readers interested in a subject with which they are not familiar, you may add color by comparing technical terms with things they are familiar. You may also avoid going too deep. If treatment in depth will be boring or confusing, you may merely skim the surface.

The following was written to inform. Read it and notice the facts you may not have known before. Notice the proportion of verifiable facts to reasonable inferences and reliable opinions. Also, notice how the writer controls personal feelings to avoid exaggeration and keep the information accurate.

In the American colonies the attitude toward sports varied a good deal from Virginia to Massachusetts. In the former, the Anglicans were more liberal in their outlook, and the more lenient southern climate fostered recreational activities. There were five horse-racing tracks in seventeenth century Virginia. Only two years after the founding of the colony, in 1609, a ruthless form of football was played. In Massachusetts, on the other hand, in addition to the colder climate, the Puritanical attitude toward life produced an atmosphere of all work and no play.

Carol Harkey

The following composition, also intended to inform, presents reliable information in a way the general reader can understand. It is not intended for the expert because it explains principles the expert would already know.

Distillation is one of the oldest ways of separating fresh water from a salt-water solution. When salt water is boiled, the dissolved salt remains behind as the fresh water vapor is boiled away. In a distillation process, water is first boiled and then the steam, or water vapor, is cooled. This cooling condenses the steam into water again. Thus, distillation involves adding heat energy to salt water in order to vaporize the water, and then removing the heat energy from the steam to condense it into fresh water.

When water is heated, its temperature increases until the boiling point is reached. While water is boiling, the steam and the boiling water are at the same temperature. However, raising water to its boiling point is not enough to cause it to boil. More heat must be added to change the water into steam. The amount of heat required to change water which is at the boiling point into steam at the same temperature is called heat of vaporization of water. The heat of vaporization is of major importance in distillation. The amount of heat required to vaporize water into steam is approximately five times greater than the heat needed to raise water from its freezing point to its boiling point.

Earl Leister

TO PERSUADE

To persuade is to urge a reader to abandon existing beliefs and accept those the writer is advocating. When you and your readers are on the same side of an issue, you may inform them by giving them more information or more reasons why they should retain their convictions. Persuasion can occur only when two people hold different positions, and one sees an advantage in trying to change the other's views.

To change readers' thinking, you may appeal to them by means of logical reasons, or a combination of logical reasons and emotional persuasion, or by inducing them to analyze something critically to make a value judgement about it.

A writer may argue the issue of giving sixteen-year-olds the right to vote by offering only logical reasons, by a combination of logical reasons and emotional appeal, or by contending that it is good or bad for sixteen-year-olds to vote based on certain specified standards. Therefore, when you want to convince, you must first know your reader. You can then decide what kinds of arguments you need and how they have to be organized to achieve your purpose.

Here is an argument against rushing ahead with nuclear power plants, aimed at those who are concerned about power shortages. To convince readers that we should "go slow" with nuclear power, the writer uses qualified sources, though the evidence in proof is not so strong as it might be.

The slowdown in orders and construction of nuclear power is probably the best thing that could happen to both the energy industry and the nation. We should proceed much more slowly for safety reasons before we accelerate our speed in the construction of nuclear power plants. We should get much more experience, and what is now on order is enough to give us that experience. We should not rush ahead without being as certain as possible about what we forsee.

Rushing to build and operate atomic plants may lead to inadequate quality assurance programs, including inspection and testing. "We rushed into space programs and incinerated three astronauts," says Phillip Sporn, former head of the American Electric Power Co. "Let's get our experience and have our accidents now, before we take more chances with more plants," he says. The fossil-fuel electrical plants still have accidents after eighty-six years of operation, and we are going to have some in atomic energy.

This "go slow" attitude is not a pessimistic one. On the contrary, it is merely a cautious one. The United States Bureau of Public Utilities predicts that 95 percent of the nation's electricity will be generated by the year 2065. But before this happens, the utility companies must get enough nuclear experience.

Jane Fiore

In the next passage the writer appeals to his readers' emotions as well as to their minds. We can detect this emotional appeal in the emphasis on the obvious: "The car doesn't get the driver drunk" and "a car can kill as surely as a gun" — both appeals more emotional than logical. The writer also has logical reasons:

Manufacturing a safe automobile is industry's concern; safe driving is everyone's business. An automobile company can completely pad the inside of a car and produce a car safer than a piece of overstuffed furniture. However, all this is useless until the driver learns that the driver is the cause of 99 percent of the automobile accidents. The car doesn't get the driver drunk and cause itself to weave all over the road. The automobile doesn't speed or run through stop signs and red lights by itself. Part of the blame rests on our ineffective laws and understaffed police force. But the major problem is to teach drivers that a car can kill as surely as a gun. Until a driver learns to respect the maiming and killing possibilities of a car and uses it strictly for transportation, no car is safe.

Gerald Kirk

There are many issues on which people are strongly emotional. These issues, which include political, labor, social, and religious beliefs, must, in many instances, be approached by emotional as well as logical appeals. It would be very difficult to convince readers to discard their cherished convictions because of logical argument alone. For this type of situation, persuasion (through a blend of emotion and reason) is most effective.

The main objective of persuasion is to promote agreement. It is not necessarily intended to arouse readers to do anything specific, only to believe. Often they don't have the skill or authority to do what they are persuaded should be done. For example, to persuade them that a war between two nations should be stopped requires only that they agree. It is hardly practical to expect them to stop the war; they have neither the power nor the authority to do that.

To Actuate

When the writer's purpose is to actuate, the communication is designed so that it arouses readers to go one step beyond persuasion and take positive action. Therefore, actuation is unlike the other purposes. Although writing to actuate is used to urge readers to do something— vote for a candidate or buy a product—it is used almost as often to direct them not to do something. Much of our greatest written expression has been penned to actuate millions of people living at the time of the writing and millions more to come. These written communications include the laws and constitutions of many countries and the great books of all religions, including the Bible, the Koran, the Vedas, and the wisdom of Confucius. *To actuate is to urge someone to perform or refrain from an action within that person's capabilities.*

Before you decide to move your reader to action, you should discover whether your readers will be able to take the desired action. If they are not capable, you should select another purpose, such as to inform or persuade. For example, readers under eighteen do not have the power to vote for a candidate or to raise a sunken ship from the bottom of the Atlantic. You must be governed by these limitations. You will be wise to redirect your message and actuate your readers to do something within their power and capabilities—to work for a candidate, or to write letters to their Congressmen urging that the sunken ship be raised.

As a dominant general purpose, the wish to actuate differs from the wish to inform or to convince, though it includes these as subordinate purposes. To actuate your readers, you must first inform them so that they can understand why they should take action. You thus convince them to accept the conclusions offered and, as a result, to act as you recommend.

It is one thing to convince your readers that you are right, but it is quite a different thing to get them to do something about it. Two techniques which play an important role in written communication to actuate are visualization and intimate relationship.

Visualization

A device which enables you to use the reward and punishment technique effectively is *visualization*. Through this device you make your readers see themselves satisfying their needs and desires or fulfilling their hopes and dreams. You stimulate your readers to create visions of themselves and their relatives and friends enjoying the possessions, position, fame, fortune, and other benefits which their devotion to duty, cleverness, skill, wealth, or power enables them to acquire. Sometimes the other side of the picture is even more effective, and you cause your readers to imagine the misfortunes which can befall them—poverty, disgrace, illness, injury, or death—if a particular action is not taken. Actuating is often used for worthwhile causes, to induce people to donate blood, to pledge financial support for charities, to support colleges, hospitals, churches, and so on. These devices are also used in all types of selling and advertising.

The following paragraph offers the readers rewards in order to actuate them. These are made vivid by enabling readers to see themselves enjoying them. The "punishment" they will incur if they do not follow the writer's recommendations is also clear: "the roar of the city," "sickening exhaust fumes," and "the killing pace." Physical comfort and survival— what better motivation for action can there be?

Leave the shadows of the city for the sunshine of the open land. Imagine yourself and your friends breathing the clean, fresh air and enjoying the benefits that only rural life provides. Make it possible for them to hear the sounds of nature in the morning instead of the roar of the city. Be like the early American pioneers who ventured courageously out into the unpopulated regions of this great nation. Give free reign to the urge to return to the joys of country living. In the country, you and your friends will be away from the sickening exhaust fumes of automobiles and the killing pace of the city. Let yourself derive strength, health, and vigor from a life close to the earth, close to nature. Move to the country.

Bill Metzger

**Establishing an
Intimate Relationship**

Often the only way to persuade readers to do something is by *establishing an intimate relationship* with them. By doing this, you let them know that you are on their side and want them to do something for their own good. You can do this by talking to your readers directly, by addressing them in the second person. You can also use "their own language." Notice the intimate conversational language in the following.

So you say you're bored with school. It's become a complete drag and you just can't take it anymore. Don't sit around and complain. Quit! Get out! Go out and have fun! There's nothing like a lazy summer afternoon in which you pitch pennies in front of the unemployment office. Or just think of the prestige you will enjoy as you walk down to pick up your unemployment check so that you can later wave it in front of the kids at the pizza parlor. So what if you blow the whole check; you'll get a check next month. What if there's nothing for you to do while your pals are slaving away over the books in school; you can always relax in front of a boob tube watching the soap operas until your friends get out. You must realize, of course, that even this perfect life out of school has its little nuisances which will last a lifetime.

Helen Kirk

When your purpose is to actuate, it is not always necessary to state explicitly the precise action which your readers are urged to perform. Often it need only be implied.

As we pointed out earlier, after you have determined your purpose, you will know why you are writing. You will then be better able to search for, think about, and select the facts, ideas, and words in which to express them, as well as the best order and organization.

**MAINTAINING THE
DOMINANT
GENERAL PURPOSE**

Sometimes a writer starts with one dominant general purpose but ends up causing the readers to respond in a different way from the one intended. You might, for example, start out to inform your readers, but your words, ideas, or manner might entertain instead and give them no important or valuable information.

In the following passage, the writer apparently doesn't really know what he intends to do. Consequently he starts out with a purpose sentence ("Parents . . . should enroll their children in self-defense courses") which indicates that he intends to actuate. But the remainder of the composition does not actuate; it merely informs. As a matter of fact, it ends up telling why the reader *should not* do what the writer started out telling him he *should* do!

Parents concerned by the crime rate in areas through which their children must pass to and from school should enroll them in self-defense courses. Most self-defense schools in Detroit teach children either judo or "self-defense," a combination of judo and other Japanese techniques for protecting oneself. In a judo class, the child learns only judo, but in a self-defense class, he learns a combination of techniques which the instructor favors. There are arguments in favor of both courses. Some people prefer self-defense classes because they believe that judo alone is too formal. Those who prefer judo say that the child in a combination technique course does not learn anything well enough to use it effectively. Self-defense training of any kind will not prepare for defense against weapon-wielding assailants. According to the Detroit Police Department, the best defense for a child is his voice and his legs, in other words, his ability to scream and to run away from danger. Therefore, why should a child take either judo or self-defense courses?

You must not only know your purpose yourself, but you must also make it clear to the readers by implication or direct statement, usually in an opening sentence. Here is a paragraph which illustrates the kind of writing which results when this is not done:

My dog is quite small because he is a cross between a dachshund and a beagle. The strangest things amuse him, such as stocking feet, leaves blowing up and down the driveway, and, most of all, rubber bands. Rubber bands amuse him because they are flexible enough to strike back at him; he thinks that they are alive. He is gold in color and has short legs, a long tail, and a chubby body, big ears, a short snout, and big brown eyes.

The following is better because the writer clearly implies the purpose. This purpose, to convey an impression, is made clear by the key phrases, "looks odd" and "behaves strangely." These phrases also convey the main impression.

My dog not only looks odd but also behaves strangely. Because he is a cross between a dachshund and a beagle, he perplexes everyone other than members of his family. He is gold in color and has short legs, a long tail, a chubby body, big ears, a short snout, and big brown eyes. The strangest things amuse him, such as stocking feet, leaves blowing up and down the driveway, and most of all, rubber bands. Rubber bands amuse him because they are flexible enough to strike back at him; he thinks they are alive. His strange appearance and antics enable him to get along well with the others of his family; that is, with my mother, father, and me.

PRACTICE in Achieving This Chapter's Objectives

Practice in prethinking and writing the appropriate dominant general purpose.

		Applications
1.	Identifying the dominant general purpose.	1, 2, 4
2.	Finding the kind of details needed to arouse the appropriate reader response.	3
3.	Detecting and correcting development inadequate or inappropriate for the intended purpose.	5, 6
4.	Writing a composition with a predetermined purpose, containing appropriate details and adequate development.	7
5.	You Be the Judge	

APPLICATION 4-1

In the blank after each of the following sentences, write the name of the dominant general purpose which the sentence suggests.

1. John Wilkes Booth shot Lincoln during a performance at the Ford Theater. _____

2. Don't give your children dangerous toys. _____

3. Grandma was a kindhearted borrower. _____

4. Children must be punished when rebellious toward authority. _____

5. The criminal was tried and convicted. _____

6. The manufacture and sale of medicine is one of the most important industries in the world. _____

7. In 1901, dust particles from a storm in Algeria were carried by a cyclone as far north as Denmark. _____

8. Are you thin enough to ride between the humps on a camel? _____

APPLICATION 4-2

Select a favorite magazine or periodical and read five articles (not short stories). As you read each one try to determine its dominant general purpose and list the characteristics of the article which indicate which of the five purposes the writer was attempting to achieve. Find one article for each of the five dominant general purposes, and attach them to your explanation of the purpose of each.

APPLICATION 4-3

The paragraph below is an anemic paragraph, with skimpy details that are not adequate for the purpose of conveying an impression. Rewrite it below, adding all the details necessary so that it does convey the impression intended.

It was a clear morning, so the children decided to walk toward the fishing harbor at the end of the bay. As they sat on the edge of the dock, they could see a small fishing boat coming into the harbor. Several gulls flew around the fisherman's catch. As the children sat and watched, they dreamed of the day when they too would have their own boats.

_____

_____

_____

_____

_____

_____

APPLICATION 4-4

Carefully read the following passages. In the blank accompanying each passage write the dominant general purpose which each is intended to achieve. Underline those words and ideas which indicate the purpose.

1. While unpacking my gear, I cannot help but admire the symmetry of the arrows lying neatly in their carrying cases: the slimness of the shaft tapering down to the geometric precision of the fletchings. The bow is graceful with its curves from one end to the other. The smoothly flexing limbs testify to the skill of the hands. Slowly, I draw the string back full to my anchor point. With a precisely controlled release, the arrow is sent winging swiftly on its way, coming to rest instantly with a decisive swish, full in the center of the target's bull's-eye.   _____

2. Although archery may not be as strenous as football or soccer, it is a sport which is wholesome not only for the body but for the important human spirit as well. Like other sports, archery will give a person a wholesome exercise. It is moderate, and consequently, suitable for many people who have reached an age when excessive physical strain may be dangerous. Drawing the bow repeatedly and walking from the firing line to the target to retrieve your arrows furnishes exercise which is not too strenuous for people of all age groups. The repeated acts of drawing and firing, trying each time to improve your shots, has the effect of relieving mental tensions. Therefore, archery is good for the nerves as well as for the muscles. As you improve your skill, the satisfaction from steadiness of hand, clearness of vision, and tranquility of thought will become manifested in the confidence of your stride and the decisiveness of your action.   _____

3. Jujitsu is an oriental sport dominated by the silence and the self-restraint of the Eastern mind. The *judoka,* the two contestants, quietly move over the 3′ x 6′ mat in the *dogo,* the small, square, simply-furnished room in which judo is practiced. The two silently watch each other's movements; suddenly, a grunt-like sound is emitted, indicating an aggressive attempt by one of the contestants against the other. Then silence prevails again as the two continue their cautious, stealthy, feline movements, each waiting for the precise opportunity to effect the decisive stroke which will make one of them slap the adversary's body against the mat. The spectators seated around the floor make no sounds, and the black-belted instructor sternly sits watching carefully the skill of the students. It is this instructor who imposes the awesome atmosphere of oriental self-restraint which pervades the room as though the content were a deeply religious ritual.   _____

4. Jujitsu is an ancient sport which has risen to the eminence of becoming one of the Olympic games. This ancient form of sport originated in Japan among the Samurai warriors and was then called *jiujitsu*. In 1882, Dr. Jigoro Kano, the father of modern jujitsu, after making a thorough study of the ancient sport, compiled a book setting forth the rules and the best techniques for practicing judo. The popularity of the sport, consequently, spread throughout the world. Today, it is one of the sports which are included in the annual Olympic games.

$\rule{2in}{0.4pt}$

APPLICATION 4-5

The following paragraph is typical of the writing which results when a writer does not predetermine his dominant general purpose. It contains details related to two different purposes. On the lines below the paragraph, first identify each purpose; then, write the sentences which are related to each under it. Doing this will give you two separate paragraphs. Draw a line through sentences which are not related to either of the main ideas.

I find it hard to believe that a car was ever invented. It is a useful and valuable invention. An automobile is more than merely a form of transportation. It is the force that keeps things going in our complex world. Without cars people would be late for work each day. People often have pet names for cars. If a car is old and undependable, Old Baxter and Old Red are likely names. If it is sporty or fast, perhaps Dynamite or Whiz would be appropriate. The reason cars can be named is their distinctive personalities. Each acts and performs differently. A car must be treated with respect, otherwise it may become stubborn and uncooperative. Some cars have bigger appetites for gas and oil than others.

Purpose _____

_____

_____

_____

_____

_____

Purpose _____

_____

_____

_____

_____

APPLICATION 4-6

The following passage is intended to inform the reader in a somewhat informal manner; however, some details in it are not related to the intended purpose. On the lines below, write the sentence(s) that contain unrelated details and identify the purpose for which they are more suitable.

If you enjoy traveling, trailers are a necessity. In the beginning there was the tent for the traveler, but the tent was too much bother, hence, the trailer. Trailers enable the tourist to travel in comfort. Their owners are not required to pay property taxes. From the first, they rapidly multiplied to serve as bottlenecks on the highways. Trailers are a blessing for people who cannot afford to pay restaurant and hotel prices for food and lodging while traveling.

_____

_____

_____

_____

_____

_____

APPLICATION 4-7

Select any topic and write a composition of several paragraphs, at least 300 words. Establish your dominant general purpose and write your composition so that it will elicit the response you intend from your reader. Be sure to indicate your purpose above the title of your composition.

   Your instructor may decide to have another student judge your composition, using the You Be the Judge evaluation form which follows, and the instructions inside the back cover of this book. Read these before you start writing this assignment so that you will know what criteria the evaluator will use in grading it. Here are two possible ideas for a composition.

1. A composition intended to entertain or to convey an impression about *windows:* department store windows, windows of a deserted house, stained glass windows, dirty windows, windows of a bar or a nightclub, school windows, and so forth.
2. Select a specific subject about which you know there is much controversy, especially one about which you feel concerned (drafting women into the army, capital punishment, and so forth) and write a composition intended to convince.

   If you have questions about grammar or other mechanics while writing, refer to the Handbook of Correct and Effective Usage.

YOU BE
THE JUDGE

Writer's name _____

Date _____ Section _____

Title of paper _____

Chapter _____ Application No. _____

General instructions on the You Be the Judge Applications, and specific instructions for Parts I and III, are printed inside the back cover of this book. Read those instructions carefully; then do Part I.

In the lines below, and on another sheet of paper, answer the questions in Part II. Then enter a grade for the paper in the space above left, and write your evaluation for Part III. Reread the composition to see how well the writer understands and applies the principles studied in this chapter. As you read the composition write any helpful suggestions that occur to you in the margins.

PART II

1. What was the writer's dominant general purpose? _____

2. How well does the first sentence imply this purpose? Explain. _____

   _____

   _____

3. Name the principal characteristic of the details which the writer uses to carry out this purpose (for example, humorous, sensuous, factual, and so forth). _____

   _____

   _____

4. Is there anything in the composition which seems to you not related to the purpose? _____

   _____

   _____

5. Is the main conclusion of the paper questionable, or does the author prepare the reader to accept it? How is this achieved? _____

   _____

   _____

   _____

_____

_____

_____

6. Does the writer need to cite qualified sources? If so, has it been done satisfactorily? _____

_____

_____

_____

_____

_____

PART III   Grade and Explanation:

_____

_____

_____

_____

_____

CHAPTER 5

THE WRITER-READER RELATIONSHIP

After studying this chapter and completing the applications that follow it, you should be able to do the following:
1. To prethink the *writer-reader relationship.*
2. To prethink how to establish reader contact: by appealing to basic needs and desires, and through the reader's background.
3. To select and maintain appropriate viewpoints: *psychological, spatial,* and *chronological.*
4. To apply these principles in a full-length composition.

ONCE you have decided whether you want to entertain, convey an impression, inform, persuade, or actuate, you are ready to think about the third major predetermined element: your relationship with your reader. Communication is a two-way street, and the writer's attitude and approach strongly influences the reader's receptiveness to the message. When you manage to establish a mood of friendliness, trust, and interest, your reader is likely to respond favorably. There is nothing like common ground to facilitate communication.

KNOWING THE READER

Knowledge of the reader, or the kind of reader, is as important as knowledge of the subject. Your reader should be as strong an influence on what to include and omit as you are yourself. For in a successful communication, every detail of content and expression will relate to the reader's needs, interests, and desires.

A writer establishes contact by discussing something the reader is already interested in or can be made interested in. You must therefore know as much as possible about human nature in general and your chosen reader in particular.

Human Needs

All human beings have basic needs and desires which are necessary to their physical comfort and survival. They also have other needs and desires which become more complex as their lives become more sophisticated. Following are the basic human needs through which you as a writer can establish contact. In using these to arouse interest, you must be aware that they vary in degree at various times in life.

Basic human needs and desires:

1. Biological needs and desires. Related to physical survival and comfort: clothing, food, shelter. Of course, quantities and qualities vary with the background and status of readers and may include comforts and lux-

uries. Anything the writer may say which promises to help satisfy these needs and desires will arouse interest.
2. Psychological needs and desires. Related to the self-concept. The reader's self-image is the person he imagines himself to be or wants to believe he is. Anything that maintains, defends, or improves the self-concept will be of interest.
3. Sociological needs and desires. Related to the needs and desires to have others accept and respect the self-concept, the social acceptance, of the persons we want to be or think we are. Anything to satisfy the need for recognition and acceptance by others will induce reading.

Following are some topics which may arouse a reader's interest because they promise to help him satisfy these basic needs and desires.

1. Biological
   a. Ways to a longer life.
   b. How to survive a nuclear war.
   c. Death on the highway: riding the left lane.
   d. New wrinkle-proof fabrics.
   e. Spraying the vegetables in your garden with poisons.
2. Psychological
   a. A miracle—your mind.
   b. You have talent; why hide it?
   c. Your mind does wonders; make the most of it.
   d. You: a unique personality.
   e. How to become the person you want to be.
3. Sociological
   a. Showing others the magic of your personality.
   b. Being a leader, not a tyrant.
   c. Everyone loves the life of the party.
   d. Conversing comfortably: the essence of charm.
   e. Satisfying the urge for togetherness.

**The Reader's
Background**

In addition to general knowledge of human nature, the writer should learn as much as possible about a particular reader or class of readers. By knowing your readers' background, interests, ability, and attitudes, you are better able to determine what they want and need, what interests and what bores them; what type of humor they will enjoy, with what kinds of experiences they have sympathy, and what kinds of information they lack. Knowing your readers are chemists, for example, tells you that an extensive discussion of an obvious minor point in chemistry with which they are thoroughly familiar would bore them.

Following are some types of information a writer should have about the background of the reader. *All the things listed below need not be known; but having any such information related to a particular composition will help you in deciding not only what to include but what to leave out.*

1. Affiliations. Membership in political, social, labor, religious, academic, and other organizations gives a hint as to what causes and movements may be supported or opposed. It may also suggest to the writer how to phrase some necessary thoughts.
2. Age. Interests vary with age. A composition about the latest dance step may interest the young, but not retirees.
3. Economic status. Economic position influences the ideas one may be interested in. Money, property, and other forms of wealth should help the writer decide what to include and what to leave out.
4. Education. A wise writer addresses the reader in a manner appropriate to the reader's educational level. You would write about international affairs, for example, in one way to a reader with little knowledge in this field, and in quite another way to a graduate student in history.
5. Occupational training and experience. The way people earn their livings is a key to many of their interests and concerns, and to how much they know about a given subject. A restaurant operator would be interested in reading about how to operate a business more efficiently or more profitably. Having such knowledge about your reader will enable you to decide how to deal with any subject.
6. Personal interests. Hobbies and other avocations (hunting, fishing, horseback riding, raising dogs, and so forth) are constantly popular, and there are many articles directed to these interests.
7. Sex. Males often have some interests which are different from those of females, but most of these distinctions are old-fashioned and are breaking down rapidly.

The following definition of an internal combustion engine is written so that it can be easily understood by readers who seldom if ever lift the hood of an automobile to see what goes on beneath it. Notice especially how the writer here relates the explanations to experiences which even a person with no technical knowledge would encounter in daily life; this is obvious from the terms as well as from the comparisons and analogies used because they are related to things with which most people are familiar.

An internal combustion engine produces power by burning fuel within a tightly closed cylinder. The carburetor of the engine performs the important twofold job of vaporizing the air and fuel and of combining them into a highly explosive mixture of about fifteen pounds of air to one pound of vaporized gasoline. By doing this, the carburetor functions much like an atomizer or an aerosol can often used around the house.

The ignition system of the internal combustion engine ignites the vapor produced by the carburetor. Because this vapor is mixed and compressed into a highly combustible spray, it is as easily ignited as the natural gas used in a kitchen gas range. To cause the explosion in the internal combustion engine, the vapor flows into the combustion chamber. Then a spark plug, which has two separated wires extending from it into the chamber, emits an electrical spark which jumps from one of these wires to the other. The ignition spark is activated by an electrical current conducted from the storage battery to the spark plug by means of wires. This spark, like a match, causes an explosion within the chamber. We can also compare this operation with that of a cigarette lighter which uses a mixture of air and lighter fluid. The spark which ignites the lighter is caused by the friction of an abrasive wheel turned against a piece of flint.

From this point, harnessing the power from the combustion chamber of the internal combustion engine to the axle of the automobile to move it forward and backward is done by a series of connected gears and shafts called the transmission. This process is not unlike the operation of the old foot-treadle sewing machine. When the seamstress rocks her foot forward and backward, the power is transferred by means of gears and shafts to the head of the machine, causing the needle to move up and down to do the stitching.

Fred Dagle

THE WRITER'S ATTITUDE

It is not enough for the writer to establish contact with the readers by choice of subject and to arouse their interests and their willingness to interact with the written word. You as a writer must maintain that willingness to read. Knowing in advance—prethinking the attitude you must take toward your subject and toward your readers—will help you to predetermine how you should express your ideas about the specific subject. *The writer's attitude is the mental posture or stance with which and from which he or she chooses to regard the subject and the readers to achieve a purpose.* To maintain the appropriate attitude for the required relationship, you must predetermine your point of view and tone.

Point of View

Point of view is the way the writer decides to look at the subject in order to achieve the necessary relationship with the reader for the desired purpose and main idea. The three points of view important for a writer to think out and maintain are psychological, spatial, and chronological.

Psychological Point of View

A puppy observed from the point of view of a biologist is a complex of organs and tissues making up a complicated living organism. From the point of view of a physicist, the same creature is a mass of particles of matter, arranged in an elaborate pattern of forces and motions. From the point of view of a small child, the puppy is a warm and affectionate playmate. You may write about the same puppy from the point of view of any of these people or from many others. So before you can decide which ideas are appropriate for a specific communication, you must decide from which psychological viewpoint you will regard the subject.

The psychological point of view is the intellectual and emotional frame through which the writer chooses to regard something related to the subject. There are three psychological points of view: the objective, the semi-objective, and the subjective.

The objective point of view is a realistic one in which the writer tries to see the subject as it is. In such academic assignments as research papers and technical reports as well as in many other kinds of informative material, you try to be objective. When you are objective, the way you look at the subject and the accuracy of what you say are more important than your feelings. You are searching for factual, reliable information; therefore, you try to restrain any emotions that might detract from your objectivity. Although it is almost impossible to keep all emotion out of writing, the objective writer allows only that kind of feeling which increases the impartiality or disinterestedness of the observations. You want the readers to realize that you are not being influenced by your biases and are discussing your subject objectively. In a sense, you are giving your readers a precise black and white photographic print of the subject. You do this because your purpose and main idea require it.

The subjective point of view is the attitude of the writer who wants the color of emotions to dominate what is said. In a sense, subjective writing produces a color print rather than a black and white print of the subject. When the writer consciously takes the subjective attitude, the intent is to allow opinions, biases, and personal beliefs to influence ideas.

A composition written from an objective point of view will contain different ingredients than one written from a subjective point of view. Objective writing will mainly consist of what you regard as fact, reasonable inferences, and reliable opinions (see Chapter 1). If you express a personal opinion, you will so indicate by direct statement or by implication. Subjective writing will be dominated by personal judgments. It will record not the actual, verifiable characteristics of the subject, so much as your reactions to it. It will contain mainly your emotional and sense reactions to the subject, rather than a realistic factually reliable account of it.

The objective and the subjective points of view in writing can be compared to a photograph contrasted with a portrait. Because of the nature of the camera, the photographer usually gets a much more objective view of the subject than the painter. The photographer has some control over the quality of the picture, but cannot change the appearance of the subject drastically. In portrait painting, the artist has complete freedom to paint the physical features of the subject so that they reflect the painter's interpretation of them. Interpreting the dominant characteristic to be strength, the painter will portray the cheeks, jaw, lips, and eyes in a way which conveys strength or show a hand resting firmly on the back of a chair, giving his subject a confident posture and stance. Unlike the more realistic picture of the photographer, the painter's portrait may show qualities which the subject lacks and ignore or play down real ones.

Following are two paragraphs on the same topic. Because the writers determined beforehand their points of view, the results are different in several ways. Can you tell which is objective and which is subjective (and why)?

OUR JENNY

Jenny is adorable. Her baby blue eyes can express love and pleasure better than mere words could ever do. When they cloud up with frustration or anger, only one crocodile tear lies on her cheek, like a dewdrop on a fresh peach. There are four dimples across the tops of the knuckles on each wee pudgy hand, and her artistic fingers can curl around your heartstrings as easily as they clutch a toy. Her hair is as fine as cobwebs and almost as wispy. Ribbons and finger-formed curls alike fall out of it as fast as they can be placed there. Two partially developed, very white, very sharp little teeth give her an appealing pixie-like grin. The soft sweet nape of her neck is the best possible place to implant a kiss of endearment.

Laura E. Smith

JENNIFER LYNN

My elder daughter, Starr, gave birth to our first grandchild on November 12, 1966, in Toledo, Ohio. The child was a nine pound girl whom they named Jennifer Lynn. She has blue eyes, fine straight hair, and two teeth. At the present time, she has progressed past the creeping state and is standing alone, preparing to take her first steps.

Laura E. Smith

The semi-objective point of view is a blend of the objective and the subjective. It is often used when the writer needs to inform or to argue about something in a somewhat informal manner. You use this viewpoint when you want to add color, emotion, casualness, or warmth to the relationship with your readers. It makes information pleasanter and often easier to absorb. It can use vivid illustrations and comparisons to make facts interesting and digestible for the readers.

You will often take a semi-objective attitude toward a subject when you recognize that the writer-reader relationship is as important as the information you intend to express. You intentionally set your mind to regard the subject semi-objectively, sometimes because you know the readers require some extra spice to keep them reading. This point of view is often used in writing not addressed to experts in a field but to readers with no compelling interest who want to be interested as well as informed. The semi-objective point of view is probably the one most commonly used. It is common in newspapers, magazines, and many other printed mass media.

Here are three brief compositions on the same subject, each written from a different psychological point of view. Notice how the amount of emotion varies and, consequently, how the accuracy of each is affected.

Objective

Disposable income is the portion of personal income which remains after the payment of personal taxes. This income is distributed between personal consumption expenditures and personal savings.

Semi-Objective

Disposable income is what you have left of your earnings after you pay to the local, state, and federal government your personal taxes. You may spend the little which you have left for anything you need. Any of the disposable income remaining beyond that you may save.

Subjective

Disposable income is the little bit of money which a person can hold on to after the politicians of the local, state, and federal governments take their share. This is what you have left with which you are supposed to buy additional food, shelter, and clothing for your family. A person usually has to borrow money to pay his taxes. Why can't we just forget about them?

John Nelson

The point of view must be appropriate to the purpose. Following are a few examples of points of view a writer might adopt to convey the right degree of objectivity or subjectivity required by the intended writer-reader relationship.

Point of View

Subject	Objective	Subjective
A car	Automotive engineer	A person hoping to buy it
A flyswatter	Its manufacturer	A fly
Toy kitten	A toy merchant	An infant
Pencil	Impersonal user	A student who received it from an admirer
Cheese	A cheese maker or grocer	A mouse
Snow	A weather forecaster	A child with a new sled
Monkey	A zoologist	Another monkey

Spatial Point of View

The writer must sometimes, especially in description, indicate from what point in space a subject is viewed. If you intend to describe the design of a 747 jet plane, you might tell the reader that you are standing fifty feet from it, looking at either of its two sides. If your main idea is the power of the plane, you might take a position just under the jet engines. But if you are concerned with the comfort of the passenger area, you will have to take the reader with you inside the plane as you describe the comfortable seats and other facilities. To develop other main ideas, you may have to assume a physical position above the plane, beneath it, or even on its wings. *The spatial point of view is the position in space from which the writer chooses to view the subject.*

Spatial description must be orderly. Otherwise it may confuse a reader. Before starting to write, you must determine from which point in space you will view your subject and whether you should use a stationary or a roving point of view (see Chapter 14) to get the best picture for the reader. In other words, you must think about space much as a photographer does.

Can you identify the point in space from which the writers of the examples below are viewing their subjects? Do the descriptions move through space in an orderly manner?

At night, Traverse City, Michigan, takes on a colorful appearance when viewed from the high ski slope east of the city. The largest hotel, with its powerful revolving search light, stands out tall and majestic over the smaller buildings which huddle around it. From this point high on the hill, a person can see the cluster of brightly flashing neon signs in the heart of the city. The harbor lights along Traverse Bay reflect off the ice like flecks of silver, adding glamour and romance to the view.

As I looked in from the doorway I saw a velvet sofa, two carved end tables, a huge stone fireplace, a bearskin rug; but my eyes rested on a Victorian chair which quietly murmured "class." It sat with pomp and dignity in its place by the hearth. Textured brocade curved gently over its stately arms in a way that invited me to sit. Once seated, I was surprised at its springy comfort. It enfolded me with its high rounded back. It extended its arms to support my arms in a regal, durable way. It proved to be a most inviting piece of furniture and the thing I remember best about the room.

Mary Laski

At the last game of the baseball season last year at Tiger Stadium, some friends and I were seated in the seats along the first base line. We were close enough to see the expressions on the faces of the Tiger players as they came up to the plate when each was at bat. When Willie Horton walked by, I looked at his face, and I knew from the expression on it that he was going to get a hit. Shortly after, I saw Willie let loose with a soaring drive into the left field seats for a homerun; the final score was Detroit 9 and the New York Yankees 1.

Jim Iaxi

The Chronological Point of View

The chronological point of view is the moment in time from which the writer regards a subject. You may stand, so to speak, in the present time and tell what happened some time in the past, perhaps a thousand years ago, fifty years ago, or yesterday. You may take a position during the Crusades and narrate what is happening all around you as though you are actually there.

Chronological viewpoint is important in all narratives, including history, biography, telling how something is done, and fiction. It also must be handled in an orderly manner if the writer is to succeed in maintaining the required relationship with the reader. Here is an example.

LUCKY TO BE ALIVE

My first haircuts weren't those of a professional barber, but after I acquired the knack, even my army buddies weren't unhappy with them. While in the service, where haircuts are an important requirement, my friends let me practice on their heads because they couldn't afford a professional barber. To start a haircut, I used scissors to trim around the ears and back of the neck to form the pattern along which I wanted to cut. Continuing with the scissors, I tapered the back and sides to the extent I thought suitable. While doing this, it was important to remember to keep an even line. Following this step, I cut the length of the hair on the top of my friend's head to what I thought he wanted. Also, when the hair was thick, I would use thinning shears. The final touch was accomplished with clippers. This crucial step was achieved by blending the sides and back with the hair on the top, doing it slowly and easily until there was no ridge dividing them.

Larry Moore

Since writing is thinking on paper, and since everything we think is always related to our mental attitude as well as to time and place, a writer should predetermine the psychological, spatial, and chronological points of view.

Tone

A final important element in the writer-reader relationship is tone, the feeling of the writer toward the reader as reflected in the manner of expression, the way things are said to accomplish the purpose and to explain the main idea. Your tone may be solemn or flip, formal or breezy, serious or ironic, emotional or coldly logical, warmly personal or icily distant. There are as many tones in writing as there are in the human voice or as there are attitudes expressed in the relationship of one person to another. Long before starting to write the first draft, you should give thought to the tone you will use. There are various ways to set and control tone in writing, most of them concerned with the careful selection of words and their arrangement. Chapter 15 discusses diction and tone in detail. You should read the section on tone in that chapter now (pages 300–314) because Chapter 6 requires that you have some understanding of the concept. You can return to it for detailed study when your class takes up the subject of diction.

PRACTICE in Achieving This Chapter's Objectives

Practice in prethinking and establishing the appropriate writer-reader relationship.

	Applications
1. Identifying the intended dominant general purpose.	1
2. Identifying the intended psychological point of view.	3
3. Identifying spatial and chronological points of view.	2, 4
4. Writing a composition demonstrating the ability to prethink and to establish and maintain the elements of the writer-reader relationship intended.	5
5. You Be the Judge	

APPLICATION 5-1

Match the sections by placing a letter and a roman numeral from the lists below in the blanks before each sentence to identify the dominant general purpose and the psychological point of view.

Dominant General Purpose	Psychological Viewpoint
A. to entertain	I. objective
B. to convey an impression	II. semi-objective
C. to inform	III. subjective
D. to persuade	
E. to actuate	

_____ _____ 1. Poverty cannot be eliminated in this manner.

_____ _____ 2. Don't fret and don't phone; just write.

_____ _____ 3. Mother and Father are still a magnificent reflection of humanity.

_____ _____ 4. The "dogs" my kids drag home beguile me.

_____ _____ 5. We can and must save the Everglades.

_____ _____ 6. Wheel alignment is easy.

_____ _____ 7. Polynesia is a lover's paradise.

_____ _____ 8. You should travel on the installment plan.

_____ _____ 9. MacArthur is an old soldier who still "lives."

_____ _____ 10. The Louisiana bicameral legislature should be made unicameral.

APPLICATION 5-2

Print an S before those items that express a spatial viewpoint, and a C before those items that express a chronological viewpoint.

_____ 1. From the plane window, the telephone poles below looked like a picket fence.

_____ 2. Standing here in the year 1492, I see three ships sailing away from the coast of Spain.

_____ 3. Charlie Johnson threw three touchdown passes in this stadium three years ago.

_____ 4. Looking across the river, I saw the Indian camp.

_____ 5. From the doorway, I saw the antique roll-top desk against the opposite wall.

_____ 6. The space program of today will seem primitive in the year 2000.

_____ 7. As I stood behind the car, I saw it move forward.

_____ 8. As far as I could see down the road, the snow was drifting into piles on the shoulder.

_____ 9. During the 1930s, there was a serious depression in the United States.

_____ 10. At precisely noon, ten years ago, the plane, with sixty people aboard, met its terrible fate.

APPLICATION 5-3

In the appropriate blank, indicate whether the viewpoints of the following passages are objective, semi-objective, or subjective. Next, underline those words and ideas which support your conclusion.

_____ 1. The clean white of winter has changed the view from our window wall across the back of our house. The slopes of the yard, tops of bird houses, barbecue, and picnic table are covered with fresh snow. Bushes, trees, and fences provide contrast in shades of brown and gray. The channel at the edge of the lawn adds a swiftly moving line of steel blue water. In the expanse of the lake to our left, two mounds of white indicate the presence of our twin islands.

Harold Lecht

_____ 2. Water power is derived from the energy of flowing water by velocity, weight, or pressure. These processes are utilized by water descending from one level to a considerably lower level. The earliest use of water power dates back to ancient times when man devised the water wheel. About the middle of the nineteenth century, all types of water wheels gave way to the invention of the turbine, which used both pressure and velocity of the water. Presently, mechanical energy seems to have taken more effect in industry, although water power is still used widely all over the world.

Glen Soleair

APPLICATION 5-4

Underline the words and groups of words which enable the writer to maintain the appropriate spatial viewpoint in the following passage.

My Grandparents' country home was a fascinating place to visit, full of surprises and mysteries. The massive grey fieldstone house stood alone with only fields and woods to keep it company. It was not a lonely place, however. The dark, damp, moldy smelling basement was one place I did not venture often—back in its catacombs could be found a wine cellar, something you'll not find in many homes today.

The main floor on ground level opened from an enclosed porch into a big, old fashioned country kitchen, complete with fireplace and black, wood-burning stove.

The second floor could be reached by large wooden steps coming up the front of the house or by narrow, winding stairs leading from the back of the kitchen. On this level was a huge center hall, and opening off of it, was a large living room with a stone fireplace reaching to the high ceiling and a large formal dining room.

The third floor held three large bedrooms as did the fourth floor. These bedrooms were without heat, but had fireplaces and each was equipped with plenty of warm quilts on fluffy feather beds.

The things that I remember most vividly about this house as I grow older and memories fade are the smell of country air mixed with the chirping of the crickets, the smell of a turkey roasting in the stove, the feel of a feather bed on a cold winter night, the piano in the living room, and most of all the love that was in that house.

Nancy Hunter

APPLICATION 5-5

Write a composition of at least 400 words, consisting of several paragraphs. Underline your main idea, and indicate your dominant general purpose and point of view in your heading. Develop the composition with ideas which appeal to the background and interests of your reader. Be sure your ideas are expressed in a manner appropriate to your purpose and to the psychological viewpoint required. Be sure to read the following You Be the Judge before starting. Another student may grade your paper. If you have questions about grammar while writing, be sure to refer to the Handbook of Correct and Effective Usage on pages 383–409. Here are some suggested topics you may wish to write about.

1. A county fair
2. A carnival
3. An amusement park
4. A small railroad depot
5. The lobby of a hotel
6. Our kitchen

YOU BE THE JUDGE

CHAPTER 5

Evaluator's Initials ☐☐☐

Date _____

Section _____

Grade _____

Writer's Name _____

Date _____ Section _____

Title of paper _____

Chapter _____ Application No. _____

General Instructions on the You Be the Judge Applications, and specific instructions for Parts I and III, are printed inside the back cover of this book. Read those instructions carefully; then do Part I.

In the lines below, and on another sheet of paper, answer the questions in Part II. Then enter a grade for the paper in the space above left, and write your evaluation for Part III. Reread the composition to see how well the writer understands and applies the principles studied in this chapter. As you read the composition write any helpful suggestions that occur to you in the margins.

PART II

1. Describe as well as you can the type of reader to whom the composition was addressed. _____

_____

_____

_____

_____

_____

_____

_____

2. How successfully did the writer establish a satisfactory relationship with this reader? What was the relationship? _____

_____

_____

_____

_____

_____

3. What was the writer's main idea? How well was it adapted to the interests of the reader? _____

_____

_____

_____

_____

_____

4. How well are the details and style of the paper adapted to the intended reader? Explain with specific illustrations. _____

_____

_____

_____

_____

_____

_____

5. What is the intended viewpoint? How well was it carried out? _____

_____

_____

_____

_____

_____

_____

PART III

Grade and Explanation:

_____

_____

_____

_____

_____

CHAPTER 6

PREWRITING: PURPOSE STATEMENT AND OUTLINE

After studying this chapter and completing the applications that follow it, you should be able to do the following:
1. To identify the parts of a correctly written *purpose statement*.
2. To write the *purpose statement* in sentence form and in list form.
3. To use the *purpose statement* in planning a composition.
4. To prepare and use the *working outline*.
5. To prepare a *formal outline*.
6. To apply these principles in writing a full-length composition.

S O FAR, we have focused on the *prethinking* stage of writing in which the writer pins down as specifically as possible the predetermined elements of the composition: the specific subject, the dominant general purpose, and the writer-reader relationship.

We turn now to the next preparatory stage, *prewriting,* which involves writing down the purpose and the plan for carrying it out, but which is still preliminary to the actual writing. In this stage you are still addressing yourself mainly, not your reader. There are two steps in prewriting, preparing the *purpose statement,* and establishing the *outline* or *plan* for carrying it out. You keep these before you as you do any further thinking, research or reading, and as you do the actual writing. You stand ready always to revise your plan and improve it as the work goes on.

It may seem at first that you are being asked to go through an almost endless procedure before you write a thing. And the first few times you go through the prethinking and prewriting stages they may seem long. But as with any other skill worth learning, the easy way is often the sloppy way and leads to nothing better than mediocrity. True mastery demands work and self-discipline. With writing, fortunately, these preliminary stages are not so hard or so time-consuming as they sound. After the first few times, once you get the hang of it and understand what you are doing, many of these processes can be completed in a matter of minutes. *The important thing is that you know most of what you want to say, to whom, and how, before you begin to write.*

**THE PURPOSE
STATEMENT**

Most creative occupations, whether tool-and-die making, cooking, or the building of a house, require some type of job description, recipe, list of specifications, or plan and blueprint to make efficient performance possible. The writer too should have some type of specification sheet. For our purposes, we will call the writer's job description or specification sheet the *purpose statement*. Regardless of how many houses a carpenter has built, each time a new one is begun the specification sheet for that particular house must be drawn up. Moreover, while many houses can be built from the same plan, no two pieces of writing are ever exactly alike. Therefore you as a writer must have something specific to help you write with precision.

Even professional writers often explicitly state or clearly imply the elements of their purpose statements. In longer, more formal types of writing, such as a textbook, the writer usually does this in the foreword or preface. Here are two illustrations:

The purpose of this essay is to introduce students of the drama to one of the great periods of English dramatic activity, the Restoration Age. . . . I have tried to define and describe the varieties of Restoration drama and to analyze outstanding examples of each kind objectively, without bias or prejudice.
from the foreword to *Restoration Drama* by John Harold Wilson.

My purpose has been to write an introduction to Byron's poetry for twentieth century students and readers in the light of what is known of the life, character and psychology of the poet, and of the intellectual and literary milieu of which he wrote. I have tried neither to over-emphasize nor to neglect the biographical interpretation, always important for the understanding of the self-revelatory poetry. . . . .
from *Byron's Poetry: A Critical Introduction* by Leslie A. Marchand.

Until you are able to keep all the factors which make up your predetermined elements in mind automatically, it is best to write them in a purpose statement which you can keep before you in prewriting until your piece of writing is completed. Later, you may include in your statement only the main factors of the predetermined elements because some of them are obvious or because they are clearly implied. For example, you will know automatically that an objective attitude requires a formal tone or that when the purpose is to entertain, usually it will call for a subjective attitude and most often an informal tone. You may not even find it necessary to identify the length of your composition by number of words. Of course these parts of the purpose statement do not have to appear in exactly the order in which they appear below, but they should be included somehow.

The purpose statement is a brief declaration or assertion in which you remind yourself what you have decided to do in a particular composition. *It identifies the predetermined elements: the specific subject (the*

*specific topic and the main idea), the dominant general purpose, and the
writer-reader relationship (the type of reader, the writer's attitudes:
point of view and tone), and the genre (kind of writing) and scope (length).*

In the following illustrations, the predetermined elements are italicized
to enable you to recognize them more readily.

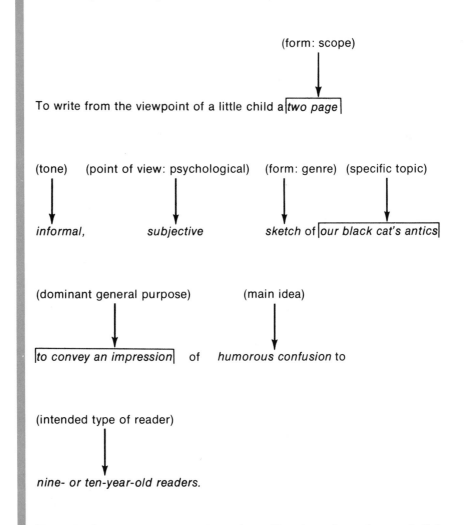

(form: scope)

To write from the viewpoint of a little child a |*two page*|

(tone)   (point of view: psychological)   (form: genre) (specific topic)

informal,   *subjective*   *sketch* of |*our black cat's antics*|

(dominant general purpose)   (main idea)

|*to convey an impression*| of   *humorous confusion* to

(intended type of reader)

nine- or ten-year-old readers.

**Writing the
Purpose Statement**

The writer's purpose statement may be written *in sentence form or in list
form.* Its parts need not be stated exactly in the order in which they are
shown in our examples. After writing two or three purpose statements,
you will be able to identify the parts without labeling them.

You may prefer to write the purpose statement in sentence form because it is more compact or because it will help in seeing more clearly the

relationships between the things which make up the statement. Following
is one in sentence form with the parts labeled.

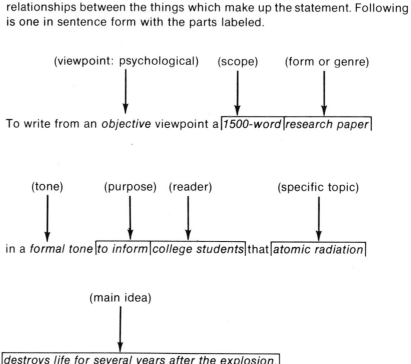

In sentence form, the statement is formulated first and the labels are
then added as a check to see that all necessary points are covered. Following is this same purpose statement in list form.

1. General and specific topic: atomic radiation.
2. Main idea: destroys life for several years after the explosion.
3. Dominant general purpose: to inform.
4. Reader: college students.
5. Attitude—point of view and tone: objective and formal.
6. Form—genre (kind) and scope (length): 3000-word research paper.

The list form of the purpose statement has one important advantage
over the sentence form: with all the headings written down first, it is
easier to be sure that each one is fully covered in the statement. But the
list also has the disadvantage that the statement itself, because it is
broken up into headings, trends to be defined more by those headings
than by the idea, whereas the sentence form lets the idea take its own
shape.

Here is another illustration of a purpose statement first written in
sentence form and then in list form.

In sentence form:

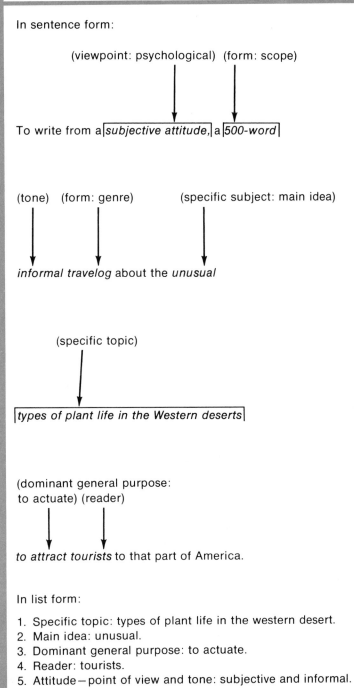

In list form:

1. Specific topic: types of plant life in the western desert.
2. Main idea: unusual.
3. Dominant general purpose: to actuate.
4. Reader: tourists.
5. Attitude — point of view and tone: subjective and informal.
6. Form — genre (kind) and scope (length): 500-word travelog.

Following are two examples of statements written without labels above the predetermined elements. This is probably the way a professional writer would write it. Although we have put labels such as tone and psychological viewpoint on these purpose statements, the experienced writer would probably leave them out because they would be self-evident. See if you can identify the various predetermined elements in these examples.

To write to local taxpayers from a subjective attitude in an informal tone, a 1500-word essay, based on personal experience, to convey an impression of the public relations wizardry of a public school principal's assistant.

To write from a semi-objective viewpoint a 1500-word article for a magazine aimed at middle-aged married couples to inform them about the daily lives of their prototypes in fourth-century Athens.

The purpose statement serves you as an important guide while thinking about what to write as well as while doing library research. Since the purpose statement serves to remind you constantly what you set out to do, you will also use it as a sort of yardstick with which to measure the relevance and effectiveness of the ideas which occur to you in your search. As these related thoughts are discovered, you will jot them down if they measure up to the specifications given in your purpose statement.

**ORGANIZING:
FIRST STEPS**

After you have gathered enough material to be able to formulate your predetermined elements, you should again check your list before you reorganize your topics into the order in which you will deal with them in the actual writing. In doing this, you will check to see whether each of your ideas is related to the predetermined elements. Those which are related you will retain, and any which are not you will discard. To illustrate this procedure, a purpose statement together with the thoughts the writer gathered follows. Notice how easy it is to select the related thoughts and ignore or discard the unrelated ones when there is a purpose statement to serve as a guide.

Purpose statement: To write a 500-word essay from a semi-objective viewpoint and in a semi-formal tone to inform the average person that being a physician is a demanding profession.

Following is the list of thoughts gathered by the writer to develop this purpose statement.

1. Although doctors have prestige and economic security, their burdens are many.
2. The hours of practice are long and unpredictable.

3. They have miracle drugs to help in treating patients.
4. Their compassion for others causes emotional strain which affects their own health.
5. They must keep abreast of new medical developments.
6. There are efficient clinics to assist in diagnosing.
7. They are always conscious that any failures cause grief and anguish to relatives.
8. Relatives of patients expect doctors to perform miracles.
9. They receive loads of free samples from drug manufacturers.
10. On their days off many physicians play golf.
11. Their formal education and training are long and expensive.

On examining this list, you can readily see that Items 1, 2, 4, 5, 7, 8, and 11 are related to the writer's purpose statement, especially to its main idea. Items 3, 6, 9, and 10, however, are not related and should be eliminated.

Next the writer must rearrange the list in an order suitable for development later into the working outline, in preparation for the writing of the first draft. Perhaps the following list will result.

1. Although doctors have prestige and economic security, their burdens are many.
2. Their formal education and training are long and expensive.
3. Their hours of practice are long and unpredictable.
4. They must keep abreast of new medical developments.
5. Their compassion for others causes emotional strain which affects their own health.
6. Their failures cause grief and anguish to relatives.
7. Relatives of patients expect doctors to perform miracles.
8. Doctors are always conscious of these failures.

For a short composition, the writer may use the preceding list as a working outline. A more detailed working outline would be more helpful if the composition is to be more than just a few paragraphs in length.

You should keep the purpose statement before you as you gather information in preparation for the actual writing. To understand how valuable this practice can be, let's assume that you are developing the purpose statement about the effects of atomic radiation (page 108). If you will look back at that statement, you will see that you want to inform; therefore, you will know that much of the material you need should consist of reliable information derived from qualified sources.

This purpose statement also serves to remind you that the readers are college students. This tells you that you can use the vocabulary of educated people when writing your notes as well as later when writing the first draft. Also, it will help in determining which technical terms may be used without having to be defined and which must be defined. Knowing your readers also tells you to what extent you must explain and expand your ideas to express them clearly.

The purpose statement about atomic radiation also reminds you of the kind of paper you intend to write along with its length: "a 3000-word research paper." Knowing the form and length not only tells you how much information you will need but also how to develop and organize that information after you have gathered it. This particular statement reminds you of the objective attitude and the formal tone which must be maintained toward both subject and reader.

Most important, this particular statement enables you to have a yardstick against which to measure the relevance of information as it is gathered. The main idea reminds you that most of the paper will not concentrate on the fact that atomic radiation destroys life; college students already know this. It will mainly be concerned with atomic radiation destroying life "for several years after the explosion." Therefore, while doing this research you will be especially watchful for material specifically related to this main idea.

**Checking
Appropriateness of
Predetermined
Elements**

By carefully examining the purpose statement, like the tool-and-die caster working from a job description, the builder from a specification sheet, or the carpenter from the architect's plans, a writer can detect some of the more conspicuous faults or weaknesses which may occur in a piece of writing long before they happen. One very important thing that can be checked in advance is the appropriateness of the ideas to the factors which make up the predetermined elements.

The predetermined elements of a purpose statement must be appropriate to each other. The following statements need some improvements if the writer is to succeed in getting the desired response from the readers. In the first one that follows, the dominant general purpose is not appropriate to the other predetermined elements.

To write a 1500-word research paper to entertain educated readers by telling them about the social implications of the mass demonstrations which are taking place in Detroit, Michigan, today.

Here is another in which the tone of the writer-reader relationship is not appropriate.

To write in a humorous tone an objective article to inform college students taking American History I of the economic disintegration of the South between 1864 and 1900.

**OUTLINES
Working Outlines**

Once you have worked out a satisfactory purpose statement, you are ready to tackle the next stage in prewriting, the working outline. There are two main kinds of outlines, the *working outline* and the *formal outline*. The working outline, as the name implies, is a rough outline which is mainly for the writer's own use. The formal outline, a refined, finished, and more complete outline, is mainly for the readers' use. It enables them to scan the paper quickly to discover its main ideas and to determine whether they want to read it. It also enables them to locate sections of particular interest to them.

A short composition of two or three paragraphs seldom requires a formal outline. An experienced writer may not feel it necessary to write any outline for so short a composition because he or she can usually remember the main points and how to develop them. But until you are experienced, it is wise to make some notes for all pieces of writing, even if only a list of ideas.

Let us assume that you have to write a paragraph tracing the development of the typewriter. After you have done the preliminary research and thinking, you might rough out a working outline by merely listing points about the typewriter as they occur to you. Following is a purpose statement and such a working outline:

To write a 150-word informative report in a semiformal tone to inform college students in secretarial science that the typewriter is not a modern invention.

1. Many surprised to learn that typewriter not modern invention.
2. In 1833, typing machine made in France with key lever for each letter.
3. In 1714, typewriter made by Henry Mill, England.
4. M's machine very clumsy and of little practical use.
5. Though perfection in typewriter came recently, machine first made over 200 years ago.
6. In 1873, American named Sholes produced machine good enough for extensive manufacture.

From this rough listing you can almost instantly see the order in which to arrange ideas for a paragraph to inform: chronological or time order. You can easily check to make sure information is reliable so your reader will understand the main idea, "the typewriter is not a modern invention." You may even write your paragraph without bothering to rewrite your outline.

Many persons will be surprised to learn that the typewriter is not, as they supposed, a modern invention. As early as 1714, a typewriter was made by Henry Mill in England. Mill's machine was clumsy and was of little practical use. In 1833, a typewriting machine was produced in France having a separate key lever for each letter. In 1873, an American named Sholes produced a machine sufficiently useful to warrant extensive manufacture. Since that time, improvements followed in rapid succession. Although perfection in the typewriter came only recently, the machine was first made over two hundred years ago.

A working outline is even more important for a longer or more complex composition. In writing a long research paper, it will become a rough map or plan which will guide you in carrying out your predetermined objectives. It will be much more detailed than the list of ideas which suffices for a short composition. You will not only follow it as you write, but as you go, you will insert into it additional facts and ideas as they occur. You will also delete from it material which you discover to be irrelevant or of minor importance and make changes in order and organization as you write. Here are some ways in which you may use a working outline.

1. To determine whether the facts and ideas you plan to develop are properly related to the parts of the purpose statement.
2. To help eliminate irrelevant or unnecessary points.
3. To keep the interrelationships of a large mass of detail clear.
4. To test the effectiveness of supporting statements.
5. To help locate and correct points lacking logical support.
6. To help locate and alter or discard illogical conclusions.
7. To help locate and correct important ideas which need further expansion to make their relationship to the main idea clearer or more emphatic.
8. To help make important changes without rewriting large sections of the paper.
9. To help test the order and proposed organizations of the paper before you write it.
10. To help you find out whether your material will enable you to achieve your predetermined objectives.

Formal Outlines

Long compositions such as investigative reports and research papers may require a formal outline or a table of contents for the convenience of the reader. The table of contents is usually merely a listing of the chapters or major parts of a piece of writing with the page number on which each part begins. Either a table of contents or a formal outline may be prepared from the working outline. Following is a table of contents:

Contents

A formal outline is often prepared after the final draft of a composition is completed. Formal outlines are usually prepared for the convenience of the readers: they provide a quick overall view of the composition. They let them see logical relationships and major and minor supporting ideas, serve as a detailed table of contents, and enable them to find quickly a particular point of interest. In some formal outlines the purpose statement is replaced by a briefer sentence which includes the main elements of the purpose statement.

Here is a formal outline with a title and a purpose statement. Before you study it, refer to the working outline on the same topic on page 111.

MEDICINE IS A DEMANDING PROFESSION
To write a 500-word essay from a semi-objective viewpoint and in a semiformal tone to inform the person that being a physician is a demanding profession.

   I. Although doctors have prestige and economic security, their burdens are many.
  II. Their formal education and training are long and expensive.
     A. As an undergraduate and medical student.
     B. As an intern and resident.
     C. As M.D. studying for specialization.
 III. Their hours of practice are long and unpredictable and include varied duties.
     A. Attending to office patients.
     B. Performing house calls.
     C. Making hospital rounds.
     D. Attending patients during emergencies.
 IV. They must keep abreast of new medical developments:
     A. In medicines.
     B. In medical techniques.
  V. Their compassion for others causes emotional strain which may affect their own health:
     A. Constant pressure of suffering and pain.
     B. Consciousness of the anxiety of relatives.
       1. Awareness that concerned relatives expect doctors to perform miracles.
       2. Consciousness that failure causes them grief and anguish.

Notice that each of the items in each section is expressed in the same kind of grammatical construction: the items with roman numerals are the same, the capitalized items within each roman numeral are the same, and the numbered items within each section are the same. Moreover, the topics, taken together, all make complete statements.

Formal outlines, like working outlines, are of different types, but there are two main kinds, sentence outlines and topic outlines.

Sentence Outlines are preferred for complex relationships. They express ideas fully, define the relationships between ideas, and relate ideas to the complete composition. Here is a sentence outline.

Qualities of Shakespeare's Plays
I. What is revealed in Shakespeare's drama?
   A. Soliloquies reveal wisdom.
   B. Dialogue reflects character.
   C. Word denotations and connotations suggest complexities of human nature.

Topic Outlines are usually made up of noun elements (single nouns or noun phrases).

Nouns:
I. Classification of Shakespeare's plays
   A. Tragedies
   B. Comedies
   C. Romances
Verbal-Noun Phrases:
II. Kinds of Shakespearean dialogue
(Gerund)
   A. Satirizing human fraility
   B. Revealing human nature
   C. Depicting human character
(Infinitive)
   A. To satirize human fraility
   B. To reveal human nature
   C. To depict human character

Formal outlines should conform to certain conventions of form, punctuation, and general appearance.

1. Center the title of the paper above the outline.
2. When a controlling sentence is required, center the purpose statement or subject sentence double spaced under the title.

3. Observe standard outline form and indent each sublevel beyond the one immediately above it:

I.
    A.
        1.
           a.
              (1)
                (a)

4. Each item should begin with a capital letter, but should end with a period only when it is a sentence.

Because the divisions of an outline indicate the logical relationships of the items to the purpose statement or purpose sentence, the level of each heading should reflect its logical relationships. Study the following examples.

LEARNING TO DRIVE

Incorrect

A. Steps in learning to drive
    1. Learning to shift gears
        a. shifting gears
        b. memorizing the gear positions
    2. Acquiring speed in shifting
B. Signals to be used before making turns

Correct

A. Steps in learning to drive
    1. Learning the gear positions
    2. Shifting the gears correctly
    3. Acquiring speed in shifting
B. Signals to be used before making turns

To keep the logical relationships between the items of the outline clear, the writer should not write the main topics as subheadings or the sub-headings as main topics.

Incorrect

I. Qualities of flight attendants
    A. Posture
    B. Disposition
    C. Body coordination
    D. Erect stance
    E. Personality
    F. Physical appearance
    G. Friendliness
    H. Courtesy

Correct

I. Qualities of flight attendants
   A. Physical Appearance
      1. Erect stance
      2. Body coordination
   B. Personality
      1. Friendliness
      2. Courtesy
      3. Disposition

PRACTICE in Achieving This Chapter's Objectives

Practice in preparing and using purpose statements, working outlines, and formal outlines.

	Applications
1. Identifying the predetermined elements in a purpose statement.	1
2. Using the purpose statement to check the appropriateness of the predetermined elements.	2, 3
3. Writing purpose statements, working outlines, and formal outlines.	4, 5
4. Writing a composition based on a purpose statement.	6
5. You Be the Judge	

APPLICATION 6-1

Above each of the predetermined elements in the following purpose statements, print the kind of element it is, for example, *purpose, reader, tone,* and so forth.

                                           scope   form   point of view
                                            ↓   ↓   ↓
Example: To write approximately a *500-word editorial* from a *subjective attitude to*

        purpose   tone   reader   main idea
          ↓   ↓   ↓   ↓
entertain informally the *average American* by a satire about the *propagandizing*

              specific topic
                  ↓
techniques of *Russian newspapers.*

1. From a semi-objective attitude, to write a semiformal two-page letter to actuate citizens

   to write to the United States Postmaster General, protesting the latest increase in

   postage rates.

2. To write from an objective attitude a 500-word news bulletin to inform priests, ministers,

   and preachers in a formal tone about the municipal ordinances governing church

   bazaars.

3. To write from a semi-objective attitude a 1000-word semiformal article to convince, by

   persuasion, young parents that camping is an inexpensive recreation for middle-income

   families.

APPLICATION 6-2

In each of the following purpose statements, the dominant general purpose is inappropriate to one or more of the other predetermined elements. List each of the elements to which the purpose is inappropriate after each purpose statement. Then indicate the purpose which would be most appropriate.

1. To write a 500-word objective, formal technical report to convey an impression upon automotive engineers of the efficient use of computers in programming production schedules of automobiles. _____

   _____

   _____

   _____

2. To write a 500-word humorous subjective article to inform a college student of the creatures from outer space who landed in Boulder, Colorado, on October 19, 1973.

   _____

   _____

   _____

   _____

3. To write a semiformal, subjective description to inform the average reader about the dedication of Dwight D. Eisenhower to the defense of his country. _____

   _____

   _____

   _____

   _____

4. To write a subjective 2000-word descriptive sketch to convey an impression to prospective students of the advantages of attending X College. _____

   _____

   _____

   _____

   _____

APPLICATION 6-3

In each of these purpose statements one or more of the predetermined elements is missing. After identifying those not included, rewrite each in sentence, outline, or list form.

1. To write in a formal tone, to inform college students concerning the nucleoprotein structure of the DNA molecule in the chromosomes of a rabbit. _____

_____

_____

_____

_____

2. To write a humorous two-page letter to commuters about the sympathy which a subway car has for the frustrated travelers who mutter weary complaints to it as they squeeze aboard twice a day. _____

_____

_____

_____

_____

3. To write a two-page personal-experience subjective article for a family magazine to convey an impression of the role which a clerk plays in creating favorable public relations for the drugstore. _____

_____

_____

_____

_____

4. To write a 1000-word persuasive article to convince young buyers of homes that a custom designed house would save them money in the long run. _____

_____

_____

_____

_____

APPLICATION 6-4

I. In the following list, find and write down the item which expresses a main idea. Outline the remaining items by first labeling major headings with the appropriate roman numerals. Then under each such item, place the minor items related to it and put the right capital letter before each. Add a title.

1. Between the shores of Lakes Erie and Michigan lies a megalopolis.

2. It has industrial resources to absorb an increasing population.

3. The great corn and wheat belts of the midwest can provide the necessary food for its teeming inhabitants.

4. The St. Lawrence Seaway contributes to its expansion.

5. It has a large amount of space for population expansion.

6. The Great Lakes provide cheap and easy transportation.

7. A megalopolis is a gigantic metropolis.

8. It enables midwest products to be exported throughout the world.

9. Detroit, Chicago, and Cleveland are almost connected industrial centers.

10. The midwest can support a megalopolis.

11. Raw materials needed from foreign countries can easily and cheaply be imported.

12. It has made the Great Lakes an inland sea.

13. Ships are reloaded with a variety of foodstuffs and finished products for distant destinations around the world.

II. Now write a composition consisting of one paragraph for each of the major (roman numeral) headings of your outline. Be sure these paragraphs are related to each other and to the specific subject (especially the main idea) of the sentence at the top of the outline. Add more material of your own if necessary.

APPLICATION 6-5

Select the sentence below which you think contains the main idea to which most of the other sentences in the list are related; then write a purpose statement. Using the purpose statement as a measure, cross out the sentences which are not related to the composition you will write. Now write a composition of five or six paragraphs developing the selected sentence in a manner appropriate to the purpose statement.

1. Much profit may be derived from toy sales.

2. Too much advertising is devoted to Christmas toys.

3. Children are not swayed by TV advertising of toys.

4. Parents should not buy toys advertised on TV.

5. Toys advertised on TV are often expensive.

6. There is an unlimited selection of toys that appeal to the creativity of a child.

7. Some toys are too expensive to maintain.

8. Toys may not be sturdily built.

9. Worthwhile toys must arouse the imagination.

10. Battery-operated toys may be a waste of money.

11. Some toys are dangerous.

12. At Christmas time, parents must reinforce their resolutions to purchase toys wisely.

13. Some toys require parent supervision while being used.

14. Toys may not be suitable for the intended child.

15. Children often prefer to play with cupboards or discarded containers.

APPLICATION 6-6

Select a topic of your own, and after prethinking your predetermined elements, prepare a purpose statement on a separate sheet of paper. Your instructor may want you to turn it in separately. Use any of the purpose statement forms discussed in this chapter. Then write a composition on your purpose statement of at least 400 words and a minimum of four paragraphs. This composition should adhere to all the predetermined elements in your statement.

Your instructor may decide to have your composition judged by another student, using the You Be the Judge evaluation form.

YOU BE THE JUDGE

Evaluator's Initials □□□

Date _____

Section _____

Grade _____

Writer's Name _____

Date _____ Section _____

Title of paper _____

Chapter _____ Application No. _____

General Instructions on the You Be the Judge Applications, and specific instructions for Parts I and III, are printed inside the back cover of this book. Read those instructions carefully; then do Part I.

In the lines below, and on another sheet of paper, answer the questions in Part II. Then enter a grade for the paper in the space above left, and write your evaluation for Part III. Reread the composition to see how well the writer understands and applies the principles studied in this chapter. As you read the composition write any helpful suggestions that occur to you in the margins.

PART II

1. In the space below formulate a purpose statement for the composition and express it in sentence form. _____

   _____

   _____

   _____

   _____

   _____

   _____

2. In the space below express your purpose statement in list form. _____

   _____

   _____

   _____

   _____

   _____

3. When you receive the writer's purpose statement, first check whether all of its parts are appropriate to the purpose. Explain. _____

   _____

_____

_____

4. Prepare an outline for the composition, using three levels of heading;
   I, A, and 1. Point out any places where you think that the paper is not
   well organized and indicate how you would correct them. _____

_____

_____

_____

_____

_____

_____

PART III

Grade and Explanation:

_____

_____

_____

_____

PART 3

WRITING: MAKING A START

CHAPTER 7

STRUCTURE: CONTROL AND SUPPORT

After studying this chapter and completing the applications that follow it, you should be able to do the following:
1. To identify each of the three main sections of a written communication and the function each is intended to perform in relation to the predetermined elements: *beginning section*, *developing and supporting section*, and *concluding section*.
2. To identify *primary* and *secondary sentences* by their relationships to the *controlling sentence*.
3. To identify the functions of a *concluding section*.
4. To write a full-length composition with each section, especially the concluding section, performing its intended function.

THE STRUCTURE OF COMMUNICATION

Almost every expository communication, spoken or written, has the same basic structure. It says something *about* something and has specific parts. Even a communication consisting of a single sentence generally has three main parts. Most sentences have not only a subject and a predicate verb which says something about the subject, but some form of completer which rounds out the meaning. Each of these parts is necessary, and, without all of them, the whole meaning could not be communicated. Here are a few examples. Notice that in a few cases a completer is not needed, but that in most it is as important to rounding out the whole meaning as the subject and the predicate verb.

Basic Structure

Subject	Verb	Completer	Extras
(You)	Help!	(me.)	
Babies	cry.	——	
Sparks	fly	——	upward.
This plane	flies	——	at 600 miles an hour.
Wellington	defeated	Napoleon	at Waterloo.
She	'll say	"Please"	9 times out of 10.

Sentences may be only one word long or many hundreds, but in order to communicate a complete meaning they must have at least two and usually three main parts or sections—subject, predicate verb, and completer—whether expressed or understood.

**The Controlling
Sentence**

A communication that consists of a single paragraph usually contains three kinds of sentences, each kind doing a particular job. Such a paragraph will usually have a main sentence which states the topic, just as the subject of a sentence states the topic of the sentence. This sentence, which we call the *controlling sentence,* is the heart of the paragraph and all the other sentences say something about it and help to develop its meaning. The controlling sentence usually comes at the beginning, though it can come anywhere in the paragraph, even at the end. Most of the rest of the paragraph is made up of *developing* or *supporting* sentences, which explain, illustrate, or prove the point made in the controlling sentence. Finally, it will have some kind of conclusion, which may be a whole sentence or may be only a part of the final sentence.

In the following paragraph the opening sentence is the controlling sentence: it states the topic of the paragraph and gives the main idea. The remaining sentences are supporting sentences: they tell why the main sentence is true. The last sentence is a conclusion.

She sat on the hill watching the storm rally its forces. The night was hot, sticky, and still, and the sky was dark. The sounds of crickets and frogs filtered through the darkness. The evening breeze caressed her, gently whispering to her. It slid around her, loosening her hair, causing it to float careless and free. Abruptly the wind became strong and demanding. With sharp scissors, the lightning began to cut out great sections of the soot-colored sky. The thunder clouds cleared their throats, and heavy drops began to fall. She made a wild dash down the hill and into the house, slamming the door as the rain followed her, to beat angrily upon the roof.

Alma Olney

This paragraph describes one reaction to a storm. The opening sentence states the writer's purpose and controls the content of the sentences that follow. Each of these develops and supports the controlling sentence by stating one or more details of the gathering storm. The final sentence completes the happening by changing the scene with the coming of the storm, thus bringing the event to a close. The meaning is completed, and every detail—every word in the paragraph—develops the main idea. The paragraph has a controlling sentence, a number of supporting sentences, and a concluding sentence.

In much the same way, a written communication of many paragraphs will usually have a beginning paragraph, one or more developing paragraphs, and a concluding paragraph, or at least a concluding statement at the end of the final paragraph. The following brief outline should help you to see the general form of a written communication, a number of paragraphs in length. Like the single sentence and the single paragraph, the longer communication will fall into three main sections, as follows:

1. The beginning section
   A. The title
   B. The opener (when needed)
   C. The main paragraph
      1. The subject sentence
      2. Explanatory sentences
II. The developing and supporting sections
   A. Primary supporting elements
   B. Secondary supporting elements
III. The concluding section

Each unit in this outline performs a very important function in the development of the whole communication. The *beginning section* establishes contact with the reader through the title and the opener, both of which are intended to arouse interest and curiosity. The title should be chosen very carefully not only to reflect the purpose, specific subject, but also to introduce the tone and viewpoint required by the writer-reader relationship which the writer wishes to establish. The opener may be a story, joke, anecdote, or experience which is itself entertaining or especially vivid, and which follows from the title and gets the reader interested enough to want to go on reading the rest.

The developing and supporting section, though it looks very short in the outline above, is actually the main body of the communication and may range from one or two paragraphs to many pages in length. This part illustrates, explains, or proves the main topic or idea, and discusses it at length after it is suggested by the title, introduced by the opener, and stated in the main paragraph. In length, the supporting section is generally over 90 percent of the whole communication. This section is made up of supporting paragraphs, each of which is constructed somewhat like the paragraph about the person watching the coming storm, that is, each has a controlling sentence, support, and a conclusion.

THE NATURE OF SUPPORT
Developing the Controlling Sentence

It is important to understand the nature of supporting sentences and their relation to the controlling sentence for this relation is the heart of expository writing. The supporting material contains the facts on which the inferences expressed in the controlling and concluding sentences are based. It is the foundation of the house, the base of the pyramid, the knowledge, observation, experience on which everything else in the communication is based. Supporting sentences may be primary or secondary. *Primary support sentences are directly related to the main idea and the controlling sentences. Secondary support sentences do not have a direct relationship to the controlling sentence. They are directly related to a primary support sentence, often the one just before; consequently, they are related to the controlling sentence only indirectly.*

Like the primary sentences which develop the controlling sentence, making its relationship to the purpose sentence stronger and clearer, the secondary support sentence does the same thing for the primary support sentence to which it is related. Each amplifies the idea its leading sentence expresses in order to reinforce its relationship to the controlling sentence of the paragraph and through it, the subject sentence of the whole communication.

Notice how this happens in the following supporting paragraph, with the controlling sentence at the beginning. The primary sentences, directly related to the controlling sentence, are preceded by a *1,* and the secondary sentences, directly related to the preceding primary sentences and indirectly related to the controlling sentence, are preceded by a *2.*

Golf has produced many great athletes who have become famous for their golfing skill. (1) Walter Hagen is one of these greats, who, some say, is the greatest all-around golfer of his time. (2) Hagen's great skill and exactitude is still talked about today in the golfing world. (1) A legend in his own time, Ben Hogan has displayed great skill and perseverance. (2) An automobile accident almost ended Hogan's career, but he managed to come back and win all the major tournaments in the United States. (1) A more recent golfing great is Arnold Palmer, a man that combines amazing skill with good sportsmanship. (2) Many people are convinced that Palmer has given golf the popularity it so badly needed in the last few years. (1) Even more recently Carol Mann, a fierce competitor, has joined the Women's Professional Tour. She has helped raise the amount of prize money awarded to women.

Harold Lenz

The following paragraph is another good illustration, showing how the primary and secondary sentences expand the main idea of the controlling sentence to amplify the main idea of the composition's subject sentence. The main paragraph of the whole composition is not shown, but the subject sentence from it is first given in italics below. The main idea of the controlling sentence in the supporting paragraph developing it is in italics.

Subject Sentence

The artist's masterpiece is a painting of the family library, a study of accumulated tranquility.

The painting is a study of *disorderly order.* (1) At one end, two musty, yellowing books of poems, bindings broken, support an antique clarinet. (2) The clarinet is distinguished by cracks blackened by time, a mellowness of wood, and only four outlets for the sound. (2) The metal pieces of this antique are dull and sparse — unlike the thousands of glistening chrome odds and ends characteristic of modern clarinets. (2) Its shortness blends well with the other features — all giving the instrument an aged appearance. (1) Towards the back, a huge dictionary strides the desk like a giant, the two hard covers planted solidly, wide apart, like two great limbs. (1) Beside it, a drab blue and white pottery jar stands, eternal sentry, thick dust settled on its enameled shoulders. (1) At the other end, its candle slanted and disfigured with drippings, a plain brass candlestick rests on two sixteenth-century history books whose faded covers are fragile because of constant, although careful, use. (2) This candlestick is green with age, and even corroded in spots. (1) Within easy reach is a well-lit, but abandoned, corn cob pipe. (2) It has fallen to one side, adding to the disorder, and the scattered, smouldering ashes have burnt holes in the summertime New York *Journal* beneath it. (1) The brilliant blue tobacco pouch resting askew by a discolored newspaper startles the viewer with vivid contrast. (2) Part of the tobacco has tumbled over the side of the box and is almost touching two smoking matches nearby. (1) Forming a narrow tablecloth beneath the pipe, the tobacco, and the local newspaper, are several musty sheets with yellow watermarks on all four sides. (1) All these aged objects lie on a sturdy old walnut desk, and in spite of their state of chaos, form a picture of comfort and tranquility. (1) And, it is with an effort that we bring ourselves to the realization that it is only a picture, its scope narrowed by a common wooden frame.

Mary Duyar

**Developing the
Purpose Sentence**

This paragraph also shows how all the elements in a good composition are related to the predetermined elements. Each of the primary and secondary supporting sentences develops the idea of "disorderly order," the main idea of the controlling sentence, and this in turn amplifies the meaning of "accumulated tranquility," the main idea of the subject sentence for the whole. It is also important to note that in this paragraph every word and every sentence is in harmony with the point of view and the tone established by the subject sentence. Every detail in the composition was deliberately selected because it was appropriate to the writer's purpose, which was to convey an impression of "accumulated tranquility."

Now that we have some idea of the nature of support and how it operates to develop a controlling sentence or idea—and of how each controlling idea and each paragraph in turn is a step in the support and development of a subject sentence for a whole communication—we are ready to look at an extended example, the framework of such a communication. This illustration gives the entire opening section, the title, the opener, and the main paragraph. But for the support section—the body of the paper—it gives only the controlling sentences. This way you will be able to see in detail how the beginning section is handled, and how each support paragraph relates to the subject sentence expressed in the main paragraph, which in this case happens to be the second paragraph.

The Beginning Section

Title

THE DEMANDS OF MEDICINE
The doctor did everything to save the child's life; he used every medical technique he knew and administered every miracle drug which he thought might help, but five-year-old Pam Lilt slowly opened her eyes

Opener

and looked beseechingly at him and let them close for the last time. While the doctor and the attending nurses watched hopefully, her little heart stopped. Now it was his duty as the family doctor to tell the anxiously waiting parents. The parents found it difficult to understand "Why?" why the doctor failed with his miracle drugs and modern equipment. The doctor also found himself asking "Why?"

Main Paragraph
Subject Sentence

Explanatory Sentence

This episode illustrates one of the many ways in which *being a physician today is a demanding profession*. The practice of medicine does offer rewards such as economic security and professional prestige; however, it also makes demands upon the physical and psychological nature of a human being, beyond that demanded by other professions.

**Developing and
Supporting Section**

Controlling Sentence #1

Controlling Sentence #2

Controlling Sentence #3

Controlling Sentence #4

Controlling Sentence #5

1. People who plan to become doctors must devote more time and effort in preparing themselves for the practice of medicine than those who plan to enter most other professions.
2. After they have put the years of study and training behind them, they must gear themselves to a life in which the hours are long and unpredictable.
3. In addition to the many responsibilities for the health of their patients, doctors must keep abreast of all of today's many medical developments not only in drugs but also in therapeutic techniques.
4. More difficult than these demands upon energy and time, however, are those obligations which they impose upon themselves.
5. Perhaps the greatest sadness which they experience is caused by their knowledge that none of their skills can help them treat successfully incurable diseases.

Concluding Section

The honors and rewards of the practice of medicine are easy to understand and sometimes even to be envied by the general public and people in other professions. Individuals are, however, often reluctant to acknowledge the many years of education and training, the long hours of work, and the continuous emotional strain which doctors must accept as a necessary part of the work if they are to remain in the terribly demanding profession of medicine.

In the following completed version of the same composition, notice that the controlling sentences are fully developed by means of supporting sentences. Examine these supporting sentences carefully to see how they expand the main idea of the controlling sentence to which each is related. By doing this, you will see how these supporting sentences amplify the main idea of their controlling sentence, making its relationship to the main idea of the subject sentence clearer and easier to grasp and remember.

The Beginning Section

Title

Opener

THE DEMANDS OF MEDICINE

The doctor did everything to save the child's life; he used every medical technique he knew and administered every miracle drug which he thought might help, but five-year-old Pam Lilt slowly opened her eyes and looked beseechingly at him and let them close for the last time. While the doctor and the attending nurses watched hopefully, her little heart stopped. Now, it was his duty as the family doctor to tell the anxiously waiting parents. The parents found it difficult to understand "Why?" why the doctor with his miracle drugs and modern equipment failed. The doctor also found himself asking "Why?"

Main Paragraph

Subject Sentence

Explanatory Sentence

This little episode illustrates but one of the many ways in which being a physician is a demanding profession. The practice of medicine does offer rewards such as economic security and professional prestige; however, it also makes demands upon the physical and psychological nature of a human being beyond those demanded by other professions.

Developing and Supporting Sections

Controlling Sentence

Primary and Secondary Supporting Sentences

People who plan to become doctors must devote more time and effort in preparing themselves for the practice of medicine than do those who plan to enter most other professions. They spend many years in college as undergraduates, as medical students, and later as interns and resident physicians in a hospital before they become licensed doctors. If they intend to specialize, they must continue their studies beyond the M.D. degree.

Controlling Sentence

Primary and Secondary Supporting Sentences

After they have put the many years of study and training behind them, they must prepare for a life in which the hours are long and unpredictable. The office hours, the house-calls, the hospital rounds, and the day or night emergencies leave them with little time for themselves to participate in activities which they enjoy, including just being with their families.

Controlling Sentence

Primary and Secondary Supporting Sentences

In addition to the many responsibilities for the health of their patients, doctors must keep abreast of today's many medical developments, not only in drugs but also in therapeutic techniques. If there is a new vaccine for virus illnesses or a new drug for diabetes, they must know the effectiveness of these drugs, the way to administer them, and the possible undesirable reactions which some patients may have to them. Keeping up with the many developments in medicine requires that they set aside an adequate amount of time for study.

Controlling Sentence

Primary Supporting Sentence

Their compassion for their fellow human beings is constantly at a high pitch because of continual association with pain, death, and the disturbed minds that so often accompany these misfortunes. These emotional stresses have an effect upon their own health.

Controlling Sentence

Primary and Secondary
Supporting Sentences

Perhaps the greatest sadness which they experience is caused by the knowledge that none of their skills can help them treat success-fully incurable illnesses. Their keenest personal distress must come from the heartbreak which comes after applying all of their skills and knowledge unsuccessfully, knowing that failure will bring grief and anguish to the relatives such as the parents of Pam Lilt, who expected the doctor to perform a miracle.

Concluding Section

Concluding Paragraph

The honors and rewards of the practice of medicine are easy to under-stand and sometimes envied by the general public and people in other professions. Individuals are, however, often reluctant to acknowledge the many years of education and training, the long hours of work, and the continuous emotional strain which doctors must accept as a neces-sary part of their work if they are to remain in the terribly demanding profession of medicine.

Reread the concluding paragraph above paying close attention to the way the sentences in it identify not only the specific subject (that is, the specific topic and main idea) of the subject sentence, but also—by im-plication—the dominant general purpose. They also retain the appropri-ate point of view and tone of the writer-reader relationship previously identified in the subject sentence. Also notice the way this concluding paragraph summarizes in very condensed form the main ideas of the con-trolling sentences of the supporting paragraphs.

In these examples we get an important glimpse of the basic structure of thought. It is composed of control and support, the same things that we called inference and fact in Chapter I, and brought together under the guiding hand of purpose. When we know what we want to say, to whom, and for what purpose, we are able to select the right facts to develop and support our controlling ideas.

PRACTICE in Achieving This Chapter's Objectives

Practice in identifying and writing main sections, controlling sentences, primary and secondary support.

	Applications
1. Identifying primary and secondary support sentences.	1, 2
2. Identifying main sections.	3
3. Writing main and concluding paragraphs.	4
4. Identifying controlling sentences.	5
5. Writing main sections with control and support.	6
6. You Be the Judge	

APPLICATION 7-1

In the blank at the left of each of the following sentences, place the letter P to identify primary supporting sentences and S to identify supporting sentences. Place an X in the blank if the sentence should not have been included in this paragraph.

(Controlling Sentence) I decided to attend Kent State University for three

_____ 1. reasons. (1) I had spent hours talking with my parents and my high school coun-
_____ 2. selor before making up my mind. (2) These hours were not wasted because I
_____ 3. am now certain Kent State is the ideal school for me. (3) First, it has fine facili-
_____ 4. ties. (4) I plan to study chemical engineering, and Kent's new science and
_____ 5. engineering buildings have the latest and best equipment. (5) Second, it has a
_____ 6. distinguished faculty. (6) My parents are both mechanical engineers, and they
_____ 7. say that I will be studying under recognized leaders in the field. (7) Finally,

Kent is less expensive than comparable universities I have investigated.

APPLICATION 7-2

Place a 1 before each primary sentence in the following or a 2 before each secondary sentence. Do not number the underlined subject sentence.

The sensory receptors of the human body arouse certain common responses. The skin receptors, located in the deeper areas of the skin and in some internal organs cause sensations of heat, cold, and pain. These receptors are the most numerous, for they are found in nearly every cell in the body. The taste receptors, found in the taste buds on the surface of the tongue and in parts of the roof of the mouth, bring about the sensations of sweet, sour, bitter, and salty. These taste receptors, however, are inherited in a definite pattern, and the degree of each specific taste varies with each individual. The receptors for smell, located in the nasal membranes, cause the sensation of chemical odors: camphoraceous, musky, floral, etheral, pungent, and putrid. These receptors for smell, like the receptors for taste, vary with each individual. The vision receptors, known as the eyes, enable sensitivity to light and sight. An eye consists of a lens, cornea, iris, retina, and aqueous humor. The hearing receptor, the ear, enables sounds to be heard. The ear consists of three portions; the outer pinna, the middle and the inner ear. Each ear's balance receptor, found in the inner ear and consisting of three canals and two small chambers, brings about a sense of equilibrium. All of these sense receptors enable human beings to develop an awareness of their environment.

APPLICATION 7-3

Referring to the pages in this chapter that discuss the main sections of a composition, above each of the three main sections in the following composition print the name of each. Also in the blanks following the composition identify what the numbered items represent.

WELL-DRESSED MEANS APPROPRIATELY DRESSED

(1) An attractive person is an appropriately dressed person. (2) This person dresses in clothing which is not only appropriate for the occasion, but is also in harmony with his or her age and physical characteristics.

(3) Being well-dressed, therefore, does not demand being spectacularly dressed—being an "attention-getter." (4) The "attention-getter" is one who dresses in a manner inappropriate to the occasion or purpose. This person's quest for attention often seems to obscure his or her sense of good taste. This person chooses extremes in selecting attire for a particular event. Thus, he or she stands out like a neon sign.

The cost of clothing does not necessarily insure its being appropriate. Just because clothing is purchased at Saks Fifth Avenue or I. Magnin does not assure its appropriateness. A $200 suit may look like a shroud on a certain type of person. This same person may buy a suit at a cut-rate department store which may be flattering because it fits properly.

To be well-dressed, a person must wear clothing that is appropriate to his or her body structure and age. Today's miniskirt may look attractive on a young teen-age girl with a trim figure, but this same skirt would not enhance the appearance of an obese matron with plump legs. Some people are cursed with an uneven distribution of body weight. These people should not wear clinging materials such as knits, jerseys, or stretch fabrics of any sort.

(5) People must learn to select clothing fashions and colors which are appropriate to their appearance, regardless of cost. Everybody, therefore, can dress in good taste whether they be rich or poor. They must merely learn to select clothing which is appropriate for pocket book as well as for age and physical characteristics.

1. _____

2. _____

3. _____

4. _____

5. _____

APPLICATION 7-4

Using the lines provided, complete the composition below by writing a main paragraph and a concluding paragraph based on the supporting paragraphs shown. *Remember:*

1. that the main paragraph has a subject sentence which clearly indicates the main idea to be developed in the composition. Underline the main idea.
2. that the concluding paragraph restates or summarizes the main ideas in the subject and the controlling sentences.
3. to be sure to write a title for the composition.

A. While spending a winter vacation in Northern Minnesota, the chances are good that you'll be able to see varieties of interesting wild life. Winter birds and wild animals are abundant. Cardinals, bluejays, and sometimes bears can be seen. These are beautiful examples of wild life seldom seen in the populated areas of Minnesota.

B. In addition to animals and birds, nature's winter beauty itself is a spectacle worth the trip to Northern Minnesota. Imagine looking out of the window of your cottage after a heavy snowfall. The sun glistens with needles of light sparkling off the fluff that covers everything. The pine boughs bend to the ground with huge clouds of snow snuggled to their breasts.

C. Also, there is the opportunity to try winter sports such as skiing, snowmobiling, and ice skating. Speeding down snow covered slopes on a pair of skis is great fun for the young at heart. Ice skating on one of Minnesota's many inland lakes will highlight a winter vacation.

Title _____

Main Paragraph _____

_____

_____

_____

Developing and Supporting Paragraph _____

_____

_____

_____

Concluding Paragraph _____

_____

_____

_____

_____

_____

APPLICATION 7-5

The following jumbled paragraph has a controlling sentence. Find it, and write it and the sentences related to it in one paragraph in the proper order.

A TOBOGGAN RIDE

It went quickly down the hill and then, hitting an unexpected bump, the youngsters were thrown off and the toboggan continued its course to the foot of the hill, empty. The six-year-old boy at the back hopped off and gave a quick push and then raced forward just in time to hop on the big ride. Thump! They looked at each other in bewilderment and then laughed as their toboggan reached the gulley below, empty. Suddenly three surprised children were sprawled out in the freezing snow. The three youngsters with their snug red woolen hats and matching mittens were aboard the toboggan awaiting winter's first ride. Yelling and screaming, the children sped down the hill.

Betty Galerno

_____

_____

_____

_____

_____

_____

_____

_____

_____

_____

APPLICATION 7-6

Select a topic of your own choice and write a full-length composition consisting of at least five paragraphs. Three of these should be supporting paragraphs containing primary and secondary sentences. Place 1 before each primary supporting sentence and 2 before each secondary supporting sentence. Here are some suggested topics: any item of food or clothing, any kind of sports equipment or sports activity, or any student social activity.

Remember that your instructor may decide to have your composition evaluated by another student, using the You Be the Judge evaluation sheets.

YOU BE THE JUDGE

Writer's Name _____

Date _____ Section _____

Title of paper _____

Chapter _____ Application No. _____

General Instructions on the You Be the Judge Applications, and specific instructions of Parts I and III, are printed inside the back cover of this book. Read those instructions carefully; then do Part I.

In the lines below, and on another sheet of paper, answer the questions in Part II. Then enter a grade for the paper in the space above left, and write your evaluation for Part III. Reread the composition to see how well the writer understands and applies the principles studied in this chapter. As you read the composition write any helpful suggestions that occur to you in the margins.

PART II

1. Read the composition straight through and at the beginning of each sentence place the appropriate letter or number according to the following key:
   S: subject sentence
   C: controlling sentence
   Co: concluding sentence

2. Point out any supporting sentences which you think do not correctly relate to their controlling ideas. _____

   _____

   _____

   _____

   _____

   _____

3. How accurately does the writer label the primary and secondary supporting sentences? Are there transitional and linking words in them to show their function? Point out any such relationships which are unclear. _____

   _____

   _____

4. Comment on the quality and amount of developing detail. _____

5. Comment on the effectiveness of the concluding paragraph. _____

PART III   Grade and Evaluation:

CHAPTER 8

THE TITLE AND THE OPENER

After studying this chapter and completing the applications that follow it, you should be able to do the following:
1. To identify the *title* and the *opener* along with the function each performs in achieving reader contact and establishing the predetermined elements.
2. To identify the basic and more complex human needs and desires a writer may use to establish reader contact and to amplify the reader's desire to read by the *opener*.
3. To identify nine common kinds of openers: *pertinent quotations; provocative questions; startling statements—exclamations, current controversial subjects, spectacular dimensions*, and *contradictions of cherished beliefs; vivid sketches —of a person*, and *of an animal; narrative openings.*
4. To apply these principles in a full-length composition.

T HE TITLE, the opener, and the main paragraph are the chief components of the beginning section of a written communication. These three parts perform the vital role of identifying and establishing the predetermined elements in the composition itself. It is not enough for a writer to know what the specific subject is in advance; the reader must also be told.

Although the title, the opener, and the main paragraph make up the first part of a composition they are not necessarily written first. A title, for example, is often written last. An opener is often taken out of the body of the completed composition during the revision of the early drafts. As you are writing the main part of your composition, attractive titles and openers are often suggested by the ideas being expressed. Usually, these are jotted down for later consideration.

THE TITLE

A composition begins with the title, not with the first paragraph. The title is the initial point of contact between the writer and the intended reader. It is therefore the part of the composition upon which you must rely for the important first impression. At the beginning, getting the readers' attention and arousing their interest in reading is your main task.

The title is a highly condensed form of the complete composition. It implies or states the main ingredients of the total composition; it serves as a specimen which you hold out for the readers to sample mentally, hoping that it pleases or challenges them enough to make them read more.

We read titles just as we read the headlines of a newspaper. Scanning the newspaper, we pick out the headlines which promise us bits of news or information about things with which we are concerned and interested. The title, therefore, must be written so that those points of interest are clearly stated or implied. What makes an attractive title? Since the reader is another human being, the writer offers to satisfy one or more of the basic human needs (See Chapter 5).

In addition to arousing the readers' interest, the title performs the important functions of helping to establish the predetermined elements in the composition. The title should be worded distinctively enough to attract the readers' attention, and it should be brief enough to be scanned quickly. Remember that there is a great deal of competition for readers' attention.

To be distinctive, the title must be brief. As the piston compresses the gases in an engine, so the title compresses the parts of the complete composition into a few words. Following is an illustration of forceful brevity in a title which arouses reader curiosity: "Churchill — Man of Steel and Ermine." This title interests the reader with a surprising contrast, and clearly implies its general purpose, to convey an impression. The words *steel* and *ermine* symbolize strength and aristocracy, determination and elegance — impressions which the article wishes to convey. The title also suggests that the attitude of the writer toward the subject is one of respect and admiration. Finally, this title suggests something important about the quality of the composition: that the writing will be lively, informal, and imaginative, not plodding and dull.

Thus, as we said earlier, in addition to capturing the interest of the readers the title performs the important function of introducing them to the predetermined elements of the composition: the specific subject, the dominant general purpose, and the writer-reader relationship. The chart on the next page illustrates how a title can explicitly or implicitly indicate the writer's predetermined elements. Here are some titles which establish reader contact by attracting attention and arousing interest and willingness to read by offering to satisfy these basic needs and desires:

Biological
    Miracle Drugs — Cautions and Hopes
    Death Is on the Run
Psychological
    Land That Job You Want
    Own Your Own Business
Sociological
    Join the Fight against Crime
    Foolproof Strategy in Selecting Fashionable Clothing

Titles Establish the Predetermined Elements

Title	Dominant General Purpose	Specific Subject		Psychol Viewpoint	Writer-Reader Relationship Tone
		Topic	Main Idea		
Achieving Soft Moon Landings	to inform	landings on the moon	how (implied)	objective or semi-objective	formal or semiformal
What Children Shouldn't Read	to actuate	reading material	"shouldn't read"	objective	semiformal
When Smoke Gets in Your Eyes, Wire Your Senators	to actuate	smoke pollution (implied)	stop (implied)	semi-objective	semiformal
De-Mothball the United States Battleships?	to persuade	battleships (U.S.)	"de-mothball"	objective or semi-objective	semiformal
Goodbye Captain Jack	to convey impression	President Kennedy	"goodbye"	subjective	semiformal
Kidney Transplants	to inform	kidney transplants	"how" (implied)	objective	formal or semiformal
Samoa—America's Show Place	to convey impression	Samoa	show place	subjective	semiformal
Nobody Loves a Chimpanzee	to entertain	chimpanzees	their antics (implied)	subjective	semiformal or informal
Unlearning the Lie—Sexism in Schools	to inform	sexism	evident in school systems (implied)	semi-objective	informal
Theodore Roosevelt—The Big Stick	to convey impression	Theodore Roosevelt	exercised his authority (implied)	subjective	semiformal
Medicare Will Work	to persuade	Medicare	"will work"	objective	semiformal

Following are some titles which appeal to the more complex human interests, representing combinations of the basic biological, psychological, and sociological needs and desires.

Acquiring and Saving
    Collecting Original Art Prints
    A House—A Lifetime Investment
Challenge, Competition, Conflict
    Mohammad Ali Will Smash Joe Frazier
    Mayors Meet in Mafia Fight
Companionship and Friendship
    The Sense of Security in Friendship
    We're in This Together
Courtship and Marriage
    I Fell in Love in Jail
Creativity
    A Haphazard, Nonchalant Look Is Best for a Recreation Room
    Build Your Own Harpsichord
Curiosity and Inquisitiveness
    A Tasty Dish—Grasshopper Stew
    Outer Space Has Ghosts
Entertainment, Pleasure, and Adventure
    Carnival on the Isle of Capri
    Try the New Sport of Sky-Diving
Fear and Doubt
    China Will Resort to Nuclear Warfare
    Our Water is Running Out
Worship and Loyalty
    Lent Is for Spiritual Rehabilitation
    Black Women Make History
Sex
    Love that Kills: Sexual Suicide
    Male/Female Roles in American Society

Most titles follow certain strict conventions. The first word and every important word is capitalized. Articles—*a, an, the*—and prepositions—*of, to, without,* etc.—are almost never capitalized, except at the beginning. A title is never put in quotation marks at the head of its own composition, but is quoted when named in another composition. A title is never followed by a period; it occasionally contains internal punctuation and may end with an exclamation point or a question mark. A good title is almost always a word or a phrase, almost never a sentence. Most titles are fairly short. Good titles are always catchy, often memorable.

THE OPENER

The opener is an interest-expander. It is a device placed at the beginning of a piece of writing to help the title hook the reader. It does that by intensifying the interest ignited by the title. You have heard after-dinner speakers start their speeches with a humorous quip, joke, or anecdote to establish a receptive attitude toward what they intend to say. The writer too uses these as well as other devices when needed to arouse and intensify the interest of the reader. In other words, the opener acts to increase and prolong the interest initiated by the title so that the reader will be eager to read on. We have already seen that the subject sentence which contains the writer's main idea will again intensify the reader's interest.

There are times when you do not need a special opener. When you are sure that you are offering something your readers need and want, you start directly with an appropriate title and an effective subject sentence. A paper entitled "Forces Which Influence Flight" would certainly arouse the interest of people vocationally or avocationally interested in aviation. When writing for them, you need only start with a subject sentence expressing a worthwhile main idea about flying.

The opener amplifies interest. In longer compositions, it is placed in one or more separate paragraphs at the beginning so that it expands, reinforces, intensifies the interest ignited by the title. In shorter compositions, you can't always afford a whole paragraph for an opener. You therefore weld the opener into the first part of your main paragraph, perhaps as a whole sentence, perhaps only as a phrase or clause.

Of course, any opener, whether it is a few words, several sentences, or a separate paragraph, should be closely related to the predetermined elements of the particular composition. It must be pertinent to the specific subject, especially to its main idea, and to the dominant general purpose. Starting a written composition with an unrelated or a vaguely related opener may distract the reader and so hinder you in your attempt to communicate effectively. Following are some of the more common types of openers which writers use to amplify the reader interest excited by the title.

Pertinent Quotation

An eloquent, forceful, and pertinent quotation from a person whom the readers admire or respect as an authority will reinforce their interest. If you have any doubt about their familiarity with the person you are quoting, enough must be said so that the quotation will have the desired effect. A quotation does not have to be from a great poet or prose writer; it may be from anyone who is qualified to speak about the writer's topic or main idea. The quotation should not be trite or overused. Here is a good example:

"The blasting noise of popular dance bands can harm the delicate nerve endings of the internal ear," said Dr. Charles W. Compton of Downstate Medical Center. Dr. Compton, who is the father of a

Opener

fourteen-year-old girl as well as chairman of the division of otolaryn-gology at the university, also pointed out that "when the noise reaches 100 decibels a person's clothes vibrate." *Dr. Compton is attempting to find a practical, inexpensive way to determine when the sounds of teenagers' amusements reach a hazardous volume.*

Provocative Question

Beginning a written composition with a provocative question starts readers thinking right away. It arouses their minds to search for their own answers to the question asked. This question will also arouse their curiosity about the writer's answers and how the conclusions were arrived at. Readers will also be curious to know whether or not their own answers to the questions agree with those of the writer.

Why are there more boys born each year than girls? Out of every 100 children born in any period of time, fifty-five of them will be boys. *A better understanding of genetics through laboratory research may someday make it possible to plan families more precisely.*

**Startling Introductory
Statement**

The writer may induce the reader to continue reading by beginning with a startling statement. The introduction may amaze, frighten, or shock the readers, who will then probably continue to read out of curiosity.

A startling exclamation:

"Oh, Baloney. There isn't any real juvenile delinquency here. That is just a word made up by a lot of goofs in politics." These are the words of a father of three sons who are now in the state penitentiary. *With the proper attitude toward the law and society parents can help reduce the crime rate in Ohio.*

Allusion to a startling controversial subject of current interest:

"Fat doctors"—people who deceive clients, promising them weight control by prescribing drugs to curb appetite—are again being investi-gated by a Senate subcommittee. *The problem in the United States is not weight control as much as it is convincing affluent citizenry not to spend money on foolish health fads.*

A startling statement with spectacular dimensions:

America is continuously undergoing plagues much more deadly than those of the Middle Ages. These diseases cause as much as 30 percent of the total number of deaths in the United States during a single year. *Many of these deaths could have been prevented.*

A startling statement which contradicts or challenges a cherished or a commonly accepted belief:

Opener

Columbus was not the first, but the last to discover America. Ample evidence indicates that Lief Erickson and, at different times, other Vikings came to Newfoundland long before Columbus. Some historians believe that Tartars traveled across the strip of land which once connected Russia with Alaska to establish colonies there. *To be given uncontestable credit for their achievements, the great must clearly record their accomplishments as well as achieve them.*

Subject Sentence

Vivid Introductory Sketches

These sketches produce vivid mental images designed to arouse the senses or the emotions of the reader. Using a sketch of a person, an animal, a place, or a thing, you help the readers to experience the subject at close range through a close-up of it. You want the readers to become involved with the subject so that they will want to continue reading. Following are some examples of this type:

A vivid descriptive sketch of a person:

Opener

Scott pressed his nose against the window glass of his room as a car drove up to the front of the Mary Heler Orphanage. He brushed down his wavy blond hair, wiped the moisture from his wide eyes, and stood up tall. His heart filled with hope when he saw a set of prospective parents enter the front door of the home. *"Maybe they'll take me home with them," he said to himself, pretending that he did not know that adults prefer to adopt infants rather than five-year-olds.*

Subject Sentence

A vivid descriptive sketch of an animal:

Opener

Lying in the gutter, the little brown puppy pleaded with his eyes for help. His hind legs dangled uselessly and blood flowed from a gash in his hip. A truck unable to stop had struck the dog and sent him agonizingly to the side of the road. Several children gathered mutely nearby. A neighbor came running with a towel in her hands, and gently she and the truck driver lifted the puppy to the cab. Now it was up to a veterinarian. The puppy would soon be out of his misery, one way or the other. *There should be legislation prohibiting pet owners from allowing their dogs and cats to roam freely only to be slaughtered on our streets.*

Subject Sentence

A Narrative Opening

A narrative—a story—is often used to catch the interest of the reader. Everyone is interested in stories. By starting your composition with a dramatic story, you can induce us to continue reading. Following is a dramatic narrative of a conflict:

Opener

Subject Sentence

In a seventh floor room in New York City's Mount Sinai Hospital, a forty-nine-year-old man with incurable brain disease lay in a coma one day last week. Alerted that death was hours away, a team of sixteen doctors who had been standing by for forty-eight hours quickly readied two other patients for kidney transplants. First, they removed the diseased kidneys of a sixteen-year-old Manhattan boy and kept him anesthetized on the operating table, the incision in his groin covered with a plastic drape. At the same time, they gave presurgery sedatives to a forty-eight-year-old New Jersey woman who had lost both kidneys to nephritis three months before. At 5 A.M., the brain-disease victim died; surgeons removed his kidneys, rushed one to each of the operating rooms. By eight o'clock, they had implanted a new kidney in both waiting recipients. *This "doubleheader" illustrates that there is nothing unusual about kidney transplants today.*[1]

Following is an article from *The Wall Street Journal* which has been adapted to illustrate an opener consisting of several separate paragraphs placed before the main paragraph and the subject sentence:

Elizabeth, a thirty-four-year-old blond clad in a mysterious brown robe, spreads a white sheet on the bare wood floor of her cramped twelfth floor apartment on New York's East Side. Clouds of jasmine and sandalwood incense swirl around her as she bends to draw a "magic circle"—intended to ban evil spirits—on the sheet with a stick of charcoal. Then, by the glow of flickering black candle, she chants:

"By all the names of the spirit princes and by the ineffable name on which all things are created, I conjure you . . ."

Elizabeth is a witch—or so she claims. On this full moonlit evening, the attractive freelance photographer with deep brown eyes is casting a love spell to win the affections of a New York City detective she has just started dating.

Main Paragraph and
Subject Sentence

The practice of witchcraft is casting its spell on thousands of men and women like Elizabeth across the country, and Americans are turning not only to witchcraft but also to astrology, spiritualism, all kinds of psychic phenomena and even devil worship.[2]

It should by now be evident that a good title, a lively opener, and a clear subject sentence provide one of the best ways of catching and holding the reader's interest. Once he has read your opening, the chances are good that he will go on.

[1] Don Moser, *Life,* 1966.
[2] Stephen J. Sansweet, "Americans Show Burst of Interest in Witches and Other Occult Matters," *The Wall Street Journal,* October 23, 1969.

PRACTICE in Achieving This Chapter's Objectives

Practice in identifying and writing titles and openers to establish and amplify reader contact and interest.

	Applications
1. Writing titles that achieve contact and initiate interest.	1
2. Differentiating types of openers.	2, 3, 5
3. Writing openers.	4
4. Writing a title and opener.	6
5. You Be the Judge	

APPLICATION 8-1

Read the following and write a distinctive title for each. Be sure that the titles state or imply the main idea and the writer's purpose. Also, be sure that the title is appropriate to the writer-reader relationship intended.

Title _____

The morning after studying until two or three in the morning comes all too soon at 5:30 A.M. It's all a person can do to reach for the lamp on the nightstand and decide to face the long oncoming day. Orange juice, toast, eggs, fried potatoes, and sausages do nothing to lift the dreary gloom. All seems lost until finally, COFFEE.

Title _____

I can still remember the first time I made coffee for a friend and fellow lover of good coffee. A new drip pot and the finest freshly ground coffee had recently been purchased. I carefully measured the coffee and poured the correct amount of water into the top of the pot. Little did I know that my roommate had put salt water into the pan to boil spaghetti. All my friend could say was "wow."

Title _____

Safety should be a household concern; most accidents happen in the home. The household medicine chest is one source for accidents. Children can climb up and open them. The next major area of concern is the kitchen. Knives should be handled carefully. Another item which may lead to accidents is cleaning fluids. They should be properly capped and stored. Ladders or tools for cleaning hard-to-reach places should be sturdy and well placed.

APPLICATION 8-2

Choose several of your favorite magazines and examine the beginnings of the articles which they contain. Copy the beginning of one article which illustrates the use of any of the following types of openers:

1. pertinent quotation
2. startling introductory statement
3. allusion to a startling controversial subject
4. vivid descriptive sketch
5. dramatic introductory narrative

_____

_____

_____

_____

_____

APPLICATION 8-3

Choose several issues of your favorite newspaper and examine the beginnings of the editorials they contain. Copy the beginning of one editorial which illustrates the use of any of the following types of openers:

1. provocative question
2. startling statement which contradicts or challenges a cherished or a commonly accepted belief or opinion
3. vivid descriptive sketch
4. narrative of a shocking incident
5. narrative of a struggle or conflict in progress

_____

_____

_____

_____

_____

_____

APPLICATION 8-4

Select one of the following types of openers and write a beginning paragraph which contains both the opener and the subject sentence. Be sure your opener is pertinent to your main idea and purpose. Underline the opener with one line and indicate the type of opener you have chosen. Underline the main idea with two lines. Identify your purpose.

1. provocative question
2. vivid introductory sketch
3. startling exclamation
4. dramatic introductory narrative

_____

_____

_____

_____

_____

_____

APPLICATION 8-5

Read each of the following openers, and in the blank opposite each, write the name of the kind you think it is.

1. I was in Damascus, Syria, where roses bloomed and nightingales sang. There, mathematics, art, and astronomy were in bloom long before the Crusades. But, today, the roses are no longer in bloom, and the country is being shaken by a social revolution.　　　　　　_____

2. "In my boyhood, the woods were full of game, and the sky was black with ducks," said Charles A. Lindbergh to an audience last week. Deeply concerned, Lindbergh now crusades all over the world in an effort to preserve the vanishing wildlife. He works closely with the International Union for the Conservation of Nature and the World Wildlife Fund.　　　　　　_____

3. There is nothing wrong with being fat. There are about 20 million fat people, one out of every ten Americans, who have been discriminated against by those who belong to the "cult of thinness." Obesity is unhealthy for naturally thin people, but many fat people are healthy only when they remain fat because of their glandular make-up.　　　　　　_____

4. How are you when it comes to flying? Do your palms perspire? Can you really relax? If you don't enjoy yourself, be assured, you're not entirely alone. Although there are only small numbers of people whose fear of flying is phobic, quite a few are extremely distressed and uncomfortable. Many well-known singers, actors, athletes, and politicians think flying is a terrible way to travel.　　　　　　_____

5. They stood by the fence and waited for the big airliner to taxi up to the terminal. Their son had finally come home from the war. He was the last one to leave the plane, for it took awhile to lower his coffin to the ground. Their hearts ached to see it end like this, even though they knew he died a hero. As the truck bearing the coffin trundled toward the terminal, their thoughts whirled back to twenty years before, to the day they first held their infant in their arms.　　　　　　_____

6. One day shortly after returning from military service, civilian life began to bore me, and I became eager to find some way to relieve the boredom. In my search, I found a want ad which seemed to reach out and grab me. It read "Wanted a bold, adventuresome man. Easy work. $7.00 an hour. Apply Fenn Building." Immediately, I drove down to the Fenn Building and started working in the most terrifying job which I ever had, perched precariously on a scaffold, washing windows ninety feet above the street.　　　　　　_____

APPLICATION 8-6

Select one of the following subject sentences, or one of your own, and write a composition 400 or more words in length, consisting of a title and an opener. The opener may be in a separate paragraph or it may be a part of the introductory paragraph in which your purpose sentence is placed.

Be sure your opener is pertinent to the main idea of your composition and to your purpose. Also, don't forget to indicate what your intended purpose is by placing it opposite the title. Here are some possible topics.

1. Language as a device for subterfuge
2. The women's movement liberates men
3. What is pornography?
4. Compulsive whistling is a symptom
5. Public dancing is therapeutic

YOU BE THE JUDGE

Evaluator's Initials ☐☐☐

Date _____

Section _____

Grade _____

Writer's Name _____

Date _____ Section _____

Title of paper _____

Chapter _____ Application No. _____

General instructions on the You Be the Judge Applications, and specific instructions for Parts I and III, are printed inside the back cover of this book. Read those instructions carefully; then do Part I.

In the lines below, and on another sheet of paper, answer the questions in Part II. Then enter a grade for the paper in the space above left, and write your evaluation for Part III. Reread the composition to see how well the writer understands and applies the principles studied in this chapter. As you read the composition write any helpful suggestions that occur to you in the margins.

PART II

1. Does the title reflect the tone and dominant general purpose of the composition? _____

_____

_____

_____

2. Does it establish reader contact by arousing interest in reading?

_____

_____

_____

3. Suggest two other possible titles and evaluate them in relation to the original. _____

_____

_____

_____

4. Does the title state or imply the subject? If so, how? _____

_____

_____

_____

_____

5. What kind of opener does the writer use, if any? _____

_____

_____

_____

_____

6. Does the opener intensify the interest of the readers and their wish to read? _____

_____

_____

_____

_____

7. Can you suggest a different type of opener which you think might also be effective? _____

_____

_____

_____

_____

PART III   Grade and Explanation:

_____

_____

_____

_____

CHAPTER 9

THE MAIN PARAGRAPH

After studying this chapter and completing the applications that follow it, you should be able to do the following:
1. To identify the parts of a main paragraph and the way they reinforce the pre-determined elements (specific subject, dominant general purpose, and writer-reader relationship) established by the title: *opener* (if needed), *subject sentence,* and *explanatory sentences.*
2. To identify and to write *subject sentences* and *explanatory sentences.*
3. To identify and to write the stated and implied *key* in the main idea of the *subject sentence* and *controlling sentence.*
4. To place *subject sentences* correctly.
5. To write effective *subject* and *controlling sentences.*
6. To apply these principles in a full-length composition.

IN LONGER pieces of writing, the main paragraph is the most important paragraph in the entire composition because it contains the specific subject sentence. This is usually elaborated by one or more supporting or explanatory sentences that clarify terms or ideas in the subject sentence and that are important to the discussion. In addition to the title and any opener, they also help the writer tune the reader in on the tone in which the ideas are being expressed so that hidden assumptions and meanings, if any, are made clear.

Along with the subject sentence and the explanatory sentences, the main paragraph sometimes has its own opener. This is especially true in a short composition of one or two pages, in which a single first paragraph does the whole job. Here is a main paragraph with all three of these parts:

Opener
Subject Sentence

Teenagers, your next smash-up will probably occur on a weekend. *The proportion of traffic accidents involving teens is highest on week end days.* On Fridays of 1968, 20 percent of the accidents involved a teenager; on Saturdays, 23 percent; and on Sundays, 26 percent involved a teenager.

Explanatory Sentence

Following is a main paragraph consisting of a subject sentence and its explanatory sentences:

Subject Sentence

Heart specialists are studying giraffes these days in an effort to prevent heart attacks. High blood pressure is dangerous to human beings. It leads to strokes and contributes to heart attacks. But sky-high pressure, pushing blood up ten feet of neck, doesn't hurt giraffes. Scientists are trying to find out the answer to this oddity and to many others in their search to save human beings from heart failure.

The subject sentence in this paragraph is striking enough to serve as its own opener, so that in effect the paragraph contains all three introductory elements.

The outline below shows once more the relationships between the main paragraph and the other parts of the whole composition.

I. The beginning section
  A. The title
  B. The opener
  C. The main paragraph
    1. The main paragraph opener (when needed)
    2. The subject sentence
      (Explicitly and implicitly introduces the predetermined elements. May also act as its own opener when no other precedes it. This is the most important sentence in the composition.)
    3. Explanatory sentences
      (Define, explain, or give background to enable the reader to better understand ideas expressed in the subject sentence.)
II. The developing and supporting section
III. The concluding section

**THE SUBJECT
SENTENCE**

By now you are familiar with the subject sentence as the *topic sentence* or *thesis sentence* of the whole communication. The term *subject sentence* is used in this text to stress the fact that this sentence does more than merely identify the topic or thesis of a composition. It establishes within the composition those elements that you identified while deciding what you should write and how you should write it. The subject sentence performs the important function of telling the readers by explicit statement or by implication what your intended predetermined elements are, that is, the specific subject, dominant general purpose, and writer-reader relationship. In a sense, it programs the readers' minds, focuses them on what is to follow.

As we said earlier (Chapter 3), the specific subject sentence includes both the specific topic with whatever qualifications the author wishes and the main idea. Here are a few such sentences with the topic in italics and the main idea in boldface:

1. *Oral expression* **may conceal your thoughts.**
2. *Inflatable field hospitals* **were vital in Vietnam.**
3. *Road maps* **are invaluable to motorists.**

Implied Dominant General Purpose

In anything but a long formal composition such as a textbook, the writer indicates the dominant general purpose by implication. That is, you indicate whether you wish to entertain, to convey an impression, to inform, to convince, or to actuate his reader. You may imply your general purpose in a subject sentence such as "Queens used to suffer notoriously from the amorous ambitions of their courtiers." The last part of this sentence, "from the amorous ambitions of their courtiers," suggests that the writer probably intends to entertain, that a humorous or satirical tone will dominate the discussion of the "notorious suffering" of queens.

Read the following subject sentences carefully to see what each implies about the writer's dominant general purpose. The main ideas are italicized. An easy way to determine the intended purpose is to locate the key word and identify the reader response it aims at. Keys are discussed on several of the immediately following pages.

To entertain:

1. The ferris wheel *is a laughing matter.*
2. Owning a fabulous diamond *can be a bad omen.*
3. A lifeguard's lecture about swimming is *"a dry subject."*

To convey an impression:

1. The words "Indian summer" *fill me with a gentle sense of felicity.*
2. The dome of the Capitol in Washington, D.C. *radiates dignity and stability.*
3. Carry Nation's life *is a legend.*

To inform:

1. The corporation *is the second most widely used form of business ownership in the United States.*
2. Lake Erie *is the shallowest of the Great Lakes.*
3. Hydroponics *is gardening without soil.*

To persuade:

1. A republic *is the most effective form of representative government.*
2. Red China *should not have been recognized by the United States.*
3. Pedestrians are *more to blame for accidents than drivers.*

To actuate:

1. When was the last time *you had your lawyer check your will?*
2. An annual physical checkup *is essential to avoid serious illness.*
3. Tell your senator *what you think about the draft.*

The sentences that follow illustrate that you the writer must know your dominant general purpose long before you actually start to write, because the wording of this sentence indicates your purpose. Notice how the

The Subject Sentence and the Implied Dominant General Purpose

To Entertain	To Inform	To Convey an Impression	To Persuade	To Actuate
The most difficult task for the lifeguards is keeping their eyes on the swimmers rather than on the sunbathers.	The most difficult task for a lifeguard is watching the twelve- to fourteen-year-old children.	The lifeguard looked like a bronze statue watching the swimmers from the tower.	Lifeguards should be paid higher wages to insure safety on the beaches.	Train your child to be a skillful lifeguard.
Driving on the left side of the road in England is a slight problem for a right-handed American.	In England, cars are driven on the left side of the road.	Driving in England is a nightmarish experience for an American.	England should change its driving rules to require automobiles to be driven on the right side of the road.	You should learn the traffic regulations of England when you intend to drive through that country.
Income can never keep pace with the speed of change in fashions.	The rapidity with which fashions change corresponds to the amount of economic prosperity within a country.	Changing fashions reflect the restless mood of a nation.	Fashions in clothing sometimes change unnecessarily.	You should not be too eager to accept fashion changes.

writer changed the wording of the following to indicate in each sentence the dominant general purpose intended.

When the spatial or chronological point of view is to be important, the writer will word the subject sentence so that it clearly indicates the point in space or time from which he or she is regarding the subject. Here are two subject sentences explicitly indicating the chronological viewpoint.

1. The lawyer remembered herself, a three-year-old watching the antics of her affluent parents at a party.
2. To a twentieth-century American, King Arthur was little more than a barbarian.

The Key of the Subject Sentence

The heart of the subject sentence is the key idea of the composition. The key is the single word or group of words which expresses the idea of the whole composition in the fewest words. It is usually located in the main idea of the subject sentence; thus the key is the central thought, the core, the nucleus. You must focus on the key before you start to write and as you write. The minds of your readers must also be focused upon the key if communication is to be effective.

To identify the key of the main idea you must ask yourself which word in the subject sentence pinpoints the most important idea. Or you may ask yourself which single word or group of words expresses the essence of what you want to share with your readers. To illustrate, in the following the main ideas are in italic and the keys in boldface.

1. Martha and Henry are *excellent* **runners.**
2. Undisciplined children **misbehave** *flagrantly.*
3. The tragedy revealed to him the *goodness* **of human nature.**
4. His parents were *elated* **by his recovery.**

Beginning with a general topic, you limit it to a specific topic, decide to discuss this with a particular reader in a particular way, in a particular tone which will establish a particular relationship. You keep narrowing the topic until you can express it in a single sentence which can be reduced to a word or a phrase—the key. No sharper focus is possible. Here are other examples.

Sometimes the key (in boldface below) is a single word with or without modifiers:

1. In performing a scientific analysis, there are **six** *basic steps.*
2. In sales *the approach is the* **key** *to success.*
3. Shopping for groceries is a **trying** *experience.*
4. Although too fast for me, jet planes are **vital** *for modern transit.*
5. *Slaughterhouse Five* is one of Vonnegut's **best** *novels.*

Sometimes the key is made up of several words in parallel construction:

1. Swimming is a sport that requires *not only* **skill** *but* **strength** *as well.*
2. The main industries of Alaska are **fishing, foresting,** *and* **mining.**

3. The author writes **skillfully** *and* **delightfully.**
4. The apprentice showed **promise** *and* **determination** to learn how to run the lathe.
5. In real life, a person can be both **barbaric** and **heroic.**

When the subject sentence has more than one clause, it may have more than one main idea. It will have a main idea with its own key in each clause.

1. Engineering was **my ambition,** but the field was **overcrowded.**
2. Watching TV is **enjoyable;** however, the news reports are often **tedious.**
3. Converting sea water to fresh water is a **challenging** *problem,* and it long **baffled** *the best scientists.*
4. Some horses raised in Argentina eat **very little,** yet they are **strong enough** to carry an adult.
5. The clerk usually spoke in an **apologetic** tone, but he **roared** *when angry.*

When the subject sentence is a question the key is usually the interrogative word, the word that pinpoints the idea the writer will develop. The keys in the following illustrations are italicized:

1. *How* did homo sapiens survive in the stone age?
2. *Where* is Scorpio?
3. *Why* do we have nightmares?

As we will see when we discuss methods of development in Chapters 10 through 13, the key often gives the essential clue to the way in which the topic should be developed.

Placement of the Subject Sentence

Unless your purpose requires you to do otherwise, the subject sentence should be placed at the beginning of the main paragraph. The beginning of any paragraph attracts immediate attention. It is in this spot that you place those ideas that you want your readers to notice immediately. Thus it is a good spot to place the subject sentence because it quickly identifies the predetermined elements. It is a good spot also because the opener leads the readers right to it before they can escape in pursuit of some other interest.

In some writing, especially when you want suspense or emphasis, it is wise to put the subject sentence at the end of the main paragraph, another emphatic position. Writers often reserve this spot for an idea which they want readers to remember.

The following paragraphs illustrate. They are almost the same, but the emphasis is somewhat different because the subject sentences are placed in different positions.

Mr. Murray is as devoted to his library books as a robin to its hungry young. He eagerly arises each morning and faithfully arrives at work at eight A.M. Earnestly working all day, he returns home late, sometimes after nine o'clock in the evening. When he arrives home, his briefcase is stuffed with work which he voluntarily completes at night, a new book to report on, a bit of research to do for a citizen who urgently needs an answer to a question. When it is necessary, he is often found poring over old manuscripts on weekends.

Arnold Katke

Mr. Murray thinks nothing of coming to work at eight o'clock each morning, staying all day, and returning home sometimes after nine o'clock in the evening. When he goes home, his briefcase is stuffed with work which he voluntarily completes late at night, a new book to report on, a bit of research to do for a citizen who urgently needs an answer to a question. When it is necessary, he is often found poring over old manuscripts on weekends. *He is as devoted to his library books as a robin to its hungry young, equally and tenderly.*

Arnold Katke

Effective Subject Sentences

Since the subject sentence is the most important sentence in any communication, it must be clear and interesting. Its focal word or phrase, the key, must be vivid and emphatic, and should not be buried in a thicket of apologetic, ambiguous, awkward, or inappropriate language. Yet subject sentences with these faults are common in the writing of beginners. Here is an example:

Since my knowledge of judo is very limited, I would like to discuss one facet of it which is not too difficult, its Shinto origin.

Can you think of anything more likely to turn a reader off? If you know so little about your subject, or if you don't obviously know what you want to say about it, why should any reader waste time reading you? You could just as well have said:

Judo originated as a Shinto ritual

and had a favorable reaction from your readers at the outset.

   Vague and wordy subject sentences also make a disastrous first impression.

Status is the condition or situation in which one individual or group of individuals is considered either by himself or themselves (or by somebody else) as being either above or below the other in condition or situation.

Only a determined reader could make much out of that. The writer could have kept his audience by writing:

Status is the comparative social standing of two or more individuals or groups.

Worthless Keys

Worthless subject sentences express worthless key ideas, those which have nothing real to say. Unless your purpose is merely to entertain, your subject sentence must offer the readers something new or interesting, worth the time and effort of reading. If the sentence merely offers something obvious, they will shrug their shoulders and pass on. Here are some examples:

1. Leaves change their color every fall.
2. The history of ancient Rome is interesting.
3. Toys which are indestructible are never broken.
4. War causes much suffering.
5. Food is a must for human beings.
6. Birds live in trees.
7. Travel is a rewarding experience.

**CONTROLLING
SENTENCES**

The same principles that apply to the writing of effective subject sentences also apply to the writing of controlling sentences since both perform some of the same functions. The subject sentence shapes the whole composition; the controlling sentence governs the development of the supporting paragraph in which it appears. It therefore has its own main idea and key to which all the supporting sentences in the paragraph must be directly or indirectly related.

The subject sentence and the controlling sentences are so vital to writing that you should go back after completing your first draft to check their effectiveness. You should especially check to see if their main ideas, especially their keys, are clearly stated.

PRACTICE in Achieving This Chapter's Objectives

Practice in identifying and writing effective parts of a main paragraph.

	Applications
1. Identifying the main idea and key of subject or controlling sentences.	1, 2, 3
2. Identifying the predetermined elements stated or implied by subject sentences.	4, 5
3. Writing effective subject or controlling sentences.	6
4. Writing main paragraphs with a subject sentence and explanatory sentences.	6
5. Writing a separate opener and a main paragraph.	7
6. Applying these principles in a full-length composition.	8
7. You Be the Judge	

APPLICATION 9-1

In each of the following, underline the main idea with one line and the key with two. In these subject or controlling sentences, the key consists of a single word. One sentence has an implied main idea and key; underline only the word that implies the key.

1. Violinists are put through extensive training.

2. An automobile is a necessity for urban or rural living.

3. Cooking lobster over an open fire is simple.

4. The per capita income in the United States exceeds that in Europe.

5. Because of the many distractions, studying in a dormitory is difficult.

6. What is hydroponics?

7. Structural steel is a durable building material.

8. I will tell you how to build your own swimming pool.

9. Neither the working hours nor the pay is satisfactory to the employees.

10. Photography, like painting, music, and writing, is an art.

11. Today's human is a superior being, supposedly.

12. An automobile transmission is a complex mechanism.

13. The abandoned old house was badly in need of repair.

14. Of all my possessions, I value my car most.

15. The cost of advertising is increasing.

16. Becoming a psychiatrist was Sally's main dream.

17. A trip to Bermuda is expensive for the newly married.

18. The saucer-shaped object was visible in the moonlight.

19. Modern medicine is a great aid in extending human life.

20. In roof construction, pitch is very important.

APPLICATION 9-2

Each of the following subject or controlling sentences has a key with more than one key word. Underline all the key words in each main idea.

1. The major causes of traffic accidents are speeding, "tailgating," and alcohol.

2. A stock-car driver is skillful and cautious.

3. Leslie is a dreamer and an idealist.

4. A vacation in Spain would be expensive but fascinating.

5. The tools of any trade must be handled carefully and skillfully.

6. Courageously and unquestioningly, the students followed the directions.

7. Skiing is exciting and dangerous.

APPLICATION 9-3

Each of the following subject or controlling sentences is a compound sentence consisting of two or more independent clauses, each of which has its own main idea with its own key. Underline the key of each independent clause. There are two keys in each sentence.

1. The flying object was saucer-shaped, and the villagers were terrified by it.

2. Intoxicated drivers are dangerous; they are a major cause of accidents.

3. Modern medicine reduces suffering; it also increases our life expectancy.

4. The Puritans were religious, but they were also bold reasoners.

5. The political martyrs appeared weak; however, they were strong.

APPLICATION 9-4

Following are ten specific subject sentences. In the blank preceding each, place the letter from the following key that best identifies the element which should play the most important role in the composition.

                         A. literal meaning
                         B. tone
                         C. point of view

_____ 1. Smoking is harmful.

_____ 2. Why do grown-ups insist on acting superior around us "little people"?

_____ 3. Many theorems proved in plane geometry can be proved by methods of coordinate geometry.

_____ 4. As a doormat, I felt well qualified to speak about shoes.

_____ 5. Bluffing is the fine art of telling white lies.

_____ 6. NaCl is a food staple.

_____ 7. The spider looked at the moth in the web and prepared for a banquet in the moonlight.

_____ 8. They sent the mysterious lady a rose.

_____ 9. My grandmother is genuinely interested in my life style.

_____ 10. Carbon monoxide causes a bit of respiratory failure.

APPLICATION 9-5

In the blank opposite each of the following subject or controlling sentences, place the letter identifying the most probable dominant general purpose. First underline the key and determine the reader response it intends.

A. to entertain   D. to persuade
B. to convey an impression   E. to actuate
C. to inform

_____ 1. Only recently has photography been considered an art form.

_____ 2. Though only a hobby for some, fishing is the main source of income for many.

_____ 3. European cars are more economical to maintain than American cars.

_____ 4. Imagine yourself sailing in a sailboat you built.

_____ 5. Shark hunting is fun.

_____ 6. Because it is a dangerous sport, boxing should be prohibited.

_____ 7. I must be a magician, I planted a tulip and got a lily.

_____ 8. Our agents are a friendly, neighborly sort.

_____ 9. Organic chemistry is the study of carbon and its compounds.

_____ 10. The beautiful yacht danced in the moonlight.

_____ 11. For me, bowling is fun.

APPLICATION 9-6

Select any one of the following subjects: skirts, trousers, foreign cars, toys, planets, bridges, fads, cactus flowers, tropical fish, or any other topic which your instructor may assign. Limit your topic by the use of modifiers or more specific nouns; limit it chronologically and spatially; and finally limit it by the phrasing of the main idea. Now write a worthwhile subject sentence suitable for achieving one of the five dominant general purposes. Indicate which of the five it is designed to achieve.

Below, write a main paragraph with its own opener. Be sure your paragraph has a well-written subject sentence with a worthwhile main idea. Use at least five explanatory sentences to clarify your main idea, purpose, and intended writer-reader relationship. Underline your key with two lines. Write a title for your paragraph.

Title _____

Purpose _____

_____

_____

_____

_____

_____

_____

_____

_____

_____

_____

_____

_____

_____

_____

_____

APPLICATION 9-7

Select a topic of your own and write two paragraphs consisting of a separated opener and a main paragraph. Be sure your opener is appropriate to the purpose sentence in your main paragraph. Also, be sure to have several explanatory sentences in your main paragraph, clarifying its subject sentence. Write a title and indicate your purpose.

Title _____

Purpose _____

Opener _____

_____

_____

_____

_____

_____

_____

_____

_____

Main paragraph

_____

_____

_____

_____

_____

_____

_____

_____

_____

APPLICATION 9-8

Write a full-length composition of about 600 words, consisting of: a title; an opener, either separate or incorporated into the main paragraph; a main paragraph, including a subject sentence and several explanatory sentences; at least three supporting paragraphs; and a concluding paragraph. Be sure to indicate your intended purpose. Read the following You Be the Judge before writing. Remember, your instructor may have your paper evaluated by another student. Here are some suggested topics:

1. College dorms
2. Parliamentary systems of government
3. The energy crisis.
4. A four-day work week
5. A racial issue

YOU BE
THE JUDGE

Writer's name _____

Date _____ Section _____

Title of paper _____

Chapter _____ Application No. _____

General instructions on the You Be the Judge Applications, and specific instructions for Parts I and III, are printed inside the back cover of this book. Read those instructions carefully; then do Part I.

In the lines below, and on another sheet of paper, answer the questions in Part II, then enter a grade for the paper in the space above left, and write your evaluation for Part III. Reread the composition to see how well the writer understands and applies the principles studied in this chapter. As you read the composition write any helpful suggestions that occur to you in the margins.

PART II

1. Identify the subject sentence.

_____

_____

_____

_____

2. Evaluate the subject sentence, and indicate whether it has any of the following faults: apologetic, ambiguous, illogical, inappropriate to one of the predetermined elements, weakly expressed. _____

_____

_____

_____

3. How many explanatory sentences are there in the main paragraph, and how does each explain the subject sentence? _____

_____

_____

_____

_____

175

4. In addition to the main paragraph, is there an opener? If so, tell what kind it is and how effective. _____

_____

_____

_____

5. Identify the main idea of the subject sentence. _____

_____

_____

_____

6. Identify the key. _____

_____

_____

_____

PART III   Grade and Explanation:

_____

_____

_____

_____

PART 4

DEVELOPMENT

CHAPTER 10

ENUMERATION, ILLUSTRATION, ANALYSIS, SYNTHESIS

After studying this chapter and completing the applications that follow it, you should be able to do the following:
1. To identify and differentiate four common forms of thought relationships: *enumeration*, *illustration*, *analysis*, and *synthesis*.
2. To identify and to write controlling sentences that allow or require development by *enumeration*, *illustration*, *analysis*, or *synthesis*.
3. To write supporting paragraphs of analysis or synthesis, consisting of *structural*, *functional*, or *causal* relationships.
4. To develop supporting paragraphs by writing *enumeration*, *illustration*, *analysis*, or *synthesis*.
5. To write these forms in developing the supporting paragraphs in a full-length composition.

EXCEPT for special kinds of writing such as poetry, fiction, and drama—with which we are not mainly concerned—almost all of our daily communication is intended to convey information and ideas in one form or another. We may want to tell what something looked or sounded like, how it was made, what happened, how it happened, or why it happened. Whatever our aim, the main body of what we have to say will tend to follow one of a few basic patterns of human thought. We list or *enumerate* things, *illustrate* them, take them apart or *analyze* them, or put them together in a new way or *synthesize* them. In this chapter we take a look at these four processes. The key will determine which developing form is used. Also, it will help the writer decide the extent of the enumeration, illustration, analysis, or synthesis that should be developed.

ENUMERATION

Enumeration is the commonest form of thought and development because it is the easiest to use. *Enumeration is a simple listing of words, groups of words, or sentences.* It builds up a discussion merely by giving the reader a series of details without explaining the relationships among them. It is much like laying a brick wall by placing one brick beside another in a series without adding cement to establish a firm bond between them. A grocery list is a simple form of enumeration. The items on it may have no connection except that they are all needed by the same person — that is, they relate to the same topic. For this reason, enumeration is especially suitable for treating broad and simple ideas that do not require or that cannot be dealt with in depth. It is often used to treat an idea lightly or superficially to create a casual effect or to entertain the reader.

The following paragraph consists of two sentences, a controlling sentence and a primary supporting sentence. Notice that the primary sentence is mostly a series of single words—nouns—to develop the key, "most versatile." As often happens, the key is the clue not only to the purpose but also to the method of development, in this case, enumeration.

Leonardo da Vinci was the most versatile of all the famous sons of Florence. *Painter, sculptor, architect, engineer, scientist, musician, inventor, mathematician*, and *cartographer*, he is much more famous for his skill today than he was in his own time.

Here is another example in which groups of words form a sentence enumeration within a supporting paragraph. Again the key, "many standard ingredients," is the clue.

The television program had many of the standard ingredients of a typical western. It had *sneaky outlaws, mean Indians, heroes with white ten gallon hats, black hatted horse thieves, covered wagons, beautiful saloon owners, smoking pistols,* and *hard liquor.*

The details of an enumeration may be not only words or phrases but whole sentences. Notice how a series of sentences is used in the following to develop the key idea, "many new problems."

The transportation of birds and animals from India and Africa has caused many new problems for the airplanes. *Crocodiles must be given a shower daily. Elephants must be fed hay or sugarcane,* depending upon whether they came from Africa or Asia. *Reptiles must be kept in a temperature of 67 degrees and above,* and *birds must have lighted cages.* These many problems make animal transportation hazardous for the animals as well as for the plane crew.

Joe Hartzman

Each sentence in this longer paragraph contains an item in a list of similar items which support the controlling sentence at the beginning.

Modern Americans would find it difficult to live without the machines upon which they have become dependent. Each morning they are awakened by alarm clocks. They use electric razors, electric toothbrushes, and electric hair stylers. Their breakfast toast and coffee are prepared by electrical devices. Their homes are automatically heated or automatically cooled. They drive to work in mechanical chariots, which are in themselves combinations of complex mechanical devices. At their offices they find a whole battery of typewriters, calculators, dictating machines, telephones, even computers. People have become so dependent upon these mechanical marvels that often they are not even aware of relying on them. If, however, they were deprived of their services, they would be astonished by how much a part of their lives they have become.

And here is a series of paragraphs — a whole section of a communication — devoted to a single enumerative series.

In his poem "Song of Myself," Walt Whitman beckons us to "stand by my side and look in the mirror with me." Peering into his mirror, we see that:
He was born here, from parents born here from parents the same, and their parents the same. He assumed that every atom belonging to him also belonged to us. He loafed and invited his soul to celebrate himself and sing of himself. He was then in perfect health and he hoped not to cease his song until death.
He ceased not even after death. For in starting to sing "Song of Myself," Whitman is still singing. Still, he celebrates himself and sings of himself. Still his soul rejoices in what it envisioned for America. Still today, Whitman's soul and body are united in song for the country he loved.

Ann Curran

Notice how in these paragraphs the writer clearly indicates to her reader that she is intentionally enumerating by the use of parallel construction. She does this by beginning each of her important ideas with the same words, expressed in somewhat the same grammatical patterns.

An enumeration may be written in any of three ways:

1. Solid enumeration: in which the items are neither numbered nor indented.
2. Numbered or alphabetized enumeration: in which each item is preceded by a number or a letter of the alphabet. In this form the items are not indented.
3. Numbered or alphabetized and indented enumeration: in which each item is indented and preceded by a number or a letter.

When there are only a few items in a series and they require no special emphasis it is usually better to write the enumeration as a solid paragraph with no indentation, numbering, or lettering. For example:

Many wood finishers consider coloring powder dissolved in water the most satisfactory stain for several reasons. Wood that has become dry will quickly absorb moisture. Water stains penetrate much more deeply into wood than do either oil or spirit stains. It is easy to secure darker or lighter shades and tints with water stains.

To gain added emphasis for each of the points or items in the series, each may be preceded by a number or a letter. Here is the same paragraph with the items numbered.

Many wood finishers consider coloring powder dissolved in water the most satisfactory stain for several reasons. (1) Wood that has become dry will quickly absorb moisture. (2) Water stains penetrate much more deeply into wood than do either oil or spirit stains. (3) It is easy to secure darker or lighter shades and tints with water stains.

To gain still more emphasis for the items in the series, the writer may use indentation along with a number or a letter before each item:

Many wood finishers consider coloring powder dissolved in water the most satisfactory stain for several reasons:

1. Wood that has become dry will quickly absorb moisture.
2. Water stains penetrate much more deeply into wood than do either oil or spirit stains.
3. It is easy to secure darker and lighter shades and tints with water stains.
4. Water stains dry quickly.
5. Water stains are less likely to "bleed" into subsequent coats of stain.
6. Brushes are easier to clean when water color is used.
7. Water stains are more transparent, revealing wood grains.

Enumeration allows you to deal with a topic over a broad range, including extensive spreads of time and space, in a greatly reduced number of words. It enables you to skim the surface of the topic by merely listing characteristics related to your key idea. It would be difficult to discuss the rock stratifications of the North American shelf, all of the ages through which the earth passed in its evolution, or the history of the Holy Roman Empire in a report of five or six pages without enumeration.

ILLUSTRATION

If enumeration is the easiest way of thinking about and developing an idea, illustration is probably the next easiest. *An illustration is a case, an example, a specimen, a "for instance."* Like the items in an enumeration, illustrations make the main statement specific. The term *illustration* is from the Latin *illustratus,* meaning "lighted up." Vivid illustrations light up important ideas and make them clear, interesting, memorable, and convincing. As you study the following examples note again how the subject sentence indicates the method of development by stating a generalization which needs to be exemplified. In this way writers make their readers aware of what they intend to do.

Illustrations may consist of single items or series of items which clarify or add feeling or vividness in written expression. An illustration may also be a narrative, lighting up an idea to clarify it in the reader's mind.

Here are some specimens. The supporting paragraph immediately following uses a series of individual items as examples. In a sense, these are specimens of the point which the controlling sentence expresses.

Military slang often includes the names of animals. The colonel may be either a *chicken* or an *eagle*, a reference to the insignia he wears on his shoulders. A *mustang* is any commissioned officer who has risen from the ranks. Or he may be an officer who has been commissioned directly in the American Navy after serving in the merchant marine. In the army or in the air force, the *dodo* is not necessarily stupid or awkward; he is merely a student pilot who has not yet soloed. *Devil dog* is a term synonymous with leatherneck or marine. In the navy a *frogman* is a skindiver who works as a demolition expert.[1]

Following is a supporting paragraph which develops its controlling sentence with a series of happenings or incidents involving well known people. These enable the writer to make the abstract key idea, "persistent investigation," concrete and easier to understand. They also add dramatic qualities that make the information more interesting.

Knowledge often results only after persistent investigation. Albert Einstein, after a lengthy examination of the characteristics of matter and energy, formulated his famous Theory of Relativity, which now acts as a basis for further research in nuclear physics. Using plaster casts of footprints, fingerprints, and stray strands of hair, a detective pertinaciously pursues the criminal. After years of work Annie Jump Cannon perfected the classification of the spectra of some 350,000 stars. Investigations into the causes of polio have provided us with the means for prevention and cure of this dreaded disease only after many years of research. As students, we too are determined in our investigation to find, retain, and contribute to the store of human knowledge.

Earl Rudolph

[1] From December issue of *Word Study* © 1968 by G. & C. Merriam Co., publishers of the Merriam-Webster Dictionaries.

Examples are often used in support of contentions. When the purpose of the writer is to convince or to actuate his reader, examples both negative and positive are often offered to support what the writer's position. Notice how this is done in the following supporting paragraph:

Not all Democratic Presidents have been active and not all Republican Presidents have been passive. Two good examples are James Buchanan and Teddy Roosevelt. James Buchanan was a Democratic President and was far from active. He did nothing about the Southern States threatening to secede from the Union or the issue of slavery in the new territories. Teddy Roosevelt was a Republican President and was far from passive. He is known for busting up trust monopolies of big business. In classifying active and passive Presidents one shouldn't class them according to party.

Richard Dailey

Everybody likes a story; therefore, narratives are often helpful not only in making writing interesting but also in enabling the writer to express clearly what he has to say. Narrative illustration is especially helpful because it enables the writer to dramatize the point he is making to express it clearly. It is very helpful when the point is an emotion or some other abstract idea. Notice how the following narrative illustration expands and makes more understandable the meaning expressed by the controlling sentence.

Often a domesticated animal's life is dependent upon the actions of his owner; sometimes, however, the opposite is true. A pet dog, especially one who lives in the city, could not survive if his owner did not provide food and shelter. Occasionally it is the dog who enables the owner to survive. Such was the case of the factory worker I know, who worked on the 10 P.M. to 4 A.M. shift. She was returning home from work one cold, wintery night when the streets were slippery and the ice was covered with a fresh layer of snow. Her little Boston bull dog habitually met her as she got out of her car to open the garage doors. On this particular night, as the woman was getting out of the car, she slipped and fell, breaking her hip. Realizing that she couldn't be heard when she shouted because of the wind howling through the trees and the sound absorption of the new snow, she knew her only chance was to instruct her dog to go into the house to get help. Sensing that his owner was in trouble, the dog obeyed the instructions and by barking and scratching at the back door of the house, he was able to awaken the woman's husband and lead him to his wife. This is one instance which illustrates that often there are good reasons why a woman becomes a dog's best friend.

Mark Muhn

The writer must select only illustrations which are appropriate to the main idea, especially the key, and to the dominant general purpose. Here is a supporting paragraph which contains illustrations that help the writer to achieve the purpose of entertaining the readers. Notice that in this example the writer does not formally introduce his illustrations with words such as *for example* or *for instance.* These introductory words become monotonous; therefore, occasionally the writer just slides in an illustration without them.

Buffalo ranchers, those who raise buffaloes, cite only one disadvantage of the buffalo – they are ornery critters. When a buffalo raises his tail, he is warning you that he is angry. One buffalo rancher likes to tell the story that one summer an angry buffalo picked up a visitor by the seat of his pants, swung him over his head three or four times and then set him down and just walked away. Another relates that once when herding a big bull and his harem with a truck, he wanted the bull to go faster, so he blew the horn and went up close to try to prod him with the truck. The bull stopped, turned around, and charged, banging the front end.

Gordon Ferisse

One type of illustration often used to make a point, especially an abstract one, is the hypothetical narrative illustration. In a sense, this type says to the reader, "let's suppose" or "let's pretend that this or that happened." Writers usually use hypothetical narratives to convince or actuate their readers.

A writer must be able to judge how much illustration and other explanation the reader needs in order to understand what is being said. An illustration need not be limited to one supporting paragraph. Often several paragraphs are used to illustrate a point, particularly in narrative illustration.

On complex subjects a writer often provides a series of supporting paragraphs with a series of examples to illustrate a point.

The firefly is shedding light on the little understood processes whereby all living organisms get their energy. By probing the process with which this insect converts chemical energy into light, dissipating very little heat, scientists are learning more about how our body cells transform food into usable energy.

A familiar example of light emission by living organisms is the "burning of the sea" in tropical water. Myriads of organisms, often one-celled, emit this eerie "cold" light when stimulated by the movement of fish or other marine life. The combined glow is often sufficiently bright to outline these fish and other marine organisms.

Other examples of biological light production include the iridescence shown by harmless bacteria growing on unrefrigerated meat and fish, and luminescence of the glow worm. In New Zealand, the ceilings of several famous caves are covered with glow worm larvae. From each of these glowing larvae is suspended a long luminescent thread that probably serves to catch food particles or to lure small insects.

These are but a few examples of biological light. Indeed, the range and diversity of bioluminescent organisms are impressive, including certain bacteria, fungi, sponges, jellyfish, crustaceans, snails, millipedes, and insects. Many fish and lower forms of plant life are luminous; however, no amphibia, reptiles, birds, or mammals automatically produce biological light.[2]

As a writer you must be able to judge how much illustration your readers need. You should avoid giving them too much or too little. If you give too much, they become bored, and if too little, they may be confused or fail to understand.

ANALYSIS AND SYNTHESIS

The philosopher John Dewey pointed out that in reflective thinking the mind starts out by establishing relationships among ideas in one of two ways; either by analysis, breaking down an idea to find its parts and see how they go together; or by synthesis, taking a given set of facts and ideas and putting them together in a new way. What Dewey is saying, in a sense, is that the mind goes two ways—from the whole to the parts by analysis, or from the parts to the whole by synthesis. It may also shed some light on the direction of these processes if we associate them with two modes of scientific thought which may be familiar to you, *deduction* and *induction*. In analysis the mind goes from the whole to its parts, and in deduction it goes from a broader concept to a series of more limited ones. Both movements are from large to small, broad to narrow. In synthesis the mind goes from the parts to the whole, and in induction it goes from a collection of single items or facts to a generalization or inference about them. In these two processes the motion is small to large, narrow to broad.

In writing, these two motions or directions of thought are clearly reflected both in phrasing and in organization or structural pattern. To show the similarities and differences between them, and to show how both are more sophisticated and advanced mental processes than enumeration and illustration, a series of specimen paragraphs treating the same subject in each of these four ways follows.

We begin with a paragraph in which a series of details is simply listed or enumerated to develop a controlling sentence:

A tropical coral reef, a self-contained community, has *a great variety of marine life*. Many kinds of colorful, exotic plant and animal life known as plankton thrive in the area within and around the reef. Snails, crabs, shrimp, oysters, clams, and a host of different kinds of

[2] O. A. Batista, "Biological Light," *Chemistry*, April 1966, p. 14, Washington, D.C.: American Chemical Society.

jellyfish live in and around it. The wiley octopus pushes his way through its waters, and the vicious moray eel weaves its way in and out, making sure that nothing goes to waste and that order prevails.

Mary Price

In this paragraph the controlling sentence, which comes at the beginning, has as its main idea "a great variety of marine life." Since this phrase implies no relationship other than simple addition—"great variety = one thing + another thing + another thing, and so forth"—the "control" implies nothing more complex than enumeration.

The following paragraph develops the point which the controlling sentence expresses through illustration.

A self-contained community is one which possesses all that it needs within its own boundaries. *One example of such a community is a tropical coral reef*, where the food supply for each form of life is provided by another form of life within the community. A typical food cycle begins with exotic plants which are eaten by snails; then the snails are eaten by an octopus, which in turn provides nourishment for a moray eel. And when the eel dies, its decomposed body is the source of nutrients for the plants.

Here the controlling sentence is a definition of the term "self-contained community," and its main idea is, "possesses all that it needs within its own boundaries." The coral reef is used to clarify that idea with a simple explanation of a food cycle. Now look at the next version, developed by analysis.

Because of the tight interdependency of the marine life which inhabits the area in and around it, *the tropical coral reef is a self-contained community*. Colorful, exotic plants which feed on marine microorganisms are devoured by fish and other sea urchins inhabiting the area. Sea snails nibble at these exotic plants, and the wily octopus devours the snails. The octopus itself then becomes nourishment for the vicious moray eel. Each form of life in the coral reef community derives its sustenance by consuming another of its members, and later, it itself becomes nourishment to maintain the cruel but beautiful balance of nature.

Mary Price

The main difference is that this paragraph contains many *thought relationships* not present in the first ones. The opening word, "because," introduces the theme of cause and result. Beyond this, the main emphasis is on "self-contained community," which in the first version was subordinate to "variety of marine life." Hence the clue is not enumeration or example but explanation by analysis of *how* that community is self-contained. The rest of the paragraph analyzes and so explains that relationship. We can say that this paragraph is developed by analysis.

Here is a fourth version of this same paragraph, this one developed by synthesis or putting the various facts together to reach a generalization about them rather than starting with the generalization.

Colorful, exotic plants which feed on marine microorganisms are devoured by fish and other sea urchins inhabiting the area in and around a coral reef. Sea snails nibble at these exotic plants, and the wily octopus devours the snails. The octopus itself then becomes a tasty banquet for the vicious moray eel. Each form of life in the coral reef community derives its sustenance by consuming another, and later itself becomes nourishment to maintain the cruel but beautiful balance of nature. Because of this tight interdependency of the marine life which inhabits the area in and around it, the tropical coral reef is a self-contained community.

Mary Price

This time the controlling sentence, coming at the end, ties everything together and states the conclusion to be reached from all these details. We can say that this paragraph is developed by synthesis—it puts it all together at the end.

Both synthesis and analysis have their special uses. Synthesis is frequently used to gain impact by withholding a dominant impression to the end, as in the following paragraph, which builds through a series of details to the final statement:

This soldier-statesman with the famous grin holds a special place of respect in the hearts of American citizens and those of the world for his endless and selfless devotion in the search for peace. Perhaps his statement, "My experience in Europe convinces me that the settlement of controversy's largely a matter of knowing how to work with people, convincing them of your sincerity, and infusing in them the goodwill and spirit of co-operation," was his guiding philosophy and the key to his popularity. His own common sense, honesty, and deep sincerity in forming decisions that were best for America were above politics and other manipulations too frequently included in policy making. His advice was sought almost to his death by those who followed him as President. So as it was said at Dwight David Eisenhower's funeral, he has fully earned, from his remarkable life, those famous words of praise, "Well done, thou good and faithful servant."

Mary Petersen

(Also, notice the use of the archaic word *thou* for special effect.)

Both synthesis and analysis can be used to explain relationships which are primarily *structural, functional,* or *causal.* An explanation which is primarily structural tells how the parts are related in space, how they are shaped, and how they fit and are connected with each other. An explanation which is primarily functional tells how things work in relation to each other. And one which is primarily causal presents the causes or the results of something. The three paragraphs which follow illustrate these three purposes:

Structural Analysis

The syringe is a device often used in medicine either to inject fluid by force or to withdraw it by vacuum. It consists of a plunger (it may also have a rubber bulb) fitted firmly to a calibrated barrel or container which is closed tightly at both ends by means of o-ring seals. The plunger and barrel assembly unit is press-fitted to a hollow stainless steel needle with a slanted point.

Ronald Wysocki

Functional Analysis

The syringe is a device often used in medicine either to inject fluid by force or to withdraw it by vacuum. When the plunger of the syringe is depressed, it transmits and equally distributes pressure to the liquid in its barrel. This pressure forces the liquid through from the barrel into the hollow of the needle and into the substance into which the point is penetrated. To withdraw fluid, the plunger is depressed into an empty barrel, creating a vacuum which sucks out the fluids.

Ronald Wysocki

Causal Analysis

Before the invention of the syringe, getting fluids into or out of the bloodstream directly was a difficult task for a doctor; consequently, many patients died. Therefore, the first syringe developed by Charles Pravas in the 1800s was a boon to medicine. Because liquids are incompressible and because force or pressure placed on fluids in a sealed container is transmitted equally in all directions, he was able to build a simple but practical syringe. When a liquid is pushed by pressure, it moves toward the point of least resistance. Because the point of least resistance in a syringe is the hollow needle, the fluid pushed by force from the plunger must pass through the needle into the penetrated substance. Of course, when extraction of fluids is desired, the pressure from the body penetrated pushes the fluid through the hollow needle toward the vacuum created by the plunger in the barrel of the syringe.

Ronald Wysocki

Enumeration makes little or no attempt to discover relationships other than addition, and illustration simply lights up a generalization with a case or an example. Analysis and synthesis go farther and explain relationships, going either from the whole to the parts or from the parts to the whole. In this movement they relate, respectively, to deductive and inductive thinking and presentation.

PRACTICE in Achieving This Chapter's Objectives

Practice in differentiating and writing supporting paragraphs of enumeration, illustration, analysis, and synthesis.

	Applications
1. Identifying enumeration, illustration, analysis, synthesis.	1, 8
2. Writing controlling sentences for enumeration, illustration, analysis, and synthesis.	2, 4, 6
4. Developing supporting paragraphs of enumeration, illustration, analysis, or synthesis.	3, 5, 7, 9,
4. Writing a full-length composition using enumeration, illustration, analysis, and synthesis.	10
5. You Be the Judge	

APPLICATION 10-1

In the blank at the left of each of the following paragraphs, tell whether it is enumeration, illustration, analysis, or synthesis. Explain your answer in the space below the paragraph.

_____ 1. Depending on the voice range of its members, a mixed choir is made up of four main sections: the soprano, alto, tenor, and bass sections. The soprano section consists of the women members who have the highest voices. The range of their voices goes up to about an *A* on the musical scale. These sopranos usually sing the melody. The altos are the women members with the lowest female voices. They sing the harmony to the melody sung by the sopranos. The tenors of the choir are male members who have the same range as the sopranos, but an octave lower. Like the altos, the tenors usually sing harmonies. The last section, the bass section, is made up of the males with the lowest voices. The members of the bass section usually sing on the root of the chord, for example, on a D chord, the basses will sing the note *D.*

Steve Cox

_____
_____
_____
_____
_____

_____ 2. Dehydrated food has progressed a long way in the last few years, both in taste and variety. Companies catering to campers have developed one-dish meals such as beef and spuds, chicken and rice, beef and macaroni. At the family grocery one can get instant rice, instant puddings in various flavors to mix with water, and appetizing dried soups such as potato-leek, mushroom, vegetable, tomato-beef. The fancy food places also sell bacon and butter in cans.

June Ina

_____
_____
_____
_____
_____

3. She strolled senuously down the path toward her destination. Her swinging sashay was spotlighted by the scintillating full moon. Her hips swivelled decisively, first to the left, then to the right. Left, bump. Right, bump. Left, bump. Right, bump. Her shoulders and freely swinging legs kept the same rhythm. Right, swing. Left, swing. Right, swing. Left, swing. But a watcher's eyes always worked their way up to her head. There, attached to her head, was the most regal horse's mane seen on any bridal path.

Martin Boyer

4. The major powers of the world today still maintain the capability of devastating biological warfare. In the arsenals of some of these nations are decapacitating agents such as equinine encephalitis, the disease that kills many animals as large as horses. Some nations keep botulism germs in stock, one ounce of which can kill every human being in North America if distributed effectively. But this biological engineering, as those who are involved prefer to call it, does not stop there. There are, for example, mutated strains of anthrax which stay alive up to seven years. This and other mutated forms of disease such as mutated undulant fever, typhus fever, parrot fever, and many others would be devastating because they are immune to present serums developed against them.

Art Glatfelter

APPLICATION 10-2

On the lines below, write three controlling sentences suitable for development by enumeration. Underline the main idea of each once and the key twice.

_____

_____

_____

_____

_____

_____

_____

APPLICATION 10-3

Select one of the sentences written for Application 10-2 and on the lines below develop it into a supporting paragraph of enumeration consisting of at least six sentences. Underline the key of the main idea in your controlling sentence with two lines, and in the designated blanks, identify the other predetermined elements intended.

Point of view: _____ objective _____ semi-objective _____ subjective

Tone: _____ formal _____ semiformal _____ informal

Purpose _____

_____

_____

_____

_____

_____

_____

_____

_____

_____

_____

APPLICATION 10-4

On the lines below, write three controlling sentences suitable for development by illustration. Underline the main idea with one and the key with two lines. Be sure to indicate the intended dominant general purpose.

_____

_____

_____

_____

_____

_____

_____

APPLICATION 10-5

Select one of the sentences written for Application 10-4 and on the lines below develop it into a supporting paragraph of illustration consisting of at least six sentences. Underline the key of the main idea in your controlling sentence with two lines, and in the designated blanks, identify the other predetermined elements Indicate the purpose also.

Point of view: _____ objective _____ semi-objective _____ subjective

Tone: _____ formal _____ semiformal _____ informal

Form of illustration: _____ individual item(s) _____ narrative

Purpose _____

_____

_____

_____

_____

_____

_____

_____

_____

_____

APPLICATION 10-6

On the lines below write three controlling sentences suitable for development by analysis or synthesis. Underline the main idea of each with one and the key with two lines and indicate the purpose.

_____

_____

_____

_____

_____

_____

APPLICATION 10-7

Select one of the sentences written for Application 10-6 and on the lines below develop it into a supporting paragraph of structural, functional, or causal analysis or synthesis, consisting of at least six sentences. Underline the key of the main idea in your controlling sentence with two lines, and in the designated blanks, identify the other predetermined elements intended.

Point of view: _____ objective _____ semi-objective _____ subjective

Tone: _____ formal _____ semiformal _____ informal

Form of analysis or synthesis: _____ structural _____ functional _____ causal _____ a combination of these

Purpose _____

_____

_____

_____

_____

_____

_____

_____

_____

_____

_____

APPLICATION 10-8

Print an E before each of the following controlling sentences that would be best developed by enumeration; an I before those that would best be developed by illustration; or an A or S before those that would best be developed by analysis or synthesis.

_____ 1. Today, cooking is done with some very efficient electrical devices.

_____ 2. The fire in the building resulted from three interrelated incidents.

_____ 3. To be accepted as a student at the university a person is required to complete several application forms.

_____ 4. My beagle hound amazes me with his intuition.

_____ 5. When he sets his mind to it, my brother can be very stubborn.

_____ 6. The violincello is mainly made of wood components held together by glue and tension.

_____ 7. The receiving department of a department store is a complex unit with three sections working together.

_____ 8. Each morning, a nurse must perform a variety of vital duties.

_____ 9. An atom has two essential structural parts.

_____ 10. To succeed in college, a student should follow these helpful suggestions.

APPLICATION 10-9

Develop the controlling sentences in the developing and supporting section below by means of enumeration in at least one paragraph and by illustration in one of the other two. Choose either or both for the third paragraph. Be sure to develop all three paragraphs in a manner appropriate to the predetermined elements identified by the purpose statement shown. Also, be sure that everything in the finished composition is related to the purpose sentence in the main paragraph.

Purpose Statement

To write a 150-word semiformal persuasion to convince young people that buying a new car is wiser than buying a used car.

Purpose Sentence And Introductory Paragraph

It is to a young man or woman's advantage to buy a new car rather than a used one. With a new car, there is no need to worry about the expense of replacing faulty parts. A common complaint of used car owners is the amount of time and extra money required. A girl I know purchased a used car for $600. Six months later, she had spent a total of $800 on part replacements and service station fees. That's $1,400 which could have been half the payment on a new car. The used car was sold for $200, showing a $1,200 loss.

Controlling Sentences

1. Unlike a used car, a new car is *dependable* in cold winter weather.
2. The up-keep of a new car is *inexpensive.*
3. A new car, of the same type, after it's broken in, will give better mileage than a used car.

Concluding Paragraph

A new car is dependable, is inexpensive to operate, and gives better mileage than a used car. For these reasons, it is wise to buy a new car rather than a used car.

APPLICATION 10-10

Write a full-length composition, consisting of at least five paragraphs, developing a subject sentence of your own choosing. Your composition should have a title, an opener if you choose, a main paragraph, four or five supporting paragraphs, and a concluding paragraph. Your supporting paragraphs should include one developed by enumeration, one by illustration, and one each developed by analysis and synthesis. In the left margin opposite each paragraph, indicate its use in the composition. If it is a supporting paragraph, tell whether you intended it as enumeration, illustration, analysis, or synthesis. Indicate your purpose in the heading with the title. Don't forget to first read the following You Be the Judge. Here are some possible subject sentences:

1. Join a club to enhance your self-concept
2. To determine whether or not he or she is ready for college, a person should do some self-analysis.
3. A considerate tenant is a courteous one
4. Here is the way to go about solving a problem
5. A flashlight has only a few main parts

YOU BE THE JUDGE

Evaluator's Initials ☐☐☐

Date _____

Section _____

Grade _____

Writer's Name _____

Date _____ Section _____

Title of paper _____

Chapter _____ Application No. _____

General instructions on the You Be the Judge Applications, and specific instructions for Parts I and III, are printed inside the back cover of this book. Read those instructions carefully; then do Part I.

In the lines below, and on another sheet of paper, answer the questions in Part II, then enter a grade for the paper in the space above left, and write your evaluation for Part III. Reread the composition to see how well the writer understands and applies the principles studied in this chapter. As you read the composition write any helpful suggestions that occur to you in the margins.

PART II

1. Comment briefly on:

    (a) the title _____

    _____

    (b) the opener, if any _____

    _____

    (c) the main paragraph _____

    _____

2. For the paragraphs developed by illustration and enumeration, answer the following questions.

    (a) How many illustrations (enumerations) does it include? _____

    _____

    (b) How well do they develop the controlling sentence? _____

    _____

    (c) How does the paragraph relate to the subject sentence of the whole composition? _____

    _____

    (d) Would either of these paragraphs have been more suitably developed by some other method? Explain your answer. _____

    _____

3. For the paragraphs developed by analysis and synthesis, answer the following questions.

   (a) Is the controlling sentence suitable for development by the chosen method? If not, explain why not. _____

   _____

   _____

   _____

   _____

   _____

   (b) Are analysis and synthesis in these paragraphs used to explain structural, functional, or causal relationships, or a combination of these? Explain. _____

   _____

   _____

   _____

   _____

   _____

PART III

4. Does the analysis or synthesis in these paragraphs stay within the limits imposed by the key in the paragraph? Explain. _____

Grade and Explanation:

_____

_____

_____

_____

CHAPTER 11

DESCRIPTION AND NARRATION

After studying this chapter and completing the applications that follow it, you should be able to do the following:
1. To identify and differentiate two general forms of development: *description* and *narration*.
2. To identify and differentiate kinds of description: *general and specific*, and *impressionistic and realistic*.
3. To identify and differentiate kinds of narration: *climatic* and *straight-line— historical*, *biographical*, and *process* or *procedural*.
4. To write controlling sentences that allow or require development by *description* or *narration*.
5. *To develop supporting paragraphs by description or narration.*
6. To write these forms in developing the supporting paragraphs in a full-length composition.

IT was once common to say that there were four kinds of writing: description, narration, exposition, and persuasion. Most of the writing that students do, both in college and after, is done to explain or persuade. Business letters, business and technical reports, public relations releases, news stories, editorials, articles for house organs, professional journals, and other magazines and newspapers, even essays, manuals, and textbooks—all will be mainly expository or persuasive and will use the same forms of development.

But writing would be dull and colorless if it never told what things look, feel, sound, smell, and taste like, or if it contained no anecdotes, biographical sketches, reminiscences, personal experiences, or even processes. So this chapter deals with *description* and *narration* not as forms in their own right but as they are used in exposition and persuasion to give eyes, ears, and a touch of everyday reality to other kinds of writing. Descriptive and narrative sentences and paragraphs are common in exposition and persuasion, and sometimes an entire communication may be an extended description or narrative.

DESCRIPTION

Description conveys the sensations, emotions, and impressions that affect a writer experiencing a person, place, object, or idea. It tells what you see, hear, smell, feel, or taste, and it often includes your emotional reactions to the physical sensations of the experience.

The sense experience which is most commonly conveyed by description is that of sight. Thus visual details, play an important part in description. Notice the number of physical features detected by sight in the following list compared to the number registered by the other senses.

Sensory:

A. Sight (often description is drawing verbal pictures for the reader)
   1. Components (or parts: face, head, body, roof, wheels, including their features or characteristics)
   2. Substance (material: brick, wood, cloth, paper, plastic)
   3. Dimensions (size: weight, height, width, length)
   4. Form, shape, design
   5. Color
   6. Decorations (embellishments, garnishments, trim, clothing)
   7. Movement (behaviorisms, mannerisms, habits, actions)
B. Sound: normal, pleasant, unpleasant
C. Smell: fragrance, aroma, stench
D. Touch: texture, softness, hardness, roughness, smoothness)
E. Taste: sour, sweet, bland, salty, pepperish)

Emotional:

A. Compassion, sorrow, sadness, anguish
B. Fear, terror, apprehension, anxiety
C. Ecstasy, joy, happiness, contentment, satisfaction, humor

In exposition, much description is in the form of support. Here is a supporting paragraph which illustrates informative and interesting description used for an expository purpose. Notice how the writer points out the characteristics that can be seen: form, shape, color, dimensions, body parts or components, to make the description vivid. Note also that the key words ("easily seen" and "harder to spot") in the opening subject sentence gives the clue to the kind of development needed.

The bighorn sheep is large enough to be easily seen upon the mountainsides, but its color blends with the snow, making it harder to spot. This sheep stands approximately 36 inches at the shoulder and measures 40 to 60 inches in length. The full grown bighorn weighs about 120 to 170 pounds, and some large rams reach as high as 200 pounds. The ram's long-haired pelage is pale buff in color. A characteristic white rump patch surrounds the short dark tail and extends down inside the hind legs. The stomach and the back of the front legs are even lighter in color, making the animal harder to see when it is lying down with its forelegs tucked under. The best known character of the bighorn which makes it a coveted animal, is the ram's huge set of curled horns. These are about 15 or 16 inches around the base. From the base, they taper sharply outward toward the tip, measuring at least 30 inches around the outer curl.

Robert Schultz

The preceding illustration is also a good example of enumeration. The following example shows how a supporting paragraph of decription may also be developed by means of functional analysis. As you read it, notice how the writer identifies and develops the functional relationships between the parts of the human eye by telling what they do and how they work together to enable the eye to see. This is a still-life description, one which has no movement.

The human eye is a compact organ. The white coating which covers and protects the eye is called the *sclera*. In front of this is a clear coating, the *cornea*. Beneath the cornea is the *choroid coat* which is made up of muscle tissue and blood vessels. Behind the cornea is the *pupil*, surrounded by circular and longitudinal fibers which are referred to as the *iris*. The iris controls the amount of light which passes through the eye. Deeper into the eye is the *retina*, made up of dark pigment and little nerve endings. These nerve endings are *rods* and *cones* which control the flow of light rays and adjust the eye to color. The *lens* is that part of the eye which enables far and close vision.

Glen Stoltz

Kinds of Description

Description may be thought of as *general* or *specific*. When your controlling sentence calls for general description, you select several of the main typical traits which characterize the subject and proceed to enumerate, analyze, or synthesize its features.

Following is a good general description of a typical quarter horse, a horse especially skillful at herding cattle. Since this paragraph focuses on the behavior and manner of the quarter horse rather than on its physical structure, it is developed by functional enumeration.

The quarter horse is really three horses in one. Originally, this horse was bred in the Southwest by ranchers who needed a working horse which could outrun, outmaneuver, and outthink the wiry, hardnosed longhorn steers. Quarter horse ancestors were small, tough, surefooted Mustang mares crossed with sleek race studs imported from the East. A quick burst of speed was what the cowboys needed, and the quarter horse is the fastest thing under saddle on a quarter mile track, hence the name "quarter horse." The cowboy also required a horse that would "use"; that is, turn, stop, back, switch ends, pay attention, and love doing it. It is the undisputed champion in this kind of maneuvering because in "horse sense" it is rated second to none. Along with its speed and maneuverability, the quarter horse is a good companion for the lonely job of herding steers. This horse is good-natured, devoted, gentle, and sensitive to affection, qualities much desired, but not always found in other breeds.

Brian Shear

The next illustration is an example of specific description. In this supporting paragraph, the writer focuses on a specific quarter horse. Thus not only the characteristics which identify this individual as a typical quarter horse, but also the characteristics of its own distinct personality are pointed out. It appears as though the differences rather than the similarities are stressed. If a writer were to describe your personality wouldn't he focus upon those characteristics which distinguish you from other persons? This writer does just that in the following description. Also notice that this is an animated description, one which points up behavior and mannerisms—not a still life.

Joe, the little chestnut quarter horse colt, with his ears pointing forward, stood near his mother under a majestic elm sniffing the air. The smell of morning tickled his nose and the brisk wind stirred the hairs in his ears. He tossed his head, snorting and squealing. He kicked up his heels and with a flick of his tail scampéred off across the pasture. His mother looked up and neighed as if telling him to be careful not to run into the fence up ahead. With a shake of her head, she galloped after the frisky colt, overtaking him in a long easy stride.

Ann Stouffer

Whether general or specific, description may be either *realistic* or *impressionistic.* Description is realistic when the topic is viewed from an objective point of view. When you examine something with the intent of gathering information about it, you try to record only what your senses detect. This kind of description is much like a black and white photograph —the camera captures only what is there. To describe realistically, you record dimensions, components, shape, behavior, and so forth as accurately as possible. Here is a realistic description. Notice how the writer maintains an objective viewpoint.

The hourglass is a primitive instrument for measuring time. It consists usually of two hollow bulbs joined one above the other, and having a narrow neck of communication, with means for placing either bulb in uppermost position. Dry sand is introduced in quantity sufficient nearly to fill one of the bulbs and fine enough to pass freely through the orifice of the connecting neck. The quantity of the sand is adjusted to the time which the glass has been constructed to indicate. In the case of an hourglass, the sand in the upper bulb takes an hour to pass into the lower-level bulb; and so on for any other definite division of time.[1]

Description is impressionistic when you regard the topic from a subjective point of view. The main purpose of impressionistic description is to share with the reader a single dominant impression which something or some thought made upon you. The dominant impression may

[1] *Encyclopedia Americana,* © 1953, American Corp., vol. 14, p. 443.

be a sense impression or an emotion. When you decide to use impression-istic description as a form for developing part or all of a composition, you usually want the readers to share something closely, vividly, and even sometimes intimately with you.

Following is a description in which the writer wants the reader to share the sensations of fabulous luxury and wealth. The dominant impression that the writer wants to convey is therefore expressed in the word *fabulous,* and there's no doubt in your mind about it. Be sure to notice that he selects only those details which are fabulous. The equipment and furnishings which are common to all ships and which do not reinforce the impression of fabled wealth and luxury are ignored completely.

Fabulous is the only word for the floating palace that awaits Aristotle Socrates Onassis. The *Christina* is 1,800 tons of sheer unadulterated luxury, 325 feet of opulence, the jewel of Onassis' far-flung shipping fleet. Her crew of forty-four is the pick of the 1,000-man German force in the Onassis fleet, and they have the latest in radar and electronic gear to aid in navigation. Stowed on her upper deck are four speed-boats, a six-ton sailing vessel, a car, and a four-place amphibious plane with a top speed of 200 m.p.h. and a range of 1,200 miles. On the stern deck is the ballroom, which in fifty seconds can be converted into a mosaic-lined swimming pool, complete with cascading fountains and underwater lightning. In addition, it has thirteen guest bedrooms, two El Greco paintings, and several gold-framed icons. Beneath the glass-topped, semicircular bar in another area of the ship is a miniature metal sea on which ships continually float by means of a magnetic hookup. Would you disagree with the word *fabulous* when applied to describe the *Christina*?[2]

Following are two paragraphs which enforce the distinction between realistic and impressionistic description. In the first the student writer described her son as realistically as she could. In the second, she picked one dominant impression of him and focused on it. Compare these two versions carefully and you will begin to see that when the writer knows in advance what he intends to do, things fall into place much more easily.

Realistic

Scott is my second son. He is nearly two years old. He weighs thirty pounds and stands twenty-nine inches high. He has a large bone structure; in fact he's stocky. He has short muscular legs, small hips, and a thick protruding stomach. He has a large head, a lot of brown hair, large ears, thick lashed big brown eyes, a small hook nose, and a thick-lipped mouth. He has nine even white teeth. He talks very seldom because his vocabulary is quite limited.

Diane Sly

[2] *Detroit News* (Oct. 19, 1968), p. 16B. Used by permission.

My second son Scott is a little devil. He is thirty pounds of energy-packed hellion. He stands only twenty-nine inches high, but oh, what those twenty-nine inches can manage to get into. His large bone structure tends to make him look like a gremlin. His short muscular legs carry him into more trouble than a person could imagine. His hips are so small that his diapers and pants are usually found somewhere in the vicinity of his knees. He has the head of a full grown man (he and his dad nearly wear the same hat size) with wicked looking hair matted everywhere except for the double cowlick which gives him the appearance of having horns. His large floppy ears and huge long eyelashed deep brown eyes can only tell one thing: he is all boy and very little saint. His little hooked nose is usually getting flattened because he has it where it doesn't belong. His cupid-bow mouth has nine miraculously whole, perfect white teeth, that manage to bite his baby brother at least three times a day. He has a quite limited vocabulary and doesn't talk too plainly, unless we don't want him to and then as clear as day he calls his Grandpa a bum and tells him to go home. A child? Yes. A devil? Yes. My son? You bet!

Diane Sly

Description must be orderly. You must arrange details by some reasonable order in space. You may have to tell the readers the distance and the angle from which the subject is being viewed. You may describe the subject in the order in which you normally observe it in space or time (see pages 95–96 and 276–279 on point of view).

NARRATION

Much of our daily communication is some form of narration. Newspapers, magazines, radio, and television programs are very largely narrative. *Narration is a chronologically arranged sequence of related incidents occurring in a unit of time.* Supporting paragraphs developed by narration mainly consist of sequences of happenings ocurring in a stated or clearly implied period of time. Narration mainly tells how something originated and developed, how it happened, or how it is done. Time, not space, is dominant, as in description. The time involved may be of any length: minutes, days, hours, weeks, months, or years.

The following narrative, though just one sentence long, has all the necessary elements: a series of happenings, arranged in an orderly time sequence.

The scholar absorbs the world around the self, meditates upon what is absorbed, places what is observed in new patterns of thought, infuses it with a part of the self, then projects it from that self so that others can detract from it and/or add to it, then pass it on to others still.

Unlike description, which draws a still-life or an animated picture, narrative projects a moving picture, a sequence of related happenings.

Narrative focuses on action. Description may use bits of action to depict mannerisms, behavior, or habits, but attention is focused primarily on the subject performing the action rather than the action itself. In description, the writer may use action to convey a dominant impression, but in narration the action itself is dominant.

There are two general kinds of narration. These are *climactic narration* and *straight-line narration.*

Climactic Narration

Climactic narration is a sequence of events which lead to a climax. Each incident in the narration is a complication in the chain of events increasing the intensity of the suspense. Each predicament or complication increases the tension of the narrative until the crisis occurs, causing the chain of events to snap and to change direction. Such a sequence may consist of a boy and girl finding each other, falling in love, then losing each other; later one of them does something or something happens that enables them to reunite. The point at which something occurs to cause the final change is the climax.

Climactic narration is extensively used in nonfiction. It is used in newspaper stories to maintain interest. Magazine articles are often made up of various kinds of climactic narrative. Here is one which could appear as a news story in a paper somewhere in the United States any day of any year. The *point of climax* is italicized.

He was driving home that bleak November night. In his careful, methodical way, he had safely maneuvered through the rush hour traffic on the expressway from Seattle. Now on Ford Road, he was eagerly anticipating being home with his family at the supper table. His speedometer hit sixty-five, the speed limit, when he approached the intersection of Sheldon Road. *The car that hit him was crossing Ford Road;* he didn't see it. He didn't arrive home for supper that night—he never came home again.

Joan Treff

The following example of climactic narration is obviously intended to entertain. Notice how each incident increases the suspense until the crisis is reached, resulting in the italicized climax. (Notice that this narrative is developed by enumeration.)

It was a most enjoyable time. I met him at the door and he smelled of Antique Spice. The evening started off with cocktails for two. We sat and talked for a while in the cozy candlelight. Later, I tossed the salad and poured the wine while he served the beef stroganoff. The wine was a very good burgundy, 1957, which I had been saving for just such an occasion as this. I turned up the stereo while we lingered over our meal. After dinner we danced, enjoying the beautiful, soft music. Then he paused and put his hand under my chin, and I raised my face to his. His warm arms gently tightened about me and just at the moment he was going to kiss me . . . *"Mamma, Daddy, my tummy hurts and my throat's sore and David keeps jumping on the bed.* Are you all done eating now? What's an anniversary, Daddy? . . .*"*

Gailyn Freeborn

Straight-line Narration

Straight-line narration is a series of related incidents which do not rise to a climax, but occur in a straight line. News reports and other types of writing which record events just as they happened are straight-line narratives. In our daily communication, we probably use more straight-line narratives than any other form. When we tell a neighbor how to get a driver's license or how to reach a certain place, we are using this type of narration. History books are extended narratives composed of many individual events. Here is a history of the invention of a device.

The origin of the mechanical clock is still obscure; however, the invention of the escapement, the most essential part of all mechanical clocks, can be traced back to the end of the thirteenth century. Since a French architect, Villard de Honnecourt, described a primitive rope escapement in about 1250, we can assume that the mechanical clock was invented then. The escapement described by de Honnecourt enabled the control of the rate of fall of a weight attached to a cord wound around a drum so that the drum rotated slowly and regularly as the weight fell. By attaching a pointer to the rotating drum, the passage of time could be measured. This was not an accurate means to tell time, but it served adequately for a while. The first practical mechanical escapement turned up in a clock erected in Milan, Italy, in 1335. Replacement of the falling weight with a coiled spring within a drum occurred in the works of a clock sometime before 1500. The invention of the pendulum, one of the most important improvements in clock making, did not occur until the second half of the seventeenth century.

Richard Newsome

Abstract ideas as well as tangible, concrete, physical objects may occur or develop in a unit of time to form a narrative. The following example covers a series of happenings occurring over a long stretch of time, from the sixth century B.C. to A.D. 1953.

In addition to religious beliefs, several theories about the origin of life have been handed down through the centuries. In the sixth century B.C., a Greek, Anaximander, said that higher living organisms developed from lower types, and that in the beginning, man was a fish. Anaximander believed that gradual evolution occurred as water was evaporated by the sun. The works of Aristotle did not become known to the Western world until the beginning of the twelfth century A.D. Aristotle said that living creatures were generated by evaporation of moisture from the earth by the heat of the sun and by recondensation of the moisture as rain. This became known as the theory of spontaneous generation. Little more than 100 years ago, Charles Darwin published his *Origin of Species*. Darwin said that all living things, including homo sapiens, have arisen through an evolutionary process. In 1924, I. A. Oparin, a Russian biochemist, suggested that the primitive atmosphere contained methane, ammonia, water, and hydrogen, and that from these gases, complex organic compounds could have been synthesized to gradually evolve into living organisms. However, serious investigation into the origin of life did not begin until 1953 when S. L. Miller passed an electric spark through a mixture of methane, ammonia, hydrogen, and water vapor to form amino acids, the most prevalent chemicals in living organisms.[3]

Biography and autobiography are both a kind of history, the story of a person's life. An autobiography is such a history written by the person himself. Notice the series of events occurring in the life of the subject in the following section of narration, consisting of three paragraphs.

I AM ON FIRE

When I was five years old, I decided the life of a firefighter would be about as good and exciting a life as any there was to be had. The thought of serving my community by risking my life at all times seemed to be quite an honorable career. The excitement which would be derived from chasing down tremendous, overwhelming fires was my idea of a worthwhile career then.

The sound of a siren, which caused a cold streak to run up my spine, always reinforced my determination. The more I heard these loud shrieks, the more the lure of the fire station attracted me. I was always eager to mount my tricycle to chase after the bright licorice-red vehicles screaming excitedly on their way to another adventure. Perhaps to save a helpless child from his parentless house, I knew, would some day prove to be my mission in life.

Yes, the thought of being one of those wonderful lifesavers of the city remained in my heart for quite a while after I grew too big for my tricycle. Even today, an accountant, I look down from my office window to the street far below to watch the red toy-like vehicle, streaking down the street, and my thoughts leave my dry numbers and race along with each fire engine to excitement and adventure.

Ralph Bly

[3] Adapted by Jan Lewis from "The Origin of Life" by Eugenia Keller, *Chemistry*, December, 1968 (Washington, D.C.: American Chemical Society, 1968).

Undoubtedly the most common type of straight-line narrative used by most people in daily communication is *process* or *procedural narration*. This is narrative which conveys a series of steps involved in telling how something is done or happens: how to wallpaper a room, how to bake a pie, or how a frog goes through the various stages of its development.

People are intensely interested in some processes they may not or cannot do themselves. They may never want to learn to fly a plane, but may be interested in how it is done. The reader may never have to construct a toboggan such as the Indian sled described in the paragraph below. But he might be glad to know the exact steps in the process as well as the tools and materials used.

Some toboggans made by the Indians are constructed of two boards, usually birch, which have been cut or split from logs with wedges. They are cut into pieces six feet long and tapered at both ends. To bend the front end of the boards into shape, these ends are immersed in boiling water and then bound into place on the toboggan with rawhide straps. The two birch boards are held together by two or three crosspieces with rawhide stitching. Grooves are cut into the boards so that this stitching is countersunk. To lash the packs securely to the toboggan, loops of rawhide are attached from one crosspiece to another. With the resulting upward curving front, the toboggan can be easily pulled over most obstacles, and still be flexible enough to absorb and withstand severe shocks which may be encountered in rough terrain.

J. Fatool

It is not unusual for a writer to use process narrative for purposes other than to convey objective information. The following was written to convey an impression. Notice that it has been given in the form of a recipe, a common type of narration.

The recipe is simple, the ingredients few, and the results surprising. Take one small girl, and one fairly intelligent father, one regulation size kite, one windy afternoon, mix well with some time and patience, and you may accomplish that rarity, a truly happy occasion. A girl and kite mix together quite readily; however, things go together more smoothly when a father's time and patience are added to the mixture. Now that the kite itself has been assembled, the next ingredient, the wind, must be added. It is necessary to have good judgment at this stage. If the wind is too strong, or too weak, the kite will not fly properly or easily. In this event, father will have to do all the work, and this gives a one-sided effect to the mixture which should be avoided. If all of the ingredients have been well chosen and carefully blended, no cooking time is required and the final product results, father and daughter sitting on the cool grass in the sun, sharing a sense of joy and accomplishment in themselves, surprisingly out of proportion to the time spent in attaining their reward.

Barbara Van Sickle

The controlling sentence of a supporting paragraph should indicate whether it will be developed by description or narration. It may also indicate which type of description or narration is to follow. Some controlling sentences may be developed in any of several ways, and you must select the one most suitable for your purpose. Here is a controlling sentence that might be developed by either narration or causation (a form of development to be discussed in Chapter 12): "The Battle of Monte Casino almost became a tragic defeat." To develop this sentence you may give the series of causes which almost made it a tragic defeat, or you may give the series of incidents that took place there.

Following are controlling sentences that clearly indicate that some form of narration is important for their development.

1. From under his master's chair, the cat waited for a chance to spring at the chattering canary.
   (This could be a climactic narration)
2. The Donner Party, with its small group of emigrants, started the long trip to Wyoming in July, 1846.
   (This probably will be a historical narration)
3. Italian wine is made in five easy steps.
   (This probably will become a process narration)

PRACTICE in Achieving This Chapter's Objectives

Practice in identifying and writing supporting paragraphs of description and narration.

	Applications
1. Identifying types of description and narration.	1
2. Identifying controlling sentences that allow or require development by description or narration.	2
3. Writing paragraphs of description and narration.	3, 4
4. Writing description and/or narration in a full-length composition.	5
5. You Be the Judge	

APPLICATION 11-1

Read the following selections carefully, and in the blank at the left of each tell whether it is description or narration. In the second blank, tell the kind it is: if description, tell whether it is realistic or impressionistic; if narration, whether it is climactic or straight-line.

Form _____

Kind _____

1. When I was about nine or ten years old and first became aware of the wonders of the world of sound, I was sure that I was destined to become a musician. I begged my parents for music lessons and would practice over and over, trying to discover a way to improve my work on the piano. When I realized Bliss, Michigan was many miles from "the big city," I decided that the fulfillment of my ambition to be a child prodigy would have to be postponed until I became an adult.

    I consoled myself by believing that the big city missed a great opportunity and that I would give the band leaders another chance when I was an adult. In the mean time, I would continue to perfect my already perfect music ability. My supply of records, which kept me informed of the current changes and trends in the music trade, was the storehouse from which I drew material for my music experiments. By imitating the beats and pauses as well as the mannerisms of the stars I had just heard or read about, I felt that I was preparing myself for a glittering career on the sound stage. I dreamed of shiny red Cadillac convertibles, heart-shaped swimming pools, yellow roses in my dressing room, and the praise and applause that is lavished on famous rock stars.

    But, as all childish dreams must vaporize into thin air, my desire to become a musician effervesced into bubbles and burst one by one as I grew older. I began to realize that the impression presented to me in my records and tapes was a superficial one which did not include the hard work behind the scenes. I learned that the world of a rock star was not all glamour and praise, but was time-consuming and arduous. I'm not sure, I told myself, and turned my sights to that of a comfortable/frustrating life of a college student.

Linda Jo Lange

Form _____

Kind _____

2. Opal is a soft gem stone and therefore must be worn with care. It may be precious, but most varieties are semiprecious. It is a semitransparent stone having a vivid display of colors. When pure, opal is colorless; when impure, it may be red, yellow, green, blue, or black. It is an amorphous form of hydrated silica containing varying amounts of water. It is composed of a series of very thin films or

layers which differ in refractivity. Opal appears to be a solidified mass of milky glass, but when light strikes the stone at certain angles, flashing colors are revealed. This phenomenon is known as opalescence. The colors are different refractivities of light in the thin layers; the thinner and more uniform the layers, the more beautiful the colors.

Ida Restino

Form _____

Kind _____

3. "Move out!" was the command whispered down the line. In the moonlight, human figures could be seen rising from the ground. As the line moved forward, rifle fire came from the right. "Keep moving!" came the command again. As the figures moved forward on their bellies, the firing increased. The drum of airplane motors rumbled overhead; then exploding bombs thundered upon a hill just ahead. As the airplanes faded into the distance, the captain gave the command to charge. Every figure sprang forward on a dead run, firing blindly from the hip. From the hill ahead came intense machine gun fire; bodies began falling everywhere. The large shells began whining overhead and exploding on the crest of the hill. "Keep moving!" shouted the captain. Just as we arrived at the base of the hill, everything stopped. It seemed as though someone had thrown a switch. The enemy had surrendered.

Bill Metzger

Form _____

Kind _____

4. The Ranch House is a Western-styled restaurant. The house itself is shaped like a big barn which is surrounded by a large fence. In front of the main entrance is a hitching post and water trough to give it that western look. Over this entrance hangs a large set of steer horns. As you walk into the building, you can almost sense the Western atmosphere. The walls are paneled with dark pinewood. A man comes up to you dressed like a ranch hand. As he shows you to your table, he speaks with a Western drawl. At first glance, your dark oak table and chairs appear very crude. It would seem that they had come directly from the old West, but at a closer examination, the furniture proves to be expertly made. As you are sitting, you gaze around the room. In front of you hangs a collection of antique guns. Each gun has a little story which tells who invented it and what importance it had in building the West. To your left, you see a few trophies—a deer head, another set of

steer horns, and a large bear head. On platforms jutting from the walls and in the corners of the room are stuffed animals like those you would see on the prairies. Such Western animals as the prairie dog, coyote, and prairie chicken seem almost real. The help who serve you are dressed like cowhands. As you slowly eat your meal in this atmosphere, thoughts of the "old West" race through your mind.

Mike Maston

APPLICATION 11-2

In the blank before each of the following, place a D if the controlling or subject sentence permits or requires development by description and an N if it requires or permits narration.

_____ 1. Sandy is direct, to the point, and able to call a spade a spade.

_____ 2. Here is how to prepare a clam bake in your back yard.

_____ 3. A wild stallion is powerful and fierce.

_____ 4. The library bubbled with excitement.

_____ 5. The room was compactly arranged.

_____ 6. Waking up "the morning after" requires careful maneuvering if one wants to survive.

_____ 7. The Hudson River-Lake Champlain route was a strategic highway for centuries.

APPLICATION 11-3

On the lines below, write a supporting paragraph of realistic or impressionistic description consisting of at least six sentences. Underline the key of the main idea in your controlling sentence with two lines, and in the designated blanks, identify the other predetermined elements intended. Here are some suggested topics:

1. a person who symbolizes vanity, honesty, tolerance, courage, or love to you
2. a summer resort
3. a florist shop
4. a cafeteria or restaurant
5. a hospital room

Point of view: _____ objective _____ semi-objective _____ subjective

Tone: _____ formal _____ semiformal _____ informal

Form of description: _____ realistic _____ impressionistic

Purpose _____

_____

_____

_____

_____

_____

_____

_____

_____

APPLICATION 11-4

On the lines below, write a supporting paragraph of climactic or straight-line narration consisting of at least six sentences. Underline the key of the main idea in your controlling sentence with two lines, and in the designated blanks, identify the other predetermined elements intended. Here are some suggested topics:

1. a humorous incident
2. how clouds, icebergs, or moss is formed
3. a happening on a date
4. an unforgetable incident
5. a nightmare

Point of view: _____ objective _____ semi-objective _____ subjective

Tone: _____ formal _____ semiformal _____ informal

Form of narration: _____ climactic _____ straight-line

Purpose _____

_____

_____

_____

_____

_____

_____

_____

_____

APPLICATION 11-5

Write a full-length composition of about 600 words, consisting of: a title; an opener if you wish, either separate or incorporated into the main paragraph; a main paragraph, including a subject sentence and several explanatory sentences; at least two supporting paragraphs, one of description and one of narration. Indicate your purpose in the heading with the title, and in the left margin opposite each supporting paragraph, indicate whether you intended it as description or narration. Write a concluding paragraph. Remember, your instructor may decide to project your composition on a large screen for class evaluation, using the criteria in the following You Be the Judge. If you have grammar questions, be sure to refer to the Handbook of Correct and Effective Usage on pages 383–404. Here are some suggested topics:

1. Travel abroad
2. A date
3. Television commercials
4. A summer or winter sport
5. Driving an automobile
6. A pleasantly peculiar person

YOU BE THE JUDGE

Evaluator's Initials ☐☐☐

Date _____

Section _____

Grade _____

Writer's Name _____

Date _____ Section _____

Title of paper _____

Chapter _____ Application No. _____

General Instructions on the You Be the Judge Applications, and specific instructions for Parts I and III, are printed inside the back cover of this book. Read those instructions carefully; then do Part I.

In the lines below, and on another sheet of paper, answer the questions in Part II. Then enter a grade for the paper in the space above right, and write your evaluation for Part III. Reread the composition to see how well the writer understands and applies the principles studied in this chapter. As you read the composition write any helpful suggestions that occur to you in the margins.

PART II

1. How appropriate is the main idea and key for development by narration and description? _____

2. Comment on the title, opener, and main topic in relation to these methods of development. _____

3. How skillfully does the writer adapt narrative and descriptive techniques to the specific subject chosen? _____

4. What kind of description is the writer using (general-specific, still-life-animated, realistic-impressionistic). Discuss. _____

_____

_____

_____

_____

_____

5. In the narrative parts of his composition, what kinds of narrative does the writer use (climactic, straight-line, historical, biographical, process, procedural)? Discuss. _____

_____

_____

_____

_____

_____

6. Does the writer use some form of enumeration, analysis, or synthesis to develop the description or narration? Which? _____
Explain, giving a brief sample from the composition. _____

_____

_____

_____

_____

_____

_____

PART III   Grade and Evaluation:

_____

_____

_____

_____

CHAPTER 12

CLASSIFICATION, DEFINITION, CAUSATION

After studying this chapter and completing the applications that follow it, you should be able to do the following:
1. To identify and differentiate three supporting forms of development: *classification*, *definition*, and *causation*.
2. To identify and write *classification* correctly.
3. To identify and write several kinds of definition: *synonym, derivative, subjective or personal, basic or classical*, and *extended*.
4. To identify and write correctly logical relationships in *causation*.
5. To identify and write controlling sentences that allow or require development by·*definition, classification*, or *causation*.
6. To write supporting paragraphs of *definition, classification*, or *causation*.
7. To write *definition, classification*, or *causation* in developing the supporting paragraphs of a full-length composition.

THE HUMAN mind constantly seeks order, and it has developed certain clear ways of finding or imposing it. Enumeration, exemplification, analysis, and synthesis are some of these ways. Three others which we shall consider in this chapter are *classification, definition*, and *causation*.

CLASSIFICATION

Classification is sorting related items and placing them in groups, classes, or categories. Almost everything we do requires some sort of classification. We classify our clothing according to the kind of material it is made of, its purpose, cost, fashion, and so on. We classify people by appearance, age, personality, sex, and the jobs they do. Every occupation requires classification. Plumbers, electricians, doctors, lawyers, or professors classify supplies, tools, laws, medicines, or students in various ways depending upon the standards or criteria required by their classification at a given time. Even writers must classify; their outlines indicate how they classify ideas.

Applying a name to a person or an object is a form of classification. When we call a person a *man* or a *woman,* an *American,* a *New Yorker,* or a *carpenter,* we are classifying that person in one way or another. Even a proper noun classifies a person. Judge Elmer Gribbs, for example, is classified by name and title as to occupation, age, sex, and blood relationship to other members of the family of Gribbs.

The class in which we place an object or an idea will always depend on the criterion and the need upon which the classification is based. This criterion is the kind of relationship which exists between one item and others in the same category. Nothing exists which fits in only one class.

Whenever we use any noun, the name of anything—*boy,* for example—we are classifying the person so described in one of several ways. Perhaps the standard is physical structure; a boy is similar in many ways to other boys, and he is certainly different from girls. To say "John is a tennis player" is placing John in a class with other persons who play tennis. Students can be classified according to many different standards; following are only a few of them.

Academic achievement
Attitude toward war, politics, and so forth
Mannerisms
Age
Race
Class—freshman, for example
Club
Physical dimensions, height, weight, and so forth
Interests: hobbies, sports
Sex

Here is a supporting paragraph developed by placing the same subject —the modern college student—in different classes based on different roles performed.

College students in the twentieth century have many roles in which they must demonstrate their expertise if they want to be acclaimed "successful students." They must be logical and critical thinkers, attentive readers and lucid writers, careful experimenters, responsible campus citizens, sympathetic roommates, and adequate test-takers. This skimpy list could be expanded if I did not at this precise minute have to read a chapter in history and outline my paper for sociology before I dash to Drama Club (and I haven't finished my treasurer's report). Then between five and six o'clock I will just barely have time to take my roommate to the bus and get a bite to eat before my six o'clock class in Chicano Literature.

To write an effective paragraph of classification, the writer can use the following procedure:

1. Clearly, and as precisely as necessary, identify the term being classified. When necessary, define it in words the reader can understand.
2. State or imply clearly the standards on which the classification is to be made. Sometimes the name of the class or classes in which the item is placed suggest the basis or standard for the classification. Classifying birds as game birds clearly specifies them as among those which can be hunted and eaten by humans.

3. Identify the names of the classes into which the items being classified belong.
4. Finally, discuss each of the classes, limiting the discussion to the standards on which the classification is based.

Following is a supporting paragraph developed by classification. The steps discussed in the preceding paragraph are indicated in the margin.

Term Classified and Defined

The Standard
The Classes

Discussion of Each Class

Vertical water wheels are devices or machines by which water power is converted to mechanical energy. Water power is generated by water's tendency to seek its lowest level, its level closest to the center of the earth. These wheels are of three classes, *depending upon where they receive the water pressure:* the *"overshot,"* the *"breast,"* and the *"undershot"* wheels. The overshot wheel is equipped with buckets attached to its rim so that as the wheel revolves, they are filled with water from a source near the top of the wheel. The weight of the water forces the wheel, and consequently, its axle to turn. The power from the rotating axle is then harnessed by means of belts and gears to the mechanism to be operated. The breast and the undershot water wheels differ from the overshot by the level at which they receive the actuating water pressure. The breast type wheel has its buckets filled from a water source slightly above or below the level of its axle. Therefore, it is especially useful in connection with waterfalls five to twenty feet high. The undershot wheel receives the water pressure below its axle; therefore, instead of buckets, it has paddles attached to its rim so that flowing water pushes the paddles as it passes under the wheel.

Russ Edwards

It is worth pointing out again that the body of a composition may consist of a series of supporting paragraphs that develop a single type of relationship. Following is part of the developing section of a much longer piece, a series of supporting paragraphs needed to develop a classification adequately and completely.

A hospital usually employs five different kinds of nurses according to their degrees and the amount of training they have had.

At the highest level are the registered nurses with college degrees. This may be a doctorate, masters, or bachelor of science degree. A degree is a prerequisite if a person desires a supervisory job or wants to teach in a school of nursing. Naturally, these jobs are the highest paid and carry the greatest responsibility.

Next are the registered nurses with an associate degree (two years of college). This is particularly suited to a person who is not quite sure about going to college. It leaves the door open to further learning and at the same time enables the person to work as an R.N. Associate degree programs are rather new and have been instituted to help relieve the crucial need for qualified nurses.

Third is the three-year diploma from a school of nursing. Upon graduation, nurses are entitled to take a state board examination. There is no degree given, however, other than R.N. These schools are rapidly disappearing from many areas as the cost of maintaining them is high, and also because state requirements insist on more attention to theory and more closely supervised clinical experience.

Licensed practical nurses have only recently become important. They usually take a twelve month course followed by a written examination required by the state before licensing. Bedside nursing is stressed and a good L.P.N. can ease the work load of the R.N. tremendously. This allows the R.N. to give medications and to carry out intricate procedures once assigned only to interns.

Aides are a valuable asset to the nursing team. Usually a few weeks on the job training with pay is all that is required. This job supplements and works in hand both with the L.P.N. and R.N.

Nancy Hunter

DEFINITION

Classification tells what group or kind of thing a subject belongs to. Definition goes one step further. *It not only places a subject in its class, but also tells how the subject differs from other members of its class.* Like classification, definition is important in education from kindergarten through college. On almost any subject, from farming to astrology, it is often necessary to define terms so that reader and writer can be sure they have the same thing in mind. Definitions are of many types, of which the following are the most common:

1. Basic or classical definition
2. Definition by synonym
3. Definition through derivation
4. Extended definition
5. Subjective or personal definition

Basic or Classical Definition

Basic or classical definition is the type used most often. Whenever someone is asked what something is or what it means, almost automatically the reply is a basic definition. Every basic or classical definition has two parts, the subject or the term defined and the predicate or the substance of the definition.

Basic Definition

Subject (Term)	Predicate (Definition)
A thermometer	is an instrument for measuring temperature.
An alcove	is a recess or partly enclosed extension connected to or forming part of a room.
To hedge a bet	is to balance it with another bet in order to limit the risk of loss.

The predicate or definition itself has two parts, the *genus* or *class,* and the *differentiation.* The first of these tells what larger group the term belongs to: a *thermometer* is an *instrument;* an *alcove* is a *recess* or an *extension; to hedge* is to *balance.* The second part of the definer is the differentiation, which tells how the term differs from others in its genus or class: an instrument *for measuring temperature;* a recess *connected to* or *forming part of;* to balance . . . *in order to limit the risk of loss.*

Three Main Sections of a Classical or Basic Definition

Term	Genus or Class	Differentiation
cumulus	a cloud formation	with a horizontal base and rounded masses piled up on each other
fulcrum	a point of support	on which a lever turns in moving something
paddock	a field of enclosure	in which horses are exercised
bonnet	a brimless hat	with a chin ribbon, worn by women and children

Basic definition must be used as precisely as the dominant general purpose requires. When the purpose is to inform or to convince, one must be much more careful than when the purpose is to entertain or to convey an impression.

The reliability and effectiveness of much written expression depends on the accuracy of its definitions. If any one of the three elements of a basic definition is inexact, the total definition suffers. The faulty sentences below illustrate how the precision of a basic definition is reduced when any one of its parts is either too broad or too narrow.

Sometimes the term chosen is less precise than the idea the writer wants to express. The cure then is to change the term:

Too broad: A *watch* is a small timepiece worn on the wrist. (The term *watch* is too broad because it includes watches which would not be worn on the wrist, for example, a pocket watch.)

Better: A *wrist watch* is a small timepiece worn on the wrist.

Too narrow: *Ruminants* are animals which feed on plants. (The term *ruminants* is too narrow because it does not include other animals which are not cud-chewers which ruminants are, for example, horses.

Better: *Herbivores* are animals which feed on plants.

Sometimes the general classes are too broad or too narrow:

Too broad: A forsythia is a *plant* with bell-shaped blossoms. (The class *plant* is too broad; it includes trees, vines, and grasses.)

Better: A forsythia is a *flowering shrub* with yellow bell-shaped blossoms.

Too narrow: A desk is a *piece of office furniture* with a flat top or sloping top. (The class *office furniture* is too narrow because it does not include desks for places other than offices, for example, homes.)

Better: A desk is a *piece of furniture* with a flat or sloping top.

And sometimes the differentiation is too broad or too narrow:

Too broad: An owl is a bird of prey *with a hooked beak.* (The differentiation *with a hooked beak* is too broad because it does not distinguish owls from other birds of prey, for example, falcons and eagles.)

Too narrow: A room is an interior space *in which people live.* (The differentiation is too narrow because it does not include rooms in which people do not live, for example, operating rooms, classrooms.)

Better: A room is an interior space *enclosed by walls.*

Definition by Synonym

A definition by synonym is the use of a word or term which means the same thing as the word being defined. It explains meaning quickly and simply. It also enables the writer to explain a word in a way which will not offend a reader who already knows it. Here are some examples:

1. The drone, the male bee, has no stinger and gathers no honey.
2. The pavis, a medieval shield, protected the whole body.
3. She wore a babushka, a head scarf.
4. Tsunamis (tidal waves) and earthquakes caused fewer than 1,500 deaths between 1900 and 1968.

Usually the writer's words will express meanings the same as or closely corresponding to the standard meanings given in the dictionary. But often, especially in writing to entertain or to convey an impression, one will use a word or a group of words in a special sense different from its dictionary definition:

5. There is a feeling within the whole community, the United States, that law and order must be maintained.

Here "the United States," is used to define "the whole community." It says that "the whole community" is "the United States," not Silver Creek, Ohio, Schoolcraft College, the State of Florida, or "any people living under the same laws and in the same district."

Definition by Derivation

Definition by derivation traces the etymology, the origin of the word, to clarify the meaning for which it is used in a particular composition. To be useful, an etymology must be related to what the writer is trying to say. This type of definition is intended to give the reader a better understanding of the word by providing some background information. Here are two examples:

Most natural hazards can be detected before they strike. But seisms (from the Greek *seismos*, earthquake) give no forewarning; therefore, like a capricious Greek god, they seem to act on impulse.

From its very origin, the word *supercilious* seems especially appropriate to its meaning. In Latin *super* means above, and the *cilia* are the eyebrows. So the word suggests not only haughtiness or arrogance but, literally, raised eyebrows.

Here is a definition by derivation which gives a great deal of background information, tracing the development of the word *tragedy* as it is used in drama, giving a more thorough understanding of the word.

The word *tragedy* is derived from the Middle English word *tragedye* which was adapted from the Latin word *tragoedia*, both of which originated from the Greek word *tragodia*. In Greek the word *tragos* means goat and *oide* means song. The word *tragedy* is derived from the Greek words which meant goat-song or goat singer. Today, the word is often used to identify a form of literature, a play whose protagonist suffers a catastrophe brought about by fate or by the moral weakness, psychological maladjustment, or social frustration of an otherwise noble person.

Andrew Loomis

Extended Definition

Extended definition is expanded definition. It is an extensive and often elaborate definition of what is meant by a term as it is used in a particular context by the writer. It is especially helpful when the writer needs to clarify an abstract (intangible) term or other complex idea.

Extended definition uses any of the other forms of development as necessary. It may use a combination of comparison and illustration, or classification and contrast, or any of the other forms which are appropriate. A common kind of extended definition combines basic definition with illustration.

Definition

Contrast

Illustration

Horse sense is judgment which reflects sound thinking. It is not a blind jump into a decision which may lead to ruin. Horse sense is not a hasty conclusion which prompts action causing deep regret later. In other words, horse sense is common sense. Anyone possessing this common sense would know better than to wear bathing trunks outdoors in December. He certainly would regret this action while recuperating from pneumonia. A sensible casting machine operator will turn off his machine before he attempts to retrieve a die which has fallen into the mechanism. A thoughtful homeowner carries liability insurance to avoid being sued by someone injured on his property. These people all use horse sense or common sense in making important decisions almost everyday of their lives. We see then that horse sense or common sense often requires sound thinking.

Earl Rudolph

Subjective Definition

What is often called subjective definition is really mood description, meant to convey the writer's personal feelings about something—a word, a date or anniversary, a place, a person, or an experience. Birthdays, holidays such as Christmas, and other anniversaries have special meanings for many people, and these are often written about. Often such subjective definitions occupy a whole article or essay; sometimes even a whole book. Some experiences can be defined in no other way; try to define the highest degree of happiness or sadness that you have ever felt. Following are two paragraphs that employ this type of definition in order to get the writer's feeling across.

The word *wilderness* has a special meaning for me. It is a sensation of intimate kinship with those who pioneered our vast frontiers. It is a feeling of closeness to Lewis and Clark, Sacajawca, Chief Joseph, and Coronado. This feeling renews my sense of discovery, my yearning for aloneness, enabling me to hear the same clear call that summoned them to climb above the timberline on Oregon's Three Sisters Wilderness and to explore the rugged mountains of Montana.

Raymond Schultz

A group of us were talking about Christmas, and Jill said that to her, the year seemed like a wreath, with Christmas at the top, where it starts and ends. Bob said that to him it was very different; it started with his Mother's birthday in September and didn't go "around" but just went forward through the weeks and months until her next birthday. Ethel said she'd never thought about it but remembered a definition of psychological time as being like a rope with knots in it held by a blind man walking along, and every knot marked some unit of time; it could be a year.

Circular Definition

A circular definition is one which uses the term being defined, or one of its derivatives, in the class or the differentiation. In such a definition, if the reader doesn't understand the term the first time, he certainly won't understand it the second. For example:

Circular

A *microscope* is an instrument used to view *microscopic* things. (Circular because *microscopic* is a derivative of *microscope,* the term being defined.)

Better

A microscope is an instrument used to view *invisible* things.

CAUSATION

Everything that exists and every event that takes place has a cause, and most things produce effects or results. Because we are endlessly interested in the present and the future we are also interested in the past from which they come; thus a great deal of our thought, talk, and writing is in search of causes and effects. Causes and effects not only rule our individual lives but they are also the stuff of science and they shape the fates of nations. *In writing, causation is the search for and explanation of causes and effects.*

In causation, the fundamental logical relationship is that one thing happened or will happen *because of* or *as a result of* another; the problem is to discover the right causes and the right effects. Here is a paragraph which attempts to explain the origin of the moon.

The moon may have been formed before the earth, a team of NASA scientists implied here Monday. The implications of some dating processes were clear. Rocks brought back from the Sea of Tranquility—a geologically "younger" area of the moon than the highlands—showed ages of between two billion to three and one-half billion years. The generally accepted age of the earth is four billion years. Later explorations of the highlands may produce rocks older than anything known on earth. Such findings would mean that the moon's origin is not connected directly with the earth—that is, the moon didn't spin off the molten earth.

When you explain complex events, you may have to identify a main cause and a series of contributing causes that lie behind it. Such a composition may be developed by showing how one cause results from a previous cause and in turn brings about still a third event. That result then becomes the cause for another result, until the main cause is explained. Notice the logical chain of causes in the following paragraph. The warm air and cold air meet and start the circular wind in motion. This wind is strong enough to topple trees and buildings.

Tornadoes are formed when warm, moist air spreads northward, meeting with cold air flowing from the north and west above it. This meeting of cold and warm air starts the characteristics of circular motion. This circular motion quickly builds up and becomes forceful enough to tear buildings apart and uproot trees. Not only are they able to move huge objects but they also occasionally do odd things, such as stripping a chicken of its feathers quickly.

J. Fatool

Causation is often used to explain an investigation conducted to find the causes of a problem and solutions for it.

My son's inability to read at a level comparable to other students caused his teacher to become concerned. During a parent-teacher conference with her, I learned that my son possesses a high ability to learn to read; yet time and time again, he failed to respond properly in reading exercises.

Our first clue in trying to solve his problem came from a series of tests administered to children his age. Although normal and above normal in three categories of the test, he fell below normal in achievement in two of them. Both of these involved hearing a story or problem read to him and requiring a correct response from him.

Perhaps, I thought, this test revealed that he was having a hearing problem. The more I thought about it, the more apparent it came to me that hearing was the cause of his problems. He always turned the TV too loud, I remembered. He didn't always seem to pay attention to me when I spoke to him and often wouldn't answer when I called him. Earaches were frequent with him. I was convinced, but I thought that I had better have these symptoms verified by a specialist.

Later, a specialist confirmed our suspicions. My son was given an extensive hearing test through which it was learned that he could not hear low decibels of sound. The doctor further explained that the cause of the hearing loss was fluid in the middle ear. Unable to drain because of swollen adenoids, the fluid placed pressure on the ear drum, hindering its vibrations.

Ann Metzger

The following supporting passage explains the principle of aerodynamics which makes it possible for airplanes to fly. Note that it is more than one paragraph in length; it is a section of causation.

There are two laws of physics that cause the airplane to fly. These laws are: For every action there is an equal and opposite reaction, and the higher the velocity the lower the pressure.

The first law deals with the propulsion of the airplane. In the case of the jet, the force of heated air out of the tail pipe to the rear causes the aircraft to move in the opposite direction. As this force remains constant, the movement of the plane is constant. As the aircraft moves, it will continue to increase speed until its speed is equal to its exhaust.

The second law — that the higher the velocity, the lower the pressure — determines the need for wings on an aircraft. The construction of the wing is so that it is flat on the bottom side and raised on the top side to taper off the trailing edge. As the thrust is applied by the engine, the aircraft begins to move through the atmosphere. The movement of the air over the top of the wing is faster than beneath the wing. This faster moving air creates a low pressure area over the wing, and when it becomes low enough as the speed increases, the aircraft is moved into the low pressure area upward.

When these two laws of physics were applied, our first airplanes were created. It is fascinating to note that such simple facts lead to the airplanes that we know today.

David Loyd

**Causation Used
to Convince**

Causation is often used to convince. When you successfully convince, you succeed in causing the readers to discard some beliefs or opinions and to replace them with those you are recommending or offering. Following are the three ways in which you may convince your readers with the kinds of reader response each aims at.

**Ways to Convince a
Reader**

Type or Causation	Solicited Reader Response
By argumentation	The reader is led *by logical reasoning* to an inevitable conclusion regardless of personal feelings. Facts and firmly established beliefs are stated, leading to a logical conclusion.
By persuasion	Causes the reader to change beliefs and opinions mainly *by appeal to emotions*.
By critical evaluation	*Induces* the reader *to accept the writer's value judgment* about something by convincing the reader that something does or does not live up to certain standards or criteria, that something is good, fair, or poor.

Here are three supporting paragraphs which were taken from longer compositions. The first is from an extended argument, the second is from an essay in persuasion, and the third is from a critical evaluation. Before you read each of these, reread what is said about the particular type under the "Solicited Reader Response" column.

The first passage is argumentation. Notice how the writer establishes logical relationships between his causes. Whenever he thinks his reader may challenge what he is saying, he supports it with sound evidence in proof.

The individual who fears to betray his or her thoughts and says little or nothing is often suffering from the same kinds of inhibitions as the continuous talker. Many times the thoughts of this more silent person are never brought to the surface because of fear of being regarded as unintelligent. This type of person often expresses these thoughts much more effectively in other ways. Geniuses such as Albert Einstein express their thoughts not by verbal communication but by expressing the workings of their minds in more concrete mathematical language.

Bob Hannigan

In the following paragraph from a longer essay in persuasion the writer tries to establish a relationship with her reader at the beginning by pointing out something on which both can agree. She uses conversational language to establish a persuasive relationship. Consequently, the paragraph appeals as strongly to the emotions as to the intellect of the reader.

A diet is no fun, I agree. It is a dull grinding chore. But we all know how necessary for good physical and mental health it is. To persuade yourself to stick to your diet, you must constantly hold a picture of yourself in your mind of how beautiful or handsome you will be. Think how pleasant you will feel when you are able to buy any suit or dress on the rack or when you come home unexhausted after playing thirty-six holes of golf. Think of living without the fear of a heart attack. Isn't that worth all of the discomfort you are suffering while on the diet?

Eleanor Schultz

Problems of Oversimplification

One of the biggest dangers in the search for causes and results is oversimplification. Particularly with very complex subjects, it is tempting to pin everything on a single cause or effect when actually there are many factors at work. This kind of fallacious thinking is common in the analysis of world affairs, and particularly in politics. Some politicians make such simplification their stock in trade: their program will cure the world, whereas their opponents' program will bring it to hasty ruin.

Another danger in the search for causes is the fallacy known as *false cause,* which we discussed in Chapter 2. It is often easy to assume that because one thing happened shortly before or after another, one caused the other, when actually there may be no relation between the two.

In causation, the subject sentence of the whole composition or the controlling sentence of each supporting paragraph determines whether the writer must or may use causation in its development. Of course, if you don't wish to write causation you have the option of rewording the purpose or controlling sentence so that it will be more suitably developed in some other way. Following are examples of subject or controlling sentences which permit or require development by causation:

1. World War I was inevitable.
2. Some people are better listeners than others.
3. Learning to write is necessary for speed reading.
4. Essay type examinations are more accurate than objective tests.
5. Do teenagers have more respect for the law than their parents have?
6. The "Wiley Nillies" is a good TV program.

PRACTICE in Achieving This Chapter's Objectives

Practice in identifying and writing supporting paragraphs of definition, classification, and causation.

APPLICATION 12-1

In the blank before each of the following, write D if the controlling sentence permits or requires development by definition; Cl if by classification; or C if by causation.

_____ 1. Democracy is a state of mind.

_____ 2. There are three kinds of classroom sleeping beauties.

_____ 3. To be successful, a person must know what success is.

_____ 4. Students have a right to dissent.

_____ 5. Some sports require as high a degree of eye-mind-hand coordination as brain surgery.

_____ 6. What are "gandy dancers?"

_____ 7. Polygamy is necessary in some cultures.

_____ 8. Students should (or should not) be allowed to smoke in the classroom.

_____ 9. Everyone has some kinds of "friends" he wants to forget.

_____ 10. Gamblers fall into several classes, depending upon what their stakes are.

APPLICATION 12-2

In the blanks before the following, tell whether each supporting paragraph is developed by classification, definition, or causation.

_____ 1. From the establishment of the first national park—Yellowstone—in 1872, the National Park System has evolved through successive congressional enactments into a system containing more than 250 parks in the fifty States and in Puerto Rico in the Virgin Islands. The system is composed of three categories of areas: natural, historic, and recreational. Natural areas contain the great scenic wonderlands—unspoiled mountains, lakes, and forests, desert canyons, and glaciers. Historical and archeological areas contain examples of ancient Indian cultures, as well as buildings, sites, and objects which have been witness to great events of American history. Recreational areas of the National Park System—together with recreational areas administered by other agencies—provide healthful outdoor recreational opportunities for a population which today is increasingly urban.

_____ 2. A republic is a state operating on the idea that sovereignty belongs to the people, and they must elect representatives and officials to act in their behalf. The word republic means "public" or rule by the people. The republican form of state may, however, be autocratic or dictatorial in nature. Rome, from 509 to 27 B.C., was a republic in which virtually everyone except slaves had a voice. When the American colonists declared their independence, they established the Continental Congress that constituted a republican form of government.

Doris Crishon

_____

3. Excessive amounts of alcohol cause one to lose one's sense of responsibility. It slows reaction time and seriously impairs depth perception. The inebriated driver is unable to make quick logical decisions and is often responsible for accidents causing serious injuries or death. Drunk drivers are dangerous; they pose a serious threat to themselves as well as to others.

Gerald Kirk

_____

4. There are three main classifications of *piles* used in the construction industry. The most common is the *bearing pile.* It transfers the heavy loads through the unstable surface soils to the denser, more stable soils below. The next is the *friction pile.* This type does not necessarily reach high-bearing materials, but does reach soil resistance to a point where the load is carried by the underlying soil and the solid pressure surrounding the pile. Friction piles thus depend on soil density and side pressure for a great percentage of their load bearing ability. The third type of pile is the *sheet pile.* It is not intended to carry vertical loads, but rather to resist horizontal pressure. The principal use for sheet piling is to hold back earth around the perimeter of an excavation.

John Grogey

APPLICATION 12-3

The following paragraphs are developed by classification. Read them carefully and answer the questions that follow each.

A. The three main types of arrows are cedar, fiberglass, and aluminum. The aluminum arrow is commonly thought of as the ultimate arrow for target or tournament shooting. The close manufacturing tolerances for the aluminum tube adds uniformity and accuracy to the arrow, thus creating this common opinion. Many people have begun using aluminum arrows for hunting, as well as target or tournament shooting. This is quite impractical though, because the aluminum arrow will bend if it should happen to strike something a little too solid while in the field. The cost of aluminum arrows is quite high. The cedar and fiberglass arrows are designed for more abuse, both in structure and cost. Although neither of these arrows are considered really good for target or tournament shooting, they are both favorites for hunting. The cedar arrow is considered especially good for hunting because it will ordinarily break after it enters the animal's body; it is then impossible for the animal to work it out. The fiberglass arrow is prized for its ability to endure both abuse and climatic conditions, unlike cedar arrows which warp if they happen to be exposed to rain or extremely humid weather. Everyone has his own opinion as to which one is the best all-around arrow. I choose fiberglass.

1. What is the subject or term? _____

2. What are the standards or criteria? _____

3. List the classes. _____

B. Sneezing, the involuntary spasmodic expirations caused either by direct or reflexive irritations of the sensory nerves of the nasal mucous membrane may be broadly divided into two classes, depending upon their causes. These are extrinsic causes and intrinsic causes.

Extrinsic causes are those which originate outside of a person's body. Many bits of foreign matter continually enter a person's nasal passage with the air he breathes. Fumes, smoke, dust, pollen are only a few of the kinds of particles which are inhaled, causing direct nasal irritations, resulting in sneezing. External causes also cause reflexive sneezing. The most common of these is the sneezing which results from the excessive stimulation of the optic nerve by strong light.

The intrinsic causes for sneezing are numerous. Any of the many internal changes within the body which cause an inflammation of the mucous membranes in the nasal passage are in this classification. Many of these intrinsic causes for sneezing are often lumped under the heading of colds.

1. What is the subject or term? _____

2. What are the standards or criteria? _____

3. List the classes. _____

C. There are four basic seismic waves: two preliminary "body" waves which travel through the earth, and two which travel only at the surface. Combinations, reflections, and diffractions produce a virtual infinity of other types. The behavior of these is well enough understood that wave speed and amplitude have been the major means of describing the earth's interior. In addition, a large earthquake generates inelastic waves which echo through the planet like vibrations in a ringing bell, and which actually cause the planet to expand and contract infinitesimally.

1. What is the subject or term? _____

2. What are the standard or criteria? _____

3. List the classes. _____

APPLICATION 12-4

Identify the kind of error in each of the following incorrectly written definitions by placing a 1 before each with a faulty term, a 2 before each with a faulty class or genus, a 3 before each with a faulty differentiation, or 4 before each circular definition. Four of these definitions are correct. Before these four, print a letter to identify the kind of definition each is. Print Sy if it is a synonym definition, D if it is a definition by derivation, Sub if it is a subjective definition.

_____   1. A gouge is something used to carve.

_____   2. Meter is the method for measuring rhythm in poetry.

_____   3. Sherbet is derived from *sharbah,* an Arabic word for drink.

_____   4. He accidentally dropped the colander, a metal sieve.

_____   5. Baseball is a game I play with my whole being.

_____   6. Definition is defining words and ideas.

_____   7. Blue, for me, is a melancholic sigh.

_____   8. A political liberal is one who believes in liberalizing politics.

_____   9. Paper is material upon which we write.

_____   10. An alloy is a mixture.

APPLICATION 12-5

On the lines below, write three controlling sentences which would best be developed by causation, three by classification, and three by definition.

Causation

1. _____

   _____

   _____

2. _____

   _____

   _____

3. _____

   _____

   _____

Classification

1. _____

_____

_____

_____

_____

_____

2. _____

_____

_____

_____

_____

_____

3. _____

_____

_____

_____

_____

_____

Definition

1. _____

_____

_____

_____

_____

2. _____

_____

_____

_____

_____

_____

3. _____

_____

_____

_____

_____

_____

APPLICATION 12-6

Select a controlling sentence from each of the groups in the preceding application and develop each on the corresponding lines below into a supporting paragraph containing at least six sentences. Be sure to indicate your purpose in the blank so designated. Also, be sure to underline the main idea in your controlling sentence with one line and its key with two.

Definition

Purpose _____

_____

_____

_____

_____

_____

_____

_____

_____

_____

_____

Classification

Purpose _____

_____

_____

_____

_____

_____

_____

_____

_____

_____

_____

_____

_____

Causation

Purpose _____

_____

_____

_____

_____

_____

_____

_____

_____

_____

_____

_____

_____

APPLICATION 12-7

Write a full-length composition of about 600 words, consisting of: a title; an opener if you wish, either separate or incorporated into the main paragraph; a main paragraph, including a subject sentence and several explanatory sentences; at least three supporting paragraphs, of which one is a definition, another classification, and the third causation; and a concluding paragraph. Indicate your purpose in the heading with the title. In the left margin opposite each supporting paragraph, indicate whether you intend it as definition, classification, or illustration. Here are some suggested ideas for development:

1. What is kleptomania?
2. Gamblers can't help themselves
3. Installment buying is a stimulant to the economy
4. The worst kind of crime is ignorance
5. Narrative poetry is the oldest text book
6. What is a "leader"?

YOU BE THE JUDGE

Writer's Name _____

Date _____ Section _____

Title of paper _____

Chapter _____ Application No. _____

General Instructions on the You Be the Judge Applications, and specific instructions for Parts I and III, are printed inside the back cover of this book. Read those instructions carefully; then do Part I.

In the lines below, and on another sheet of paper, answer the questions in Part II, then enter a grade for the paper in the space above left, and write your evaluation for Part III. Reread the composition to see how well the writer understands and applies the principles studied in this chapter. As you read the composition write any helpful suggestions that occur to you in the margins.

PART II

1. Comment on the effectiveness of the title, opener, and main paragraph, including the subject sentence. _____

_____

_____

_____

_____

_____

_____

2. How appropriate is the topic to development by definition, classification, and causation? Discuss. _____

_____

_____

_____

_____

_____

_____

3. What kinds of definition are used (synonym, derivative, subjective, basic, extended). Explain by analyzing the paragraph. _____

_____

_____

_____

_____

_____

_____

_____

4. What topic is explained by classification and how is it done? Are the classes clearly separated, defined, identified, illustrated, discussed?

_____

_____

_____

_____

_____

_____

_____

_____

5. Is the causation paragraph mainly inductive or deductive? Is it developed by enumeration, synthesis, or analysis? _____

_____

_____

_____

_____

_____

_____

_____

6. How appropriate is this paragraph to development by causal analysis?

_____

_____

_____

_____

_____

_____

_____

_____

PART III   Grade and Explanation:

_____

_____

_____

CHAPTER 13

COMPARISON, CONTRAST, ANALOGY

After studying this chapter and completing the objectives that follow it, you should be able to do the following:
1. To identify and differentiate three more supporting forms of development: *comparison*, *contrast*, and *analogy*.
2. To identify and distinguish kinds of comparison and contrast: *simultaneous*, *alternating*, *block*, and *implied*.
3. To identify and write controlling sentences that allow or require development by *comparison*, *contrast*, or *analogy*.
4. To write supporting paragraphs of *comparison*, *contrast*, or *analogy*.
5. To write *comparison*, *contrast*, or *analogy* in developing the supporting paragraphs of a full-length composition.

ONE USEFUL way of learning about something new is to find out how it is like or how it is different from something we already know about. When we point out similarities we *compare* things. When we point out differences, we *contrast* them. There is also a special type of comparison, called *analogy*, which compares things which are very different from each other except for one striking quality that they have in common.

COMPARISON

As a writer you may use comparison to help your readers move from an understanding of something with which they are familiar to something with which they are not. In the following paragraph the writer compares certain features of the surface of the earth, with which the readers have some familiarity, with corresponding features of the surface of the moon, about which until recently they could have had no real information. In this way, the comparison helps the readers use their knowledge of a known member of the class of heavenly bodies, the earth, to increase their knowledge of one they know less about, the moon.

Space scientists agree that the most abundant elements forming the surface of the moon are the same as the most abundant ones composing the surface of the earth. Studies of the data returned by the astronauts indicate that the atomic composition of the lunar surface is composed of basalt, a volcanic rock common on earth. These studies also reveal that the moon is composed of a soil containing 58 percent oxygen and 18.5 percent silicon. This is close to the average composition of the earth's crust. The lunar surface contains less than 3 percent carbon and less than 2 percent sodium. At least 3 percent of the atoms are iron, cobalt, or nickel, and some leading physicists and chemists agree that the lunar surface is composed of these same elements and in similar proportions to those composing the earth's crust.

J. Fatool

Note that this comparison does two things. It compares specific points of one subject with the same points as they relate to the other. Thus, it compares earth and moon for the presence of basaltic rock and for percentages of certain chemical elements in the crusts of both bodies— oxygen, silicon, iron, cobalt, and nickel. The point of the comparison is that the contents of the two are strikingly similar. The second thing to note about this paragraph is that the comparison mentions only those items which are covered in the controlling sentence: the abundant elements in the crusts of both bodies.

As with any other form of development, the writer of a comparison needs to follow some ordered plan or procedure. There are four plans that can be used:

1. Simultaneous comparison
2. Alternating comparison
3. Block comparison
4. Implied comparison.

Simultaneous Comparison

Simultaneous comparison occurs when the writer states the points of similarity together. This type of development is used when you don't want to discuss the likenesses in depth; you therefore go over them rapidly in compact form. You will often use simultaneous comparison when you have several or many points of similarity that you want to list in developing the main idea in the controlling sentence.

To develop this form of comparison you use words, especially pronouns, that simultaneously identify the items involved in the comparison. In the following illustration these words are in boldface; other devices are italicized.

Both bees and ants demonstrate how insects live in large highly organized colonies. The homes of **either** of these insects contain separate rooms designed for special purposes whether they be to store food or to raise the offspring. **Both** have queens that have no other task but that of laying eggs. The chief work of *the drone bee, like that of the male ant,* is to mate with the young queens and then to die soon after mating. The *workers of* **both** *colonies* do all the work, securing food, feeding their queen, and keeping the living quarters clean. From the time each *bee or ant* is hatched, it seems to know whether it is a worker or a queen and for which tasks it is responsible: hunting, maintaining order, or nursing the young.

Ann Curry

Notice that this comparison mentions several points of similarity merely by enumeration and does not treat any of them in depth. This of course is all the controlling sentence of this paragraph requires for its development.

**Alternating
Comparison**

Alternating comparison, as the name suggests, is achieved by first identifying a characteristic of one item in the comparison and following it immediately with a similar characteristic in the other item. This type of comparison is built up in layers, from first one subject, then the other. Alternating comparison is commonly used to stress points of similarity. It is like putting two things side by side and pointing first to one and immediately to the same characteristic in the other.

The following supporting paragraph is developed by alternating layers of comparison. First, a characteristic of "modern man" is given; then a similar trait in "early" or "primitive man."

Despite centuries of change, human beings still retain many traits of their primitive ancestors. Primitives fought life-long battles with neighboring tribes. Today, nations are unable or unwilling to avoid wars to resolve conflicts. Primitives proved themselves through their powers as hunters and providers. Today, men and women gain the same kind of recognition by displaying wealth, business acumen, and technological achievements. Primitives feared death and other mysterious happenings; they turned to myths and legends for their answers. People still explain the unknown by resorting to astrology or to a variety of mystics for their answers to life. Really, have we progressed so far from our primitive ancestors during the centuries separating us? Do we now have greater possibility for happiness than they did?

Robert Hannigan

The preceding is a good example of alternating comparison dealing with two periods of time. Following is one which points out likenesses between two different places, a hospital and a home.

The same qualities that make people good *house guests* make them good *hospital patients*. Good *house guests* can expect a reasonable amount of service and effort on their behalf, and *hospital patients* can also. *Guests* have to adjust to what is for them a change, and certainly *hospital patients* must do the same. No one appreciates a complaining, unpleasant, unappreciative *house guest*, and the hospital staff is no exception. *House guests* who expect vast changes to be made for their benefit are not popular for long. Certainly nurses and other personnel with their routines feel the same way about *patients* in their care. Just as *house guests* must make adjustments to enjoy their visits, so *patients* must make adjustments to make their stays reasonably pleasant and satisfying under the circumstances.

Robert Friedman

Block Comparison

Block comparison is suitable when the writer wants to treat points of similarity in depth. In this way each point is drawn out so that its relationship to another point being made is quite clear. This type of comparison is often used when the points of similarity discussed are fewer, more complex, and require more explanation.

Block comparison is achieved by stating and expanding a set of points of comparison of one of the subjects and then doing the same for the other. Often there is only one set of similarities for each term in a written communication.

Here is a supporting paragraph that first points out all of the characteristics that the writer wants to name about Ulysses S. Grant, and then follows it with a block on parallel items in the life of Robert E. Lee.

Although Ulysses S. Grant and Robert E. Lee were fierce adversaries during the Civil War, their lives, both military and nonmilitary, had a great deal in common. Grant descended from a family whose members participated in the American Revolution. He received his commission of second lieutenant from West Point and served in the Mexican War. He was later summoned by President Lincoln to assume command of the Union Forces during the Civil War. After the Civil War, Grant suffered financial problems and was forced to declare bankruptcy. Lee also descended from a family which engaged in the American Revolution. He, too, received his commission from West Point and later fought in Mexico during the Mexican War. His fame as a military strategist during the Civil War, when he was the commander of the Confederate armies, is well known. Although it is not always pointed out by historians, he, like Grant, had financial difficulties after the Civil War and was compelled to declare bankruptcy. By securing a post as president of Washington College, he was able to avoid additional poverty.

Gordon Sacris

Implied Comparison

Implied comparison is used when the writer needs to focus on only one term of a comparison and the other is so well known that it need not be discussed. Sometimes, in the interests of compactness and succinctness, one of the terms of the comparison is merely mentioned because you are sure that it is unnecessary to deal with it further. Perhaps you know that the reader is already familiar with the characteristics of one of the subjects. In the following passage, the writer does not elaborate the points of her comparison as they pertain to the United States, because she knows that the reader will be adequately familiar with them. This enables her to emphasize the characteristics of the other term, ancient Rome. This type of comparison is often used when the writer wants to inform or to convince the reader about points of similarity with which the reader may be unfamiliar.

Although the last days of the Roman Empire may at first appear very different from those of the United States today, there are ominous likenesses. Ancient Rome possessed tremendous military strength, not of the magnitude of our air power, true, but enough to maintain its control over almost all of the known world. Because of the vast expanse of its rule, however, much of its strength was devoted to maintaining order in areas other than within its own borders. Just as in the United States today, Rome was so intensely occupied with establishing and maintaining its political principles in areas other than those within its own borders, its rulers were blind to the full significance of the ominous changes taking place at home. Much of this change consisted of internal conflict induced by the indifference of the affluent Roman to the suffering of the less fortunate. This apathy of the wealthy caused the poor to resort to violence to attract attention to their complaints. This is not unlike our own time when dissenters shoot someone of renown to penetrate the stone wall of indifference.

Lauri Dee

Development by comparison need not be limited to one supporting paragraph. A writer may use several supporting paragraphs or even a whole composition to develop a single comparison. In block comparison, writers often develop one of the blocks of similarities in one paragraph and the other block in a separate one.

Comparisons of more than one paragraph may also be of the *simultaneous* or *alternating* types. Following is a simultaneous comparison mixed with a bit of alternating comparison.

Neither badminton nor table tennis requires a large playing area. Both sports are played on courts. Badminton requires an outdoor court usually twenty feet wide and forty feet long on which two or four players may play at one time. Table tennis is usually played indoors on a table court four feet wide and eight feet long; also two or four players.

Both games use somewhat the same kinds of equipment; both require nets strung tightly across the courts. In both games, paddles (called rackets in badminton) are used to bat an object back and forth over the net. In badminton the object batted is a small feathered ball. At one time a feathered cork called a shuttlecock was used. The object batted back and forth in table tennis is a small ball about the same size as that used in badminton but without the feathers. The table tennis ball is made of plastic or cellophane.

Paul Treuhaft

CONTRAST   Contrast points out or explains dissimilarities — unlikenesses — between two or more ideas or things which belong to the same class and which therefore can be logically contrasted.

Like comparison, contrast can add vividness and clarity. It also has one advantage over comparison: it can be more emphatic. Using contrast enables you to stress a point, because it lets you express your ideas in sharp relief, like placing white chalk marks on a blackboard. Notice how the writer makes the impression that he is conveying about the "old woman" in the following illustration more vivid by contrasting old age with the youthfulness of her babushka.

On a fresh spring morning last April, as I waited at the bus stop, I observed an old woman on the way to market. Her step was halting but determined, her attire was somber, and her lined face was testimony to the passage of many years. Blue eyes watery with the myopia of time, everything about her signified advanced age, except for her headwear. Crowning her head was the most colorful babushka that I have ever seen. The pinks, yellows and greens contrasted so greatly with her black coat and dress that it was obvious that her choice of scarf this particular morning was a tribute to youth. Although physically she was in the winter of her life, her spirit was attuned to the time of the year when the earth renews itself.

Tom McHale

As in comparison, the extent to which contrast is developed is indicated by the key idea of the controlling sentence. Writers don't merely point out differences between the items being contrasted; they point out only those differences pertinent to the key idea. Notice how the writer limits the points of contrast in the following to the "ease" of mining a quarry and a lode. Neither what is taken out of them nor the cost of working them is contrasted because neither of these points would be relevant.

A quarry is easier to mine than a lode. A quarry is an open excavation from which various types of rock and stone are mined for processing into building material. Both a quarry and a lode have definite boundaries separating them from the adjoining land mass, but since the quarry is open the entrance into it is usually a road built down to its bottom. Heavy trucks may move down to the huge shovels working the quarry to be readily loaded with the raw material and to drive quickly away to the nearby processing machinery. In contrast, the lode, which is completely underground, usually has a narrow passageway or shaft through which only much smaller machinery can be moved to the area being worked; therefore, working the lode and hauling out the unprocessed resources is slower and more difficult.

Robert Haas

Contrast, like comparison, must also be developed by orderly patterns, otherwise a confusing hodgepodge of differences between items could result. Since it is impossible to point out the difference between two things simultaneously, there is no way that you can develop simultaneous contrast. You can, however, use the remaining three forms of development used in showing comparison. These are:

1. Alternating contrast:
2. Block contrast.
3. Implied contrast.

Alternating Contrast

Alternating contrast is used when you want to point out several differences without discussing them extensively. You merely point out a trait of one item and then state how the other item differs from it in respect to that trait. In a sense, this pattern builds up layers of contrast.

The television western of several years ago differs greatly from the western of today. Ten years ago, for example, the swindler or bank robber in a western could be identified not by the crimes he committed so much as by the color of the clothing he wore – which was black. Today the television western reveals the villain by mannerisms and personality. At one time, every western had a superhuman, invincible "good guy" with whom the viewers could identify because he too lived out on the farm. Currently, the central figures of the west are average people who may live on a middle-class street in any part of the country. They are characters like the bus drivers, mailclerks and accountants who live next door to you in suburbia. At night they come in off the streets, buckle their holsters, and mount their horses to ride the television range. They become persons who respect others, drink and smoke only just a bit, and are able not only to outshoot the "bad guy," but also to outsmart him with good common sense.

Ron Sengal

Block Contrast

Block contrast is produced when you first discuss certain traits possessed by one of your subjects, and then discuss the same set of characteristics for the other subject, stressing the ways in which the two sets differ. Block contrast is often used when you want to focus on only a few important differences so that they can be described more extensively.

Following is an example of block contrast. The writer obviously selected this form because it provided room in which to explain these more complex contrasting points in the writings of Hemingway and Faulkner.

The writing styles of Ernest Hemingway and William Faulkner insure their literary greatness. Hemingway's sentences are usually short, simple, and straightforward; consequently, they are remarkably lucid. He doesn't overwhelm the reader with long, "purplish" words nor with complicated sentence structure. Much of what he expresses is conveyed by understatement. Faulkner's writing, on the other hand, is much more involved. He uses an elaborate stream-of-consciousness technique to reveal the psychological conflicts within his characters. His sentences are often long and complex; sometimes he carries his reader through several time periods within the same sentence. Along with their distinctly different styles, the works of both Hemingway and Faulkner contain a richness of meaningful substance and other qualities and ingredients which help maintain their places among America's greatest writers.

John Ganim

Just as comparison is often used to point out similarities between two periods of time or two different places, contrast is often used to emphasize the differences between times and places. Here is a paragraph which stresses the differences between two houses located in two different parts of the country and built at different times in different styles.

Our old house in Connecticut and our present one in Phoenix, Arizona, are quite different. Our Connecticut home is a two story wooden colonial almost one hundred years old. It has a full sized attic and cellar and a barn which can accommodate two cars. The fifteen year old yellow brick ranch in Phoenix has only an attic and a crawl space for a basement. Each of the colonial's four bedrooms can easily accommodate two twin beds. In our three bedroom ranch, only one bedroom can hold a double bed. Each house has a living room fireplace, but the colonial has another one in the other living room, the front "sitting room." Finally, the ranch kitchen uncomfortably seats only two, whereas the colonial seats at least four and has a separate formal dining room.

Mary Petersen

Implied Contrast

Implied contrast is developed by focusing on only one of the terms involved. By stressing and developing one term, the writer implies the differences which characterize the other — and usually the familiar — term in contrast. Following is an example of implied contrast involving "living on the farm" in contrast to "living in the city." In the first paragraph, the writer emphasizes the characteristics of life on the farm and implies the opposite characteristics of life in the city. In the second paragraph the opposite is true.

After living on the farm, people will never wish to go back to the city. The farm is surrounded with green fields, fresh air, and refreshing breezes. Country residents enjoy quiet afternoons and a more casual pace of living. They live closer to the earth and experience an intimate feeling of oneness with the earth and the universe.

Leslie Smith

In contrast to living on the farm, living in the city is an intense struggle to survive in a concrete wasteland. Miles and miles of pavement
are covered with swarms of determined people shackled to an inflexible system of life. Visitors from the country are bewildered by the
actions, sounds, smells, and pace of city life. Eagerly they return to the
quiet, comfortable life in the country.

Leslie Smith

Here is another implied contrast. This one only mentions "a gun" and
implies how it differs from jujitsu in providing self-defense. This technique
enables the writer to stress the advantages of relying on jujitsu instead of
a gun for self-defense.

Jujitsu is more effective than a gun for securing self-defense. First,
it is not necessary to secure a permit to practice judo. The malicious
person who plans to attack you cannot see any bulges in your pockets
to show that you are carrying a weapon. Judo is a weapon which cannot be taken away from you, leaving you without a means of defense.
It is a defense which both men and women can use with equal skill.
Accidental deaths are rarely caused by leaving it lying around the
house within the reach of children. For these reasons and others,
jujitsu is more practical than a gun for self-defense.

Robert Thacker

ANALOGY

*Analogy is tracing a striking likeness or unlikeness between things which
do not belong to the same class.* It is not "logical" to compare or contrast
an iceberg with the influence of a parent on a child, for the two subjects
belong to very different kinds or classes of things. But used in analogy,
the iceberg vividly expresses the idea that the influence a parent exerts
on a child is 90 percent submerged in the unconscious part of the child's
whole life.

Since an analogy is a comparison or contrast between two or more
things that do not belong to the same class, it frees you from restrictions
that limit you to forming class relationships and provides a larger assortment of ideas from which to select points of comparison that are colorful
or meaningful to the reader. Consequently, analogy is more effective than
ordinary comparison or contrast when you want vivid images or when you
must more effectively adapt your ideas to the past experiences of the
reader. Analogy is especially useful in enabling you to give concreteness
to an abstract idea which cannot be detected by the senses. An apt
analogy almost always has a hint of persuasion in it; it points out a
perceived truth about the subject, and then makes an extended case for
that truth. For example, look ahead to the first paragraph of the following
chapter.

In one sense an analogy is an extended metaphor (Chapter 15). Metaphor is used in all forms of poetry and prose to give a quick flash of
description, especially when an expression of intense emotion is to be

conveyed at the same time. We have all made statements such as "Your eyes are stars" or "That car is a lemon" to express emotion rather than to give accurate information. Analogy is different from metaphor in that it is often used to inform by clarifying meaning.

Following is a clear illustration of how a writer may use analogy to adapt informational material to the reader's experience. He developed this supporting paragraph after assuming that his reader would probably be more familiar with the nature of water than with that of electricity.

Electricity is transferred from one place to another in much the same manner as water. A water pipe performs the same function as a length of wire. The pipe carries water to its point of use in the same manner as wire carries electricity to its point of use. A blown fuse results from the same thing as a burst water pipe. Both give out due to extreme pressure applied to the walls of the carrier. A switch is to electricity what a faucet is to water. Both of them control the flow of the substance. Since electricity and water have some common properties, understanding the job of the plumber will help understanding the work of the electrician.

John Brower

Analogies are especially helpful in enabling you to make an abstract idea concrete; that is, taking an idea which cannot be experienced through the sense of sight, smell, hearing, touch, or taste, and relating it to a sense experience to facilitate easy and clear understanding. Human beings have more difficulty understanding things which they can experience only intellectually. Notice how the writer clarifies the meaning of "personality" in the following by forming an analogy with the peculiarities of a river, something which can be sensed.

Like a river, with its many bends and curves, the human personality has its own peculiarities, too. As a river may flood its banks one year and be low the next, so too can the personality be at a higher tension at different times. Once a river's problems are corrected with dams and locks, it runs at a much smoother pace. Also a human being develops, personality changes through environment and experience. A person must deal with the underlying problems of disorganized life. Conflicting impulses, desires, and emotions must be coordinated in order to obtain self-control and security of mind. In this way, the personality too will run a much smoother course.

Eleanor Parvic

Analogy, like any other form of development, need not be limited to a single paragraph. Depending on the complexity of your ideas and the intended length of the composition, you must judge to what extent your readers will require its development so that they will respond as you want them to respond.

The wording of a controlling sentence will suggest to you whether it should be developed by comparison, contrast, or analogy. Although these may not be the only ways to develop it, one of them may be the most appropriate to the main idea, your purpose, or the relationship you want to maintain with the reader.

The following are controlling sentences which clearly suggest development by one of these forms of development.

Comparison:

1. Venice, Italy, and Toledo, Ohio, are both glass centers.
2. Soccer is as important a sport in Europe as football is in the United States.

Contrast:

1. There is more hard work in writing than in physical labor.
2. More misconceptions exist about the writing of fiction than about the writing of nonfiction.
3. Ballet is a more exhausting art than gymnastics.

Analogy:

1. Think of your mind as a beam of light searching for the truth.
2. Objective writing is a photograph; it records only what the writer sees.
3. My conscience was a nag constantly fretting at my doing the pleasant rather than the right thing.

Comparison and contrast are often combined in developing supporting paragraphs. Following are controlling sentences which call for development by a combination of comparison and contrast:

1. Doctors and officers of the law, unlike bankers, are often expected to work beyond the call of duty.
2. "Friendship," like "love," is often discussed but seldom understood.
3. The Lebanese culture is more closely related to the French than to the American.

PRACTICE in Achieving This Chapter's Objectives

Practice in identifying and writing supporting paragraphs of comparison, contrast, and analogy.

APPLICATION 13-1

From the following key, select the letter that best identifies the supporting form most suitable for the development of each of the controlling sentences below and write it in the appropriate blank.

A. comparison
B. contrast
C. analogy

_____ 1. Though both are forms of humor, comedy is different from satire.

_____ 2. A political campaign is like a Broadway performance.

_____ 3. In 1990 the world will surely be different from what it is today.

_____ 4. There is no gathering the rose without being pricked by thorns.

_____ 5. Fashions in furniture change just as clothing fashions do.

_____ 6. Per capita earnings in the United States exceed those in Europe.

_____ 7. At Shiloh, the Confederate and Union forces used similar military strategy.

_____ 8. The patient would rather have been the dentist.

_____ 9. Buying a car requires as much skill as selling one.

_____ 10. Dating is like mountain climbing.

APPLICATION 13-2

In the blanks to the left of each of the following, tell whether it is mainly comparison, contrast, or analogy. If it is comparison or contrast, tell whether it is simultaneous, alternating, block, or implied on the first line. If it is analogy used to make an abstract idea concrete, tell what the abstract idea is on the second line.

a. _____

b. _____

1. Tornadoes and hurricanes are very similar in their make-up and in their ability to seriously damage or destroy property and life. Both are violent whirling winds, characteristically accompanied by a funnel-shaped cloud, which moves frequently and rapidly for miles. Like the hurricane, tornadoes are velocity winds blowing circularly around a low-pressure center, known as the eye. Because of the velocity of high winds, they are able to pull trees out of the ground, blow houses from their foundations; they are literally able to destroy anything that gets in their path.

Yvonne Pluta

a. _____

b. _____

2. As they build on some of the same emotional responses from their readers, Sylvia Plath and Maya Angelou have become renowned twentieth-century artists. Both of these poets capture the sensitivity of the real world and put it into words that are explosive, defensive, revengeful, wry, bitter, and joyful at the same time. These two writers know how to make people feel and respond to the world around them.

a. _____

b. _____

3. The view of Lake Superior from the deserted light house at Copper Harbor had almost a picture postcard resemblance to sections of the ocean drive at Newport, Rhode Island. On a windy day the distant whitecaps of Lake Superior gave way to waves that crushed the shore. Just as on the Atlantic shore the pebbles and stones grumbled in retreat with the pull of the undertow, only to be pushed forward again with the next wave, the Lake Superior sounds are the same. The vastness of the dark blue-green lake sparkling in the sunlight and its wave-splashed rocky coast are similar to several areas of the drive bordering the New England Coast. Even the large commercial tankers and ships down to the smallest pleasure crafts are as familiar as those which ply the ocean. Perhaps the only thing missing that day at Copper Harbor was a smell, the distinctive smell of saltwater seaweed.

Mary Petersen

a. _____

b. _____

4. Both the tent and travel trailers are escape castles in the world of camping. The trailer hitch is the drawbridge spanning the moat of humdrum everyday routine. When this drawbridge is lowered onto its tow vehicle, the family is off towing this wheeled castle up to the woods to enjoy the splendor of nature. These trailers of today can be likened to castles for they afford the owners probably more luxury than the knights of old could even dream of, and they make your kingdom out of whatever park site you choose for them.

Ed Zupanic

a. _____

b. _____

5. Love is like the sea. It can be deep and dark or shallow and light. It may be calm at times and turbulent at other periods. It comes and goes with the tides of life. It is ever changing.

Sharon L. Traub

a. _____

b. _____

6. Although Ulysses Grant and Robert E. Lee were both considered to be the great generals of the Civil War, there were tremendous differences between them. While Lee was a handsome, tall, vigorous man with a commanding appearance and manner, Grant was short and stocky with a quiet, almost shy manner, lacking any appearance of a leader of

men. Even though they both won appointments to West Point as young men, their attitudes toward studies emphasized the vast differences between them. While Lee was extremely serious in his studies, showing great devotion to duty (graduated second in his class), Grant was remembered as lazy in his studies and careless in his drills, disliking the military way of life. Their personal differences were perhaps most markedly evident at the surrender. Lee was the epitome of military regulations with his sword at his side, contrasted to a dusty, dirty Grant in his fatigue uniform, carrying no side arms at all.

Tony Shiekh

a. _____

b. _____

7. Clothing fashions today are not new; many of them were in vogue more than forty years ago. In the twenties dresses were short and pleats were the rage, and the same holds true today, although the dresses are even shorter. Women's shoes had short, chunky heels as do shoe styles at present. Fur coats were fashionable. Again, this is true today. Long beads or chains worn around the neck were popular, a current fad. Even today's men's clothing styles have changed to many of the popular fashions of the 1920s. Pin stripes, double breasted suits with narrow lapels, and wide ties are now the thing to wear in men's attire. Fashions in clothing are never really new; they usually are borrowed from styles previously worn sometime, somewhere in the long history of the human race.

Geraldine Nicoll

a. _____

b. _____

8. If you have a camera, you know something about how the eye works. The eye is like a camera that constantly adjusts itself to take and develop an endless stream of pictures at a speed greater than a high speed movie camera. Light rays are reflected from an object toward the eye. They pass first through a clear shield, called the cornea, which forms and protects the front of the eyeball. The colored object behind the cornea is the iris. The pupil is the opening through which the light rays pass. Its size is controlled by muscles that make the pupil small when the light is bright and big when light is dim. Behind the pupil is the lens. Muscles control the shape of the lens, thus focusing it to view objects at different distances.

Stewart L. Hildebrand

a. _____

b. _____

9. Although Peggy Fleming and Janet Lynn have both become famous skaters, their individual styles of skating are quite different. In taking a close look at their techniques, it is evident that, while both artists are equally graceful, Peggy Fleming's maneuvers are more creative and artistic than Janet Lynn's. Peggy moves smoothly from one spin to another, very

conscious of her body movements, her upper torso, and the extension of her arms at all times. Janet Lynn, whose skating is just as techniquely accurate as Peggy's, skates with much more emphasis on the athletic influence than does Peggy. Janet is aware of her physical structure, her dominance on the ice, and the strength of her limbs rather than of the smoothness of her movements. But both are masters of a fine art when they interpret sound and feeling on ice.

APPLICATION 13-3

Beneath each of the supporting forms listed below, write two controlling sentences which call for development by that particular form. Then select one of these sentences and develop it into the supporting paragraph intended.

Comparison

1. _____

_____

2. _____

_____

Contrast

1. _____

_____

2. _____

_____

Analogy

1. _____

_____

2. _____

_____

Supporting Paragraph

_____

_____

_____

_____

_____

_____

_____

_____

_____

_____

APPLICATION 13-4

Select one from each pair of controlling sentences you wrote in Application 13-3 and develop it into three paragraphs, that is, one for comparison, one for contrast, and one for analogy.

APPLICATION 13-5

Write a full-length composition of about 600 words, consisting of a title; an opener if you wish, either separate or incorporated into the main paragraph; a main paragraph, including a subject sentence and several explanatory sentences; at least three supporting paragraphs including a comparison, a contrast, and an analogy. Finally, write a concluding paragraph. Be sure to indicate your purpose in the heading with the title. Also, in the left margin, opposite each of the supporting paragraphs, indicate whether you intended it to be a comparison, a contrast, or an analogy. Remember, your instructor may have another student evaluate your paper, or he may project it on a screen for class evaluation. If you need help with grammar while writing, refer to the Handbook of Correct and Effective Usage on pages 383–404. Here are some suggested ideas:

1. A house and a home are two different things
2. A childhood memory
3. Illusions and delusions
4. A corporation is a family
5. A doer and a thinker
6. The FBI and Scotland Yard
7. Television programs and radio programs
8. Human life and the sea
9. Clouds and ships
10. Human eating habits—yesterday and today

YOU BE THE JUDGE

Evaluator's Initials

Date _____

Section _____

Grade _____

Writer's Name _____

Date _____ Section _____

Title of paper _____

Chapter _____ Application No. _____

General Instructions on the You Be the Judge Applications, and specific instructions for Parts I and III, are printed inside the back cover of this book. Read those instructions carefully; then do Part I.

In the lines below, and on another sheet of paper, answer the questions in Part II. Then enter a grade for the paper in the space above left, and write your evaluation for Part III. Reread the composition to see how well the writer understands and applies the principles studied in this chapter. As you read the composition write any helpful suggestions that occur to you in the margins.

PART II

1. How suitable is the topic for development by comparison and contrast?

_____

_____

_____

_____

_____

_____

_____

2. How well do the title, opener, and main paragraph introduce the pre-determined elements? _____

_____

_____

_____

_____

_____

_____

3. Are comparison and contrast used mainly to develop the main idea by description, narration, or causation? Explain. _____

_____

_____

_____

_____

_____

4. Is the comparison material primarily simultaneous, alternating, block, implied, or a combination? Explain. _____

_____

_____

_____

_____

_____

_____

5. Is the contrast material primarily alternating, block, implied, or a combination of these? Explain. _____

_____

_____

_____

_____

_____

6. For what purpose is the main analogy in the paper used, to describe, define, explain, or persuade? Explain. _____

_____

_____

_____

_____

7. Comment on the effectiveness of the materials discussed in Questions 3, 4, and 5. _____

_____

_____

_____

_____

_____

8. What is the abstraction the analogy is meant to clarify or support?

_____

_____

_____

_____

_____

_____

PART III   Grade and Explanation:

_____

_____

_____

_____

PART 5

SPECIAL SKILLS

CHAPTER 14

ORDERLY DEVELOPMENT– COHERENCE

After studying this chapter and completing the applications that follow it, you should be able to do the following:
1. To identify and differentiate *degrees* or *order of development* and *coherence*.
2. To identify and use connecting or linking words correctly and effectively: *conjunctions, prepositions, pronouns*, and *linking verbs*.
3. To identify and use repetition effectively: *the same word, derivative words*, and *synonyms*.
4. To identify and use transitional words, sentences, and paragraphs effectively: to maintain orderly *time progression, space progression*, and *logical progression*.
5. To identify and to maintain orderly arrangement: orderly *spatial arrangement* and orderly *chronological arrangement—stationary, panning, roving*, or *mobile*.
6. To identify and maintain logical relationships.
7. To identify and avoid common errors in orderly development.
8. To apply these principles in maintaining coherence in a full-length composition.

A WRITTEN communication is like a freight train. Though its cars may all contain valuable merchandise and though all may be placed in the right order on the same track behind a locomotive intended for a certain destination, they cannot get where they are going unless they are securely connected to each other and to the engine. In written communication, even though ideas are logically related, writing cannot do what it is intended to do until certain kinds of linking words and devices are inserted to hook up the ideas into orderly and connected trains of thought.

As a writer, you must be constantly aware of the gap in time and space between your thoughts and the minds of your intended readers. An associative or logical relationship clear in your own mind may not be clear to your readers. So your thoughts must be mechanically connected by words, by punctuation, and by the order in which they are arranged so that they will be readily understood. The process of achieving such a tightly knit, orderly arrangement in written communication is called coherence. *Orderly development—coherence—is the process by which the details of a composition are connected and organized to show their relationships to each other and to the predetermined elements.*

To achieve coherence, you must effectively link the details within sentences. Within paragraphs, you must also link the sentences to each other and to the main idea expressed in your controlling sentence. And, you must relate the paragraphs to each other and to the predetermined elements established in your purpose sentence. Following are some of the main devices by which this linking is done.

A. Connecting or linking words
   1. Conjunctions
   2. Prepositions
   3. Pronouns
   4. Linking verbs
   5. Repetition
      a. Of the same word
      b. By derivatives of words previously used
      c. By synonyms for words previously used
B. Transitional words, sentences, and paragraphs
   1. To maintain orderly space progression between words, sentences, and paragraphs
   2. To maintain orderly time progression between words, sentences, and paragraphs
   3. To maintain orderly logical progression from one supporting form to another
C. Orderly arrangement
   1. Spatial
   2. Chronological
   3. Logical

**CONNECTING OR
LINKING WORDS**

The italicized words in the sentences which make up the following paragraph illustrate how relationships are established between words and sentences by linking or connecting words. Usually, these words link one idea to another. Unlike the transitional elements we will discuss next, they do not move the idea in time or space. Mainly, these connectors allow the writer to join or stick or connect one idea to another, as a popcorn ball is made by sticking one kernel of popped corn to another until a ball is formed. Following are the kinds of connections used in the next passage:

C conjunction
P pronoun (or pronominal adjective)
R repetition of same word
S repetition by synonym
D repetition by derivative
(Prepositions have not been marked intentionally.)

A true sports car differs from an average automobile. First, in a *sports* [S] *vehicle* [C] the engine is more compact *and* [C] lighter in weight. *Conse-* [R] *quently*, the *engine* [P] is designed to receive more gas per cylinder. *This* [R] tends to make the *car* [R] less powerful *but* [C] enables *it* [P] to attain higher speeds. The *speed* [R] at which a *sports car* [R] can travel is important in determining its value. Second, a full sized sedan can seat four to six people comfortably, *but* [C] the smaller, more agile *sports vehicles* [R][S] can seat only one or two. Most of the space in the regular *auto* [D] is taken by the passenger compartment, *but* [C] the *motor* [S] is the main space filler in the *other*. [P] Third, the body design of the *sports car* [R] is proportioned *so that* [C][S][P] at high rates of speed the *vehicle* [P] will knife *its* [P] way cleanly through air currents *that* [P] cause vacuum pockets *which* [P] can slow down *its* [P] speed. Manufacturers carefully build *it* [P] low enough to keep *its* [P] center of gravity from causing *it* [P] to overturn. *These* [P] factors contribute to *its agility*. [S] Fourth, the large size of the wheels and tires affords faster pick-up and traction. *And* [C] fifth, the purpose for *which* [P] a person buys a regular *automobile* [S] is for transportation or for luxury. *When* [C] *one* [P] purchases a *sports car* [R] it is for the thrill of driving.

Examining this paragraph with all its connectors emphasized is like looking at a garment inside out, with its seams showing. Readers may be like customers who buy a piece of clothing because they admire its color, texture, and design. Writers, however, must always be like the tailor, fully aware of the effects which will be created by different kinds of essential stitches. In a sense, writers must periodically turn the garment inside out to check the effectiveness of the connectors. They must know about the different kinds of connectors and how each functions if they are to use them deliberately and well.

Most of these connecting devices are often used between paragraphs as well as within and between sentences. Here is a passage showing how repetition is used to connect paragraphs.

Television has become one of the most *influential* forms of communication today. It affects the lives of everyone from the diaper set to the senior citizen. The *influence* of this powerful medium ranges widely from most beneficial to extremely detrimental.

The *influence* of television is seen in the classroom. Distance has been spanned through this medium. The beautiful presentation of Johanna Spyri's classical *Heide* is almost as good as a visit to Switzerland. The magnificent African Veldt, with its fascinating wildlife, has become a real place through special programs. The mysteries of the sea have been unveiled and polar regions have been explored. Through television, the dry pages of text books have been given the warmth of life.

The *influence* of television is seen in the grocery store as the consumer purchases the laundry soap that gets clothes whiter and the peanut butter that smells like fresh peanuts. Even the toddler, riding in the cart, demands a particular brand of peanut butter.

The *influence* of television was seen in the protest marches which for a while became a standard part of society. Without television these incidents could not have been brought "live" into the home, thus affecting everyone.

Television has become such a powerful *influence* that programs must be selected carefully. This medium might be used to induce uncooperative elements in our society to participate more constructively. It can be a powerful *influence* in enabling all of us to be proud once again to be Americans.

June Inna

TRANSITIONAL ELEMENTS

In addition to repetition, synonyms, and the other devices which we have just seen, coherence is also achieved by the use of specific transitional words and phrases that establish not just the fact of connection but the nature of specific relationships between ideas. In addition to making ideas stick together, these may describe relationships in time or space, and may indicate logical relationships.

The word *transitional* is derived from the Latin word meaning to go across. Notice how the transitional sentence in the third paragraph allows the idea in the first and second paragraphs "to go across" from the discussion of the relationship between animal names and "an unpleasant quality" to a discussion of the relationship between animal names and "specific occupations."

Subject (or Controlling) Sentence

Often animal names are used to characterize a person with some peculiarity or unpleasant quality. Stupidity or foolishness in one may result in his being called an ass, a baboon, a calf, a dodo, a donkey, a goose, a monkey, a pigeon, or a yak.

Cowards are called chickens, and the very timid are known as sheep or rabbits, both vegetarian animals which are likely to be consumed by carnivorous beasts. Any disliked person may also be an ape or a gorilla, or perhaps a louse, a polecat, a skunk, or a rat. The grossly impolite person may be a bear or a boar. A person who preys on others may be a hawk or a spider or a caterpillar, or, if that person is cunning or clever, and not necessarily malignant or voracious, a fox. The dirty person is a pig or a hog, but these terms are equally applicable to a selfish person or a person who indulges in a large appetite.

The classification of people by qualities of character or as members of groups accounts for the use of many of the animal names; however, several such names are employed in reference to specific occupations. A professional gambler may be a pigeon or a shark. A singer may be a nightingale or a thrush. A slang dictionary of 1864 lists a snipe as a "long bill or account; also a term for attorneys – a race remarkable for their propensity to long bills." The train conductor is often known as the big ox.

You must use words, phrases, and clauses deliberately as transitional elements to achieve orderliness. You also may use whole sentences to effect transition between the parts of your paragraphs. In addition to the transitional elements consisting of single words or groups of words, the following passage contains two complete sentences (italicized) which are transitional elements. The first of these enables the writer to move from the time devoted to preparing for the show to the time when "the show begins." The other transitional sentence enables the writer to move in space from the acts taking place on the ground to those in the air, on the trapeze.

The circus is a thrilling and unforgettable form of entertainment. Weeks before it comes to town, gaily colored posters showing clowns, lions, tigers, and elephants are pasted upon billboards, buildings, and in the windows of stores. These posters promise that the circus will be "the greatest show on earth" and tell about its star acts. The circus comes into town on its own railroad train, and workmen begin to unload the cars at once. The occasional noisy trumpeting of a disturbed elephant mingles with the roaring of lions and the rumble of the tractors that pull the heavy wagons through the streets to the show grounds. *Soon the tents are set up, and it is time for the entrance parade to start and the show begins.* Elephants march out, wearing bright velvet coverings. Beautiful horses, their coats groomed until they shine like satin, prance by with pride in every movement. Meanwhile, the clowns go through all their hilarious antics. Dozens of them may pile out of a small car, or set a small house on fire and then put the flames out with a miniature fire truck. Some clowns make themselves appear enormous by wearing costumes which are blown up by air. *There is much more than one person can see or do.* Overhead, the trapeze artists fly through the air or risk their lives riding bicycles on high wires. No circus would be complete without pink lemonade,

Transitional Sentence

Controlling Sentence

spun-sugar candy, and popcorn or peanuts to feed the elephants after the show. Who can forget the gaiety, color, and thrilling excitement of a circus?

Sue Dodd

A large number of transitional words and phrases may be grouped according to three principal purposes, to indicate changes in time, to indicate movement from one place to another, and to indicate logical relationships. Here are some characteristic transitional elements of each kind.

1. To indicate passage from one time to another:

immediately	lately	last
temporarily	since	now
afterward	later	finally
thereafter	after	at length
meantime	first	up to now
soon	second	from that time on
hours before	meanwhile	

2. To indicate movement from one place to another:

nearby	below	next to
across	against	on the other side
beyond	to the left	in the same place
overhead	to the right	as far as
above	in the distance	returning to

3. To indicate logical relationships:

and	nevertheless	therefore
but	still	consequently
yet	hence	as a result
for	since	in spite of
also	because	accordingly
so	besides	

Spatial Transition

It is important—particularly in description—that readers be able to follow the progress of what you the writer have seen as you moved from place to place in a room, over a building, or across a landscape. To this end you will often state or imply the *physical point of view,* that is *the position from which the subject is being viewed.* In addition, you will also indicate by a series of spatial transitions just when and how you are moving from point to point as you change the focus of your description. You must do this in a manner which is both orderly and clear so that the readers can follow. That is, you may not jump about confusingly from one place to another, but must move in an orderly way—for example, from left to right, near to far, or top to bottom. You must also indicate just when and how you change position.

**Stationary Point of
View**

Perhaps the simplest technique to use in description is the stationary point of view, in which you do not move as you cover your subject, but select a spot from which you can best view the subject for a particular purpose and clearly indicate to your readers by direct statement or by implication that you will view the object from that particular place.

Next, you may indicate the range from which you view your subject. *Range is the approximate distance between the writer and the subject.* Like a still photographer, you describe a distant view of the subject, a close-up view, or a view somewhere in between, depending upon what your writer-reader relationship requires.

When using the stationary viewpoint, the writer establishes the range and doesn't change it while discussing the same subject. As the name of this viewpoint implies, you remain stationary, in one spot, and you indicate this either by clearly saying it or by clearly implying it.

You must also decide upon the angle from which you will view your subject to make your discussion of it clear. *Angle is the point of direction from which an item is viewed.*

Whatever range or angle you select for your stationary spatial viewpoint, you must not write about something which you cannot see from the viewpoint established. Your view may be limited by hills, walls, trees, distance, or angle, and your range may not enable you to see something; therefore, it would only confuse the readers to discuss details beyond your view.

Note that in the following passage the writer maintains the range, angle, and sequence of his view by means of the italicized transitions.

Range and Angle

Last fall I sat for several hours in a duck blind on the edge of a large Missouri inland lake. *Twenty yards to my right* was a drinking hole to which a variety of animals came to drink as I sat there with my gun loaded, waiting for the ducks. *First* came a doe and a buck which stood sentinel duty while the doe took a long drink. *Then* a fawn ran from behind some brush alongside the doe and licked the water. *After* the deer family moved back into the woods, a spotted skunk came to the same water hole. *Later,* two wild pigs, peccaries, also came and put their snouts into the cold water. *As I sat* there in the blind, I became so fascinated by the procession of animals moving to the water hole that I failed to watch for the flocks of ducks that fly overhead or settle on the nearby water. I didn't fire at the ducks because I knew that the sound of my rifle would frighten the other animals waiting in the woods to take their turn at the water hole. I knew that I was enjoying watching the animals drink more than I would enjoy the roast duck later.

J. Fatool

Panning

When your subject is too large or too broad to be handled adequately from one angle, you often must alter your angle of vision without moving from the spot from which you started. You do this by what we call panning, a term adopted from the movies and television. Camera operators pan by setting their cameras in one spot and by moving the lenses of their cameras about in an orderly manner, focusing first on one thing and then on another, so that they are able to get the whole picture. You can do somewhat the same type of thing when your subject is large. When you pan a description you maintain a stationary range, but by means of transitional words, phrases, or sentences, you move your angle of vision in an orderly manner. The following passage is an example, labeled according to this key:

1. Spatial viewpoint of author
2. Range
3. Panning (transitional element)
4. Angle (transition)

One hundred yards off shore, I dropped anchor. From where I sat, I could see approximately *three miles of bleached sand* around the rim of the lake. *As my eyes moved from left to right along the beach*, I first saw a small dock that appeared to have been there for five or six years. Along its right side, it was half submerged. *Directly opposite me*, the beach was empty, but *to my right*, there was a sandbar with three long-legged birds standing motionlessly upon it. *Farther to my right and as far as I could see*, birch and hemlock trees came down close to the white sand of the beach. From these trees, I concluded that there must be a river that ran back into the interior of the island.

Fred Grise

Roving Point of View

In the roving (or mobile) spatial viewpoint the writer varies both range and angle. Thus it is different from panning, in which only the angle is altered. This roving viewpoint is more difficult to use in writing because you must clearly indicate your movements from one spot to another at the same time that you are making your observations. When using the stationary viewpoint, you merely indicate the single point from which you are look-ing at the subject. When necessary you also indicate your range and angle of view. Since the roving viewpoint gives an effect more like that of a motion picture camera than a still camera, you must, when necessary, indicate all of these: the initial point at which you start your observations, the angle, and the range as each changes when you move from point to point. It must be stressed that it is not necessary for you to state these things explicitly each time a change in observation is made. *Often one, two, or even all of these are clearly implied by the context.*

It is essential that you move about in space in an orderly manner. For the readers to understand what is being said, it may be necessary to mentally take them by the hand and lead them carefully from one spot to another. Consequently, transition plays a vital role in writing description with a roving viewpoint.

Here is an example of the roving spatial viewpoint developed in an orderly way by the use of transitional expressions.

While considering the purchase of a farm in Arkansas, I thought it wise to ride about it to examine the buildings, the fences, and the amount of cleared land which it contained. I started *at the south end*, where the house stands against the side of a large hill. *Southwest of the house* was a small corral which was used for singling out specific horses whenever that was necessary. *To the north of the corral*, along the west line of the farm, stood a large barn with two floors. This was the horse barn and the equipment storage shed. *On the second floor*, the hay, grain, and other feed was stored. The pasture ran across *the north end of the farm. Along its east side* was a stand of woods which contained riding trails. These trials rose *from low marsh land in the northeastern edge of the farm to the wooded hills* surrounding the house *on the southern side of the farm.*

Gary Bartosik

Chronological Transition

Just as description depends heavily on spatial transitions, narrative uses many words and phrases expressing chronological transition—time and changes in time. Common time words are *now, then, next, yesterday, today, tomorrow, first, second, last,* and an endless variety of phrases from such stock examples as *in the first place* and *once upon a time* to those made up for the occasion, such as "When Queen Elizabeth stepped onto the balcony" and "After the flash, I recall nothing."

The same principles apply to the use of time transitions as to transitions in space. The important thing is to keep the chain of events clear, to denote the passage of time, and especially in a narrative of process, to make it plain which step comes first, which next, and why. Notice how the writer uses time transitions in this paragraph:

LUCKY TO BE ALIVE
As far back as I can remember, I have often come close to serious injury or death. *When I was six years old*, I narrowly escaped death for the first time. I was then ill with some minor respiratory ailment

for which the simplest cure was sulfa. The doctor, having no knowledge that I was allergic to the drug, prescribed sulfa tablets. *Shortly after* giving me a pill, my mother returned from work to find me gasping for breath. She called the doctor who hurried back to my home. He saved my life by administering oxygen. *Not long after that incident*, I swallowed a chicken bone which became lodged in my throat. I was rushed to the hospital emergency ward in time to save my life. *When I was eleven*, I was bitten by a dog. *As I look back*, I recall that the wound was not as painful as the series of shots which followed. Now, having all these narrow escapes behind me, I consider myself fortunate to be alive today.

Steve Belman

In the following process narrative, the writer makes careful use of time words and expressions not only to show that the steps in the procedure must be taken in a specific order, but to group them in related clusters.

In starting an outboard motor, certain steps must be taken. *First*, lower the motor from its horizontal position into the water. To make this possible, pull the pin at the left of the motor frame, and holding the motor casing at the rear with the right hand, lower it gently. *When* the motor is upright, you are ready for the *second series* of steps, connecting the gas line. *First* be sure the cap of the tank is screwed on tight. *Then* attach the bulb end to the valve on the tank, pinching the clip and pushing hard to make a tight seal. *Third*, attach the other end of the line to the similar valve on the motor, *again* being sure the connection is tight. *Finally*, squeeze the bulb several times until it is firm. This indicates adequate air pressure to force gas from tank to motor. *You are now ready* to start the motor.

This process narrative carefully marks each step with a time transition and also groups the steps into subprocesses within the larger one. All these transitions make it easier for the reader to understand and remember what is supposed to be done and exactly when.

Logical Transition

One of the most demanding kinds of logical relationship that a writer must handle is the relationship of cause and effect. There are many transitional words and phrases to express these relationships. The following paragraph illustrates some of them.

There can be little question that one of the turning points in the twentieth century was the great stock market crash of 1929. The crash was *brought on by many reasons*, including the fact that many people had bought stocks "on margin," that is, by paying only a fraction of the real cost in the hope the stocks would go up and they would make a profit, *whereas* many of them went down and they couldn't cover their losses. *Why* did the stocks go down? *One reason* was simple panic: people got scared, and began to sell. *Because* many sold, prices went down. *This caused* others to sell, and *as a result* prices went down still further. In a few months paper profits melted away like ice in July, fortunes were lost, and purchasing power dropped sharply. *Because* people stopped buying, business generally collapsed, *causing* more failures and fewer markets, *so that* factories slowed down or closed down, more jobs were lost, and the great depression was under way.

Here is a paragraph which illustrates a variety of logical relationships and the transitional expressions which may be used to express them.

The North Atlantic Treaty Organization (NATO) has become ineffective. Its usefulness to our allies in Europe has disappeared because the Soviet Union has equalled or surpassed the United States in nuclear strength. European nations are now strong enough to protect themselves against each other and, collectively, against Russia; *consequently*, they no longer need nor want American troops stationed in their lands. In joining NATO, the United States did not commit itself to becoming a permanent defender of its European allies. Nor was it committed to facing Russia "eyeball-to-eyeball" forever. *As a result* Europeans no longer accept the argument that Soviet invasion of Europe is imminent, and *therefore*, American troops must remain in Europe to deter such as invasion. *As a matter of fact* they are now less concerned with the political problems of the cold war than they are with the problems caused by troops committed to NATO. *Consequently*, the chronic irritations within NATO dramatizes its obsolescence as a protector of the weak and as a keeper of the peace in Europe.

Harry Patterson

ORDERLY ARRANGEMENT

Transitional expressions by themselves won't do everything. Unless the elements in a piece of writing follow a clear and logical order to begin with, all the transitions in the world won't make them really clear and lucid. You should determine the best spatial, chronological, or logical order before you write. If a discussion skips around in time and space, confuses causes and effects, mixes the members of one classification with those of another, or uses an example without telling what it shows, you are finished before you start.

The following illustration shows the importance of orderly arrangement to achieve coherence. The first list consists of a group of details arranged in a haphazard spatial order. The second list contains the same details arranged in a more appropriate spatial order, in which a viewer would naturally see them in space. Following is the controlling sentence which these details are intended to develop. *Here is the way we made our store attractive for Christmas.*

1. Colorful goods in show window.
2. Most attractive Christmas goods placed on the counter nearest entrance.
3. Imitation snow sprinkled on floor of the show window.
4. Santa Claus standing just outside the main entrance.
5. Red and green lights flood show window.
6. Christmas greens decorate the store interior.
7. Instrumental trio playing Christmas carols from balcony at rear of the store.
8. Ceiling festooned with bands of red and green crepe paper.

4. Santa Claus standing just outside the main entrance.
1. Colorful goods in show window.
5. Red and green lights flood show window.
3. Imitation snow sprinkled on floor of the show window.
2. Most attractive Christmas goods placed on the counter nearest entrance.
6. Christmas greens decorate the store interior.
8. Ceiling festooned with bands of red and green crepe paper.
7. Instrumental trio playing Christmas carols from balcony at rear of the store.

Common Errors in Orderly Development

To maintain order, you must clearly indicate any important changes to your readers. For example, if you start by indicating that you intend to view the subject from one point in space and later move to another without making that change clear, the readers will be confused.

In the following paragraph, the writer describes some things impossible to see from the spatial point of view first established, and the writer does not clearly indicate change in position to be able to view what is described.

Standing on my front porch across the street I enviously could see only the rear of my neighbor's new car as it stood parked in his driveway. The evening sun added to the shine of its pastel yellow finish. The rear of the car was short and stubby, a fastback. The front was long and low, like that of a streamlined sports car. When my neighbor came out of the house, I told her how much I admired her car.

This description can be improved if the writer clearly indicates the change in angle and range of vision by transitional words:

Standing on my front porch, I enviously could see only the rear of my neighbor's new car as it stood parked in her driveway across the street. The evening sun added to the shine of its pastel yellow finish. The rear of the car was short and stubby, a fastback. Later, I walked across the street and looked at the front of the car. The front was long and low, like that of a streamlined sports car. When my neighbor came out of the house, I told her how much I admired her car.

**Placement of
Transitional Elements**

It is also possible to go wrong by overdoing a good thing. While it is important to maintain order through transitions, one of the easiest ways to lose a reader is through boredom and monotony. Putting transitions in the same position in every sentence in a paragraph, such as the beginning, can make writing seem mechanical and wooden. The following passage has this defect although the order of the sentences is good.

My brother's bedroom is a reflection of his adolescence. It consistently reminds me of a second-hand store down on Weird Street. I just can't manage to stand erect when I look into his room. *Leaning wearily against the doorjamb,* I am inevitably struck by a huge picture of Elton John plastered on the wall opposite the entrance. All the other walls of the room are splattered with bright yellow tubular decals against a background of brown, the real color of the walls. *Just to the right of Elton John,* a charcoal drawing of my brother Sam himself startles me accusingly. His facial expression shouts out "I'm frustrated, inhibited, and no one understands me." *On the other side of Elton John* is a window with brown drapes and a radio protruding precariously from its sill. *To the left of this window* is a mirror, with love beads and chains suspended desperately on its corners. *Above this mirror,* a sign reads "Make Love, Not War." *On the same wall,* a variety of traffic signs are saying such things as "Sock it to me zone," "One way—My way," and "Stop! Here come the Judge!" *Placed against the middle of the wall directly opposite the one splattered with signs,* the dresser is covered with bottles, including wine bottles of all shapes and sizes. *Next to the dresser,* a desk has books and papers intentionally stacked haphazardly upon it, contributing to the chaos. *Next to the desk* is the unmade bed with papers and magazine clippings entangled in the sheets. *To the right of the doorjamb against which I'm now slouching,* a small table on which rests a little incense burner and some matches reminds me that Sam is just being himself.

Notice how the effect is improved by varying the placement of the transitional elements, some at the beginning, some in the middle, and some at the ends of the sentences.

My brother's bedroom is a reflection of his adolescence. It consistently reminds me of a second-hand store down on Weird Street. I just can't manage to stand erect when I look into his room. *Leaning wearily against the doorjamb,* I am inevitably struck by a huge picture of Elton John plastered on the wall opposite the entrance. All the other walls of the room are splattered with bright yellow tubular decals against a background of brown, the real color of the walls. A charcoal drawing of my brother Sam himself, *just to the right of Elton John,* startles me accusingly. His facial expression shouts out "I'm frustrated, inhibited, and no one understands me." A window *on the other side of Elton John* has brown drapes and a radio protruding precariously from its sill. *To the left of this window* is a mirror, with love beads and chains suspended desperately on its corners. A sign *above this mirror* reads "Make Love, Not War." A variety of traffic signs *are on this same wall,* saying such things as "Sock it to me zone," "One way — My way," and "Stop! Here come the Judge!" The dresser, *placed against the middle of the wall directly opposite the one splattered with signs,* is covered with bottles, including wine bottles of all shapes and sizes. A desk, *next to the dresser,* has books and papers intentionally stacked haphazardly upon it, contributing to the chaos. The unmade bed, with papers and magazine clippings entangled in the sheets, is *next to the dresser. To the right of the doorjamb,* against which I'm now slouching, a small table on which rests a little incense burner and some matches reminds me that Sam is just being himself.

Unnecessary Shifting of Tenses (See pages 396–397)

Another common error which detracts from the sense of orderly development is needless shifting in the tenses of verbs. To go from present to past and back again when there is no actual shift in the times of the actions being discussed is distracting. Readers can't help trying to find a reason for the changes when actually there is none. They are thus distracted from the ideas the writer is trying to communicate. Consider the following:

The doll collection that *stood* on the corner shelves *is* representative of many countries. We *have followed* a custom of bringing our children a doll from each country *we had visited.* The room is *filled* with evidences of children's interests: a mirror *stood* on the dresser, a hair brush and comb *lie* on the night stand beside a copy of *Winnie the Pooh.* This *was* a room where children *reign.*

The tenses in this paragraph shift all over the place: from past to present, and past perfect to present perfect. This could be greatly simplified if the writer realized that only two time frames are being dealt with, that of the time at which the paragraph is being written, and that of the earlier time at which the dolls were purchased. For the purposes of this paragraph, both have the same quality—they precede the time of writing. Two tenses are needed, one of which must precede the other. The one that governs can be either present or past. Thus the controlling sentence could read, "The doll collection that *stood* on the corner shelves *was* . . . or "The doll collection that *stands* on the corner shelves *is* . . . If the former, with controlling verbs in the past tense, the perfect verbs will be past perfect, that is, *had followed, had visited.* If the latter, the paragraph will read like this:

The doll collection that *stands* on the corner shelves *is* representative of many countries. *We have followed* a custom of bringing our children a doll from each country we *have visited.* The room is *filled* with evidences of children's interests: a mirror *stands* on the dresser, a hair brush and comb *lie* on the night stand beside a copy of *Winnie the Pooh.* This *is* a room where children *reign.*

*Unnecessary Shifting
of Pronouns
(See page 395)*

Another distracting inconsistency is unnecessary shifting of pronouns in person: *I,* then for no reason a shift to the second person, *you,* and then to the third, *he* or *she*—and then from singular *he* or *she* to plural *they.* The switches in the following paragraph take the readers' minds off the message and make him wonder far too much about what the pronouns are likely to do next.

According to what we read and hear today, a major problem in the United States is the problem of dieting. *I* have observed many of my friends and relatives become dieters—and as much as *they* strive *they* never succeed. A person just cannot diet successfully unless *he* recognizes that will power is *your* most important tool. The dieter succumbs to each new diet but *he* never develops the will power to eat sensibly the rest of *their* lives.

Here is a more consistent version of the paragraph which does not shift unnecessarily from one person or number to another, and which lets the reader focus on what is being said.

According to what *we* read and hear today, a major problem in the United States is the problem of dieting. *I* have observed many of my friends and relatives become dieters—and as much as *they* strive, *they* never succeed. *They* just cannot diet successfully without recognizing will power as *their* most important tool. Dieters succumb to each new diet, but *they* never develop the will power to eat sensibly for the rest of *their* lives.

You must be continuously on guard to detect disorder. You should try to establish and maintain coherence and consecutiveness when you write your first draft. Yet much of orderliness or coherence is established in revision. In revising, you must train yourself to sit as a stranger who has never seen that composition before and to read it critically and objectively. As a stranger you must ask, "Are the parts clearly connected to each other? Do the thoughts move through time and space in an orderly manner? Are the logical connections clear? Can the reader easily comprehend the relationships?" If you can correctly answer yes to these questions, you have succeeded in establishing and maintaining order.

PRACTICE in Achieving
This Chapter's Objectives

Practice in identifying and writing connecting elements, transitional devices, orderly arrangement; and in detecting common errors in coherence in order to achieve orderly development in written communication.

	Applications
1. Identifying linking and transitional elements.	1, 2, 3
2. Detecting and avoiding common errors in orderly development.	4, 5, 6, 7 8
3. Writing a composition with orderly arrangement and development.	9
4. You Be the Judge	

APPLICATION 14-1

The following paragraph uses synonyms as linking elements. Underline the synonyms which serve to link the ideas.

War subjects humanity to endless trouble. Destruction of cities and countryside brings distress to people and animals alike. The sufferings of victims in a state of continued attack or temporary occupation test an endurance almost inconceivable in peace time. Sickness resulting from contamination of water supplies, and poverty brought about by a strategy calling for total war create a misery for which reparations never fully compensate. And the agony of mind and body suffered by men and women in the front lines is at times beyond the power of the human spirit to endure.

APPLICATION 14-2

The following paragraph uses derivative words as transitional elements. Underline the derivative words so used.

The house was well built. To add extra strength to the foundation, the contractor had reinforced the concrete with steel mesh. The whole structure had been strengthened by means of steel beams laid at points of greatest stress. Strong wood joists were used throughout; in fact, the contractor ordered whatever strengthener could be used to advantage.

APPLICATION 14-3

Underline the pronouns and the pronominal adjectives which link the ideas in the following paragraph.

The senator rose to deliver her speech. Most of the spectators paid little heed to her; a few fixed their eyes intently upon her. She stood tall and erect, inflexible against the hostile neglect. Staunchly she faced the opposition, who had defied her crusade; patiently she waited their attention.

APPLICATION 14-4

Although the following paragraph is orderly and coherent, it is monotonous because the transitional elements all come at the beginnings of the sentences. In the space below, rewrite the paragraph, varying the placing of these transitions.

Upon entering my apartment, I stand in the living room. To the left of me is the skeleton of an early American couch which has been handed down through the family. At one end of the couch is a portable stereo on top of a console television set. At the other end of the couch is our fabulous library consisting of a set of encyclopedias. Along the wall opposite the couch is the antique sewing machine, which we use as a table. Against the far wall is a large reclining chair which was recently reupholstered. Above it hangs an oil painting done on black velvet. To the left of the couch, the hallway leads back to the bedrooms. To the right of the dining room is a corridor leading to the kitchen. This apartment represents the beginning of our dream, a home, a family, and a future.

_____

_____

_____

_____

_____

_____

_____

_____

_____

_____

_____

APPLICATION 14-5

The following sentences lack coherence because of unnecessary shifting in person (first, second, and third). Rewrite them correctly.

1. One can improve our study habits if they try.

   _____

2. A driver should be alert if you want to avoid accidents.

   _____

3. Anyone has to study if they are hoping for high grades.

   _____

4. A basketball player should be in shape before they play games.

   _____

5. A person must try if you wish to succeed.

   _____

APPLICATION 14-6

The following contain unnecessary changes in the tenses of the verbs. Rewrite each correctly.

1. We take the dog to the hospital and the veterinarian will examine it.

   _____

2. You will win if you would try harder.

   _____

3. The bricklayer started the job, but he sees it will take awhile.

   _____

4. She will earn much money if she tried.

   _____

5. The dog will see the cat, but he didn't chase it.

   _____

APPLICATION 14-7

The following is weak in order because of unnecessary shifting in person of nouns and pronouns. Rewrite the passage below; be sure to avoid unnecessary shifts.

Health and Too Many Calories

You may not be healthy if you are overweight. An obese person is seldom healthy. If a someone is thirty pounds overweight for his size and age his body is burdened as if he were constantly carrying a thirty pound bundle or package. Consequently, his heart is overtaxed. His breathing becomes a difficult chore. They slow down on exercise and other activity because he tires so easily. We become lazy as a result of this inactivity and continue to add weight.

Most overweight problems are caused by a person's eating habits; they eat too much and exercise too little. He must cut down on the calorie intake and must eat a nutritionally balanced diet to lose weight.

_____

_____

_____

_____

_____

_____

_____

_____

_____

_____

_____

_____

_____

_____

_____

_____

_____

_____

APPLICATION 14-8

Find the controlling sentence in the following and underline the main idea with one line and the key with two. Rearrange the sentences so that they are in proper space order. Below, write an orderly composition using these sentences to develop the controlling sentence.

1. Twenty heavy oak tables have comfortable chairs for readers.

2. Encyclopedias and other reference books are located at right of the main entrance.

3. Our college library is designed and furnished for serious study or pleasant reading.

4. Specially reserved books in revolving bookcases are at the left of the head librarian's desk.

5. Atlases are on a special desk in a quiet corner at the far end.

6. Well-lighted rooms on the second floor easily accommodate one hundred students at a time.

_____

_____

_____

_____

_____

_____

_____

_____

_____

_____

_____

APPLICATION 14-9

Write a full-length composition of about 600 words with a title; an opener if you wish, which may be separate or incorporated into the main paragraph; a main paragraph, including a subject sentence and several explanatory sentences; at least two supporting paragraphs, one mainly using spatial transitional elements and the other chronological; and a concluding paragraph. State your purpose. Here are some suggested topics:

1. A brief autobiography, which includes a short description of one home in which you have lived
2. An accident you observed and a brief description of the consequences
3. A brief description of a cultural event including a description of the place in which it was held

YOU BE THE JUDGE

Evaluator's Initials ☐☐☐

Date _____

Section _____

Grade _____

Writer's Name _____

Date _____ Section _____

Title of paper _____

Chapter _____ Application No. _____

General Instructions on the You Be the Judge Applications, and specific instructions for Parts I and III, are printed inside the back cover of this book. Read those instructions carefully; then do Part I.

In the lines below, and on another sheet of paper, answer the questions in Part II. Then enter a grade for the paper in the space above left, and write your evaluation for Part III. Reread the composition to see how well the writer understands and applies the principles studied in this chapter. As you read the composition write any helpful suggestions that occur to you in the margins.

PART II

1. Evaluate and comment on the structure of the composition as a whole (title, opener, main paragraph, conclusion). _____

_____

_____

_____

_____

_____

_____

2. Identify and name any types of repetition the writer uses (same word, synonyms, derivatives, and so forth). _____

_____

_____

_____

_____

_____

_____

_____

3. If there is unnecessary repetition, give examples. _____

_____

_____

_____

_____

_____

4. Point out, name, and describe any disorder or discontinuity you find.

_____

_____

_____

_____

_____

_____

5. Comment on the effectiveness of the paragraph using spatial point of view. _____

_____

_____

_____

_____

_____

6. Comment on the effectiveness of the paragraph using chronological point of view. _____

_____

_____

_____

_____

_____

PART III Grade and Evaluation:

_____

_____

CHAPTER 15

LANGUAGE AND TONE

After studying this chapter and completing the applications that follow it, you should be able to do the following:

1. To identify and differentiate the three tones of written communication: *formal, semiformal,* and *informal.*
2. To select the tone appropriate to the predetermined elements and to develop it consistently.
3. To identify and use *diction* appropriate to the tone intended and to avoid deliberately that which is inappropriate: *illiteracies; clichés* and *platitudes; colloquialisms* and *slang; denotation* and *connotation; general* and *specific.*
4. To identify and use figurative language effectively: *simile, metaphor, personification.*
5. To identify and use concrete and abstract details effectively.
6. To apply these principles in consistently developing the tone of a full-length composition.

A WRITER clothes thought in language, and language like clothing should suit the purpose and occasion. To use language well a writer must know certain things about words, expressions, and various grammatical structures that are commonly described as correct or incorrect; we shall come to these later in this chapter. More important and generally more useful, the writer should know when certain *kinds* of words, expressions, and grammatical structures are appropriate and suitable to a specific purpose.

TONE A good place to begin the study of this fairly complex subject is with the idea of tone, for tone determines the kind of language a writer will use in any given piece of writing. *Tone has been defined as the manner in which a writer regards the reader as this manner is reflected in the language used.* To take a simple example, one may say, "Let all parents bring their kids up the American way." One may also express the same thought this way: "Let all parents rear their children with the democratic freedom bestowed upon them by our forefathers, the founders of our country." In the two sentences the basic message is the same, but the tone of each is very different. In the first, it is informal, personal, and close. In the second it is more formal, less personal, and more distant. The first is easy and everyday. The second suggests a lecture platform. "Bring up" and "kids" are informal; "rear" and "children," formal. The allusions to "democratic freedom," "our forefathers," and "the founders of our country" ring familiar emotional bells which suggest formality and solemnity.

In learning to choose and use the right tone for the subject, reader, and purpose, you must think very carefully about the predetermined elements of your composition, your specific subject, your dominant general purpose, and the writer-reader relationship you wish to establish.

Your topic may suggest the appropriate tone. For example, a funeral, a circus, a tennis match, and a diplomat by their nature suggest specific tones. You would probably treat a funeral with solemnity, a circus in a gay, light-hearted way, a statesman with interest and excitement, and a tennis match with reverence and respect. It is also possible to think of exceptions to each of these obvious treatments—exceptions which would require different tones.

Tone may also vary with purpose—the desire to entertain, convey an impression, inform, persuade, or actuate. We use impersonal words to inform, emotional ones to persuade, forceful ones to actuate. Finally, in selecting tone, it is necessary to carefully take your reader into account. We automatically speak one way to our parents, another to our teachers, a third to our brothers and sisters, a fourth to our peers. In selecting the right tone for any piece of writing, the subject, the purpose, and the reader should all be given careful thought.

Ranges of Tone

Broadly speaking, there are three ranges of tone in writing, *formal, semi-formal,* and *informal;* the following three paragraphs illustrate. In the first passage, the formal one, the writer uses the technical language of the subject, does not inject his own personality, and has no interest in jeopardizing the precision of his statement even to make it more interesting or easier to grasp. The assumption is that the reader is capable of understanding and no concessions are made. Most writing is not so severely formal.

With the execution of a lease, the lessor is not obligated to maintain the leased premises. Nor is there any implied covenant constraining repair or restitution of property damaged by fire or other causes. The lessee must accept the premises *in statu quo* and cannot compel the lessor to make repairs without the consent of the latter. Avowal made by the lessor to rectify a condition after the lease has been executed cannot be enforced. However, in certain states, a promise to repair defective leased property is binding, providing the lessee notifies the lessor that he will vacate such premises unless such repairs are made. Statutes in a few states provide that the lessor shall keep premises intended for human habitation fit for human occupancy; otherwise, the lessee may vacate the premises without incurring liability or payment of future rent after rendering notice of his intent.

Sally Lasch

In the next example, semi-formal in tone, the writer seems as much concerned with interest and reading ability as with accuracy and precision. So she uses words and expressions with which the reader will be more familiar. She also uses a few contractions and some colloquial—that is, conversational—expressions. She avoids technical terms, except those with which this reader can be expected to be familiar. Clearly, this reader is not in the same category as the one above and is shown more personal consideration.

If a renter doesn't have it in writing from the landlord, the landlord isn't legally bound to repair the premises. No implied understanding by the renter can force the landlord to repair damages, regardless of their cause. A renter must accept the property as is. A promise to repair made after the lease is signed will not hold up in court. In some states, laws require that a promise to repair is binding, providing the landlord is notified that the renter intends to move out unless the repairs are made. Other states legally require landlords to keep all buildings used for human residence fit for human occupation. If they don't, renters may move out without paying future rent, providing they notify the landlord of their intentions.

Sally Lasch

In the following paragraph, distinctly informal in tone, the writer goes all out to interest and help the reader. Accuracy of expression is still important, but not quite so much as expression in simple everyday language with which this third type of reader will feel at home. The ideas are expressed in very colloquial and idiomatic language, full of familiar expressions, contractions, and even slang. The language is also far less specific and precise legally than that in either of the versions above.

If you don't have it down on paper in black and white, the owner doesn't have to fix the building you're renting. Nor can you take it for granted that anything damaged by fire or by anything else will be fixed up. You have to take the property as is. What a landlord says will be done and what is later done are two different things. You can't have anything repaired without an OK. After you have put your John Hancock on the dotted line, even if the owner takes a solemn oath that, something will be mended, you can't make it happen. In some states, however, if something is wrong with the property and the landlord promises to take care of it, that promise has to be kept, providing you give warning in advance that you'll move out if it isn't. In a few states, the laws say that the owner of a building in which people are to live has to keep it fit for habitation. Otherwise, the renter can take off legally without paying any more rent.

Sally Lasch

If, as we said, tone is the way you clothe your ideas in order to carry out your purpose, you tend to use different vocabulary levels for formal, semiformal, and informal writing. Many of the formal words are of Latin or Greek origin; they are often long and tend to be abstract. They are seldom part of the everyday vocabulary. At the other end of the range, the informal elements in the vocabulary tend to be short words, familiar in everyday speech, part of the vocabulary which everybody possesses. Formal language is learned; informal language is common and does not require special learning. The language of semiformal writing is in between. There are of course endless gradations between the extremes, besides the clear-cut categories that are always easy to recognize. To help make the distinctions clear, the following table is worth study.

The Three Ranges of Formality

Formal	Semiformal	Informal
equivocation	hedging	pussyfooting
rectify	correct	set straight
frankfurter	wiener	hot dog
perfunctory	indifferent	devil-may-care
intermittent	periodic	on-and-off
abdomen	stomach	tummy
magnanimity	generosity	big-heartedness
promulgate	circulate	pass around
humiliate	embarrass	put to shame
subdue	conquer	lead by the nose
cessation	intermission	break, breather
discern	understand	see through
extirpate	exterminate	blot out
concur	agree	see eye-to-eye
deduce	think	figure out
spouse	wife or husband	better-half
specter	ghost	spook
cease	stop	bring to an end
modicum	small amount	a dab, a smidgen
authentic	real	matter of fact

Choosing An Appropriate Tone

Before an appropriate tone can be selected, you must know the intellectual and educational level of the readers or types of readers to whom you are directing your remarks. Much of the content as well as tone of any piece of writing is determined by the writer's assessment of the readers' interest and ability to try to understand. A large part of a readers' willingness to make the effort of understanding, as well as their ability, depends on how much education they have had and what kind, especially in the area of the writer's subject and material. If, for example, you are addressing a group of doctors, the nervous and endocrine systems can be discussed in technical language without fear or hesitation. It would also not be necessary to expand every complex and technical idea by definition, illustration, comparison or contrast, and so on. You would not feel compelled to lighten the mixture by colloquial words or expressions or to simplify in any way. So you might write a paragraph like this:

The two chief regulatory mechanisms for functional integration of the organs and the organ systems within the human body are the endocrine system and the nervous system. The nervous system receives internal and external stimuli and instigates the appropriate responses in the body structures. The hormones exercise a more general type of control such as growth, digestive activities, and sexual preparedness.[1]

In the following treatment of the same ideas, the writer uses fewer technical terms. Those used are defined or expanded by analogy ("telegraphic apparatus," "a chemical broadcasting system"), shorter sentences, less formal diction ("message" and "orders"), all of which help to give the writing a lighter texture. By these devices, the material is written so that it is within a different reader's range of comprehension.

The human body has two chief control systems. These systems enable the various organs or organ systems to work harmoniously together. Broadly speaking, the nervous system functions after the fashion of a telegraphic apparatus; it receives "messages" from the inside or outside of the body and then sends "orders" to the various organs, causing them to respond by making appropriate adjustments. The endocrine system produces certain hormones, chemicals which enter the bloodstream. These hormones exercise a more general type of body growth, development, digestion and sexual preparedness. The endocrine system is in effect "a chemical broadcasting system."

Maintaining A Consistent Tone

The tone of a piece of writing must remain consistent throughout. The following passage illustrates what can happen when you forget to adapt what you are saying to the limitations of your particular readers. The first two paragraphs are obviously directed to an audience with little technical knowledge or vocabulary. But the writer gets so involved in the subject that in the last three paragraphs the readers' limitations are forgotten. The writer becomes more technical in both language and the details included—so complex that the interest of the reader may be lost entirely.

Do you know what the source of energy that drives a steam engine is? Before diesel engines, all locomotives were powered by the conversion of water to mechanical energy. Certainly, you know that boiled water in a teakettle turns to steam and causes the whistle in the cap to blow. That steam that blows the whistle on the teakettle is the same steam that drives the locomotive. In a locomotive, a large fire pit is located beneath a huge closed tank of water. The closed or sealed water tank is called a boiler. The boiler has an opening at the top, just as the tea-

[1] *Encyclopedia Americana,* © 1953, Vol. 10, p. 320.

kettle does. The purpose of the openings is for pressure relief. Without these openings, both the locomotive and teakettle would blow up when the steam pressure reached a certain point.

Now that we know the purpose of the steam engine boiler, let's see how the steam power is harnessed to drive the locomotive. The opening on a steam engine is controlled by a valve which allows the steam to escape or, if the engineer wants power for locomotion, he diverts it to pipes which direct the steam pressure to a chamber and piston located near the wheels.

The piston at one end of the cylinder reciprocates, changing the inside area of the chamber. As the steam is directed into the chamber through one of the ports, the pressure builds up and forces the piston to the far end of the cylinder. When it reaches the other end, it crosses another port, causing the steam pressure to decrease and allowing the piston to retract.

In double-acting engines, the power is communicated to a revolving shaft, driven by a crank and connecting rod with or without the intervention of a beam. In stationary engines, the shaft carries a fly-wheel to equalize irregularities in the action of the power by its inertia.

As a summary of our discussion of tone, the following table lists a number of devices and methods commonly used at the various levels of formality.

Methods and Devices Used to Create and Control Tone

Diction (word usage)	Formal Tone	Semiformal Tone	Informal Tone
Connotation	Some	Many	Very many
*Abbreviation(art.-article) Contraction(I'd-I would) Shortened forms(phone-telephone)	Few, if any	Some	Many
Pun or "Play on words"	Few, if any	Some	Many
Colloquialism(conversational word)	Few, if any	Some	Many
Substandard word	None	Few	Many
Cliché, Platitude	Few, if any	Some	Few
Formal English words (usually derived from Latin or French)	Many	Some	Few, if any
Technical term without added definition	Many	Few, if any	None
Technical term with added definition	Some	Many	Few, if any
Non-English words(*Habeas Corpus, et al., ad hoc*)	Some	Few, if any	None

* It must be pointed out, however, that in scientific and other forms of technical writing, standard abbreviations are often used in formal as well as in informal writing, for example, P & L for profit and loss statement, or AOAO, the Advanced Orbiting Astronomical Observatory (as used in the pamphlet "Astronomy in Space" by NASA, the National Aeronautics and Space Administration).

DICTION: THE INSTRUMENT OF TONE

Since you produce tone through words, *diction* or use of language is the key to success. It is important that you know as much as possible about words—their exact meanings, their overtones, and how to put them together.

Right Meanings

The first and most important thing to know about words is their meanings: how they are used and what people understand them to mean. Most of us grow up with wrong ideas about the meanings of certain words; we learn many words by guessing their meanings in context, and sometimes we guess wrong. More common is the misuse of a word. This is known as *malapropism,* named after a character in a play who kept saying things like "an *allegory* (for alligator) on the banks of the Nile," or a *"crude* awakening" for a "rude awakening." It is very common to remember a word just a little wrong:

the course was *stiltifying* (for stultifying)
he dropped out of his own *violation* (volition)
couldn't *mustard* the energy (muster)
candlelight is so *rheumatic* (romantic)
acted like a *bustard* (bastard)
a *bladder*-mouth (blabber-mouth)
a war *mongrel* (monger)
sending the package by *partial* (parcel) post

Whenever you have the least doubt about the meaning of a word, consult a good dictionary. Your English instructor has probably urged you to buy a dictionary and recommended one or several to you. You should have one, keep it all through college, and use it often. It is a mine of information on many subjects, and one of the most interesting books you can own. A thesaurus is also very helpful.

Illiteracies

Quite different from the occasional misuse of a word through misunderstanding its meaning or not remembering it quite right, is a level of language known as *illiteracy.* Illiterates are people who never properly learned to read or write and who have been brought up among others of the same kind. They habitually use nonstandard forms of verbs and other words, and they often use nonstandard word formations. Here are a few obvious examples:

You should of seed all the stuff he'd got.
They might of knowed the baby would be light complected.
My parents can't work like they used to could.
I disremember just whereabouts I seen it.

Few college students are unconsciously guilty of more than an occasional illiteracy, if that. But the skillful *intentional* use of illiteracies in writing can sometimes be very effective when the aim is to recreate the tone and effect of rustic or backcountry speech.

**Clichés and
Platitudes**

Good writing seems fresh and original, not tired, stale, and shopworn. You should therefore avoid *clichés* or *trite expressions,* phrases which have been used and used until their original force and vividness has been entirely lost. Many clichés are metaphors, similes, personifications (see the discussion of imagery); others are simply common expressions once expressive but long since overused. Here are some representative specimens:

tired but happy
last but not least
against my better judgment
in the last analysis
I could have died
hard as a rock
strong as an ox
ran like a flash
bright as a new dime
the staff of life
as sober as a judge
as gentle as a lamb
"something is rotten in the state of Denmark"
money talks
the last straw

Usually it takes only a little thought to find a fresher way of saying these ideas. Sometimes it is easier to find a new phrase than to recognize that a familiar phrase is as worn out as it is.

Closely related to clichés are *platitudes;* these are whole statements that express old truths or observations on such subjects as life, fate, death, love, the weather, and human nature. Here are a few typical ones:

It is not that you won or lost, but how you played the game.
Opportunity knocks but once.
Look before you leap.
A bird in the hand is worth two in the bush.
A penny saved is a penny earned.
Experience is the best teacher.
An apple a day keeps the doctor away.
He who hesitates is lost.
Crime doesn't pay.
Let the punishment fit the crime.
Majority wins.

Whenever you are tempted to use such statements as these, think twice and ask yourself whether this is really what you mean to say or whether it is just something to fill space—taking the place of an original thought. Again it is usually possible to do a good deal better with a little effort.

**Informal Diction:
Colloquialisms
and Slang**

Since there are three main ranges of tone in writing, it follows that informal expressions such as slang and colloquial or conversational terms can be appropriate in writing with an informal or perhaps semiformal tone, but not in writing with a formal tone. Here are a few examples:

colloquial	*formal*
kibitzer	onlooker
gumption	initiative
pan	criticize
yen	desire
pal	friend

Because few students have any difficulty in deciding between these pairs of words, it should not be hard to make the right choice when questions of tone come up. When you can't decide, consult your dictionary or thesaurus.

**Denotation
and Connotation**

We come now to a most important point. Most words have two kinds of meanings, *denotation and connotation.* Denotation is the explicit, literal, matter-of-fact meaning of a word. The denotation of *cat, dog, man,* and *pig* are the specific animals to which these words literally refer. Connotation, on the other hand, is not literal meaning, but associative meaning. All four of the animals named above have rich and varied connotations or associative meanings in addition to their literal ones. Here are some of them:

cat   mean, malicious, often jealous person; in recent black English, modish and admirable person: "So I says to the cat . . ."

dog   various meanings as in "dirty dog," "gay dog," "sea dog," "that girl was a dog," "dog-tired," "dog-eared."

pig   slovenly, lazy, or gluttonous person; piece of iron as in pig iron; police officer

man   human being; human beings as a class; person; male person of courage, strength, virtue; husband; lover; vassal to a medieval lord; form of address, as in "Hey, man!"

In the creation of tone, words used in their denotative meanings tend to be factual, unemotional, detached, objective, and thus most appropriate in writing to inform. Words used in their connotative senses arouse strong associations in the reader's mind. Connotation is thus important in writing to persuade and also in writing to convey impressions, such as literary description and narration—in any writing where it is important to evoke emotions, memories, sensations. Many words will be mainly denotative in one context, and mainly connotative in another. The word *sea* in a factual and objective discussion will simply represent the unemotional fact of a large body of water. But in a different context it may call up any number of emotional or sense reactions suggesting beauty, romance, homesickness, loneliness, and such sensations as fog or mist

Denotative and Connotative Meanings

Word	Meaning	Sense Association	Emotion Association
schooner	a sailing vessel with two and sometimes three masts	sound of slushing surf, cold wet mist, feeling of swaying deck, sound of creaking mast, touch of wind	excitement, thrill of adventure, romantic feeling
jewel	a precious stone	diamond ring, glittering surfaces, smoothness	opulence, wealth, well-being, love, enchantment, marriage
evening	the end of the day and early part of the night	hushing city sounds, dusk, smears of orange of setting sun	restfulness, reminiscence, calmness, peace
death	the end of life	blackness, stillness, smell of funeral flowers, wet tears, coldness of death	restraint, sorrow, despair, loneliness, nothingness, fear
autumn	the period between summer and winter	warm sun, colorful leaves, smell of ripening fruit, stacked corn stalks, smell of burning leaves	patience, contentment, gaiety
snow	soft, white crystalline flakes	coldness, sheets of stark whiteness, snow-covered evergreens, sound of bells	holiday happiness, excitement of new sights, snugness
lane	a narrow way between hedges, walls, fences	snugness, tightness, kiss, flowery path, strolling	loneliness, seclusion, excitement, security, contentment
shimmer	shine with an unsteady light, glimmer	lake, reflecting sunlight, rippling water, shivering jello, heat waves from a corn field, desert sands, light in a person's eyes, a tear drop	joys of summer, refreshing assurance, pleasure, tranquility, infinity, happiness, deep sorrow
squash	beat or press into a soft flat mass, crush	crunching sound, stepping on a crab with bare feet, stomp, caterpiller crush, sound of crunching, egg shells, stepping on ants	sharp pain, anger, unpleasantness, embarrassment, helplessness

on one's face, the sound of lonely horns or bells, the murmur of surf, the dazzle of sun on water.

It has often been said that using a word for its connotation is like dropping a stone in water—the ripples spread through a reader's memory as on a pond, to the very edges. Ripples close to the center represent feelings and sensations commonly associated with the word. Those farther out are more personal and individual. Thus with the word *fireplace* the inner ripples suggest the usual associations with warmth, comfort, and contentment. Those farther out suggest memories of individual fireplaces, rooms, houses, people and personal experiences. The list on page 304 represents the reactions of students in one composition class.

General and Specific Diction

For almost any desired meaning, you may have several words in your consciousness competing for attention. Which one will you pick? As always, the choice should depend on tone. If you are dealing with broad ideas, principles, rules, truths, large quantities, you may want the more general word. If you are dealing with particular facts, sense impressions, individual things, you will want the more specific word. *General* means *broad. Specific* means *narrow.* On most topics there are many degrees of generality or specificity. For example:

Nouns

General	*More Specific* ——————→			
instrument	musical	drum	tom-tom snare tympani	
	surgical	knife	scalpel scissors	
plant	flower	rose	American Beauty	
textile	cloth	cotton silk wool	seersucker crepe de chine worsted flannel	
sustenance	food	meat	beef pork	roast steak chop cutlet
	drink	water beverage	 tea coffee	 iced instant hot drip percolator
building	residence	house apartment	bungalow cabin condominium	

General	More Specific — — — — — →	
smooth	sleek	glassy
slow	sluggish	lazy
soft	pliable	molten
heavy	fat	obese
sly	cunning	sneaky
nice	pretty	winsome

Adjectives

General	More Specific — — — — — →	
rest	sleep	nap
oppose	rebel	mutiny
insert	inject	inoculate
separate	cut	dissect
consume	eat	gulp

Verbs

General	More Specific — — — — — →	
intentionally	deliberately	obstinately
willfully	voluntarily	conscientiously
unhappily	pathetically	agonizingly
unwisely	hazardously	perilously

Adverbs

For many ideas there is a variety of possible words, and you should choose the one that is general or specific enough to express your meaning. Many times you will want to be as specific as possible. But sometimes you will want a more general word. The purpose should govern the choice.

The two paragraphs below illustrate how writing can be made more vivid by the use of concrete words when they are what is required:

The night was windy and rainy. The old house was of Victorian architecture with shutters that hit the outside wall. Inside the house, the rooms were covered with dust. A stuffed chair was the only piece of furniture in the room, and light was provided by a candle whose flame flickered with the wind. I tiptoed through the room.

The *dark, moonless night* was made worse by the *driving rain* and *howling wind*. The *strange, old house* was of *Victorian architecture* with *loose shutters* that *crashed* against the *drab, peeling paint* of the outside wall. Inside the house, the rooms were *shrouded* with *thick blankets of dust.* A *musty-smelling chair* was the only piece of furniture in the den, *meagerly lighted* by a *small thin candle* whose *flame* flickered when the wind blew. *Floorboards creaked* with age as I gingerly tiptoed around the room. Upstairs the *wind whistled* through the *cracked window* and a *mouse* scurried across the floor.

Debbie Westfall

Figures of Speech

No doubt you have heard people say, "I am at a loss for words," or "I just can't tell you how I felt." These are occasions for figures of speech. *Figures of speech* are words and phrases which compare one thing to another, usually by describing something fairly general or hard to express in terms of something more specific and familiar. In this way they add vividness to writing.

Simile

The simplest figure of speech to use and the easiest to recognize is the *simile* which openly compares one thing to another, usually by use of the words *like, as,* or *so.*

1. *Like a lump of mud,* the *toad* squatted on the ground before us.

2. The mountain *range* was *like a caravan of camels* marching across the far horizon.

3. The *atmosphere* of the house was *like that created by a death* in the family.
4. *Crafty as a wolf, quick as a tiger,* and *deadly as a cobra,* the *shark* is the most bloodthirsty of sea animals.

You can see at once how these similes—the comparisons beginning with *like* or *as*—help to describe their subjects and make them more vivid: the toad *like* a lump of mud, the mountains *like* a line of camels because of their humps, the house that felt *like* death, the shark compared to three animals, each for its special quality.

Metaphor

The simile clearly says A is *like* B. More subtle is the *metaphor,* which makes the same kind of comparison, but omits *like* or *as* and says that A *is* B. Thus metaphor is both more compact and less obvious than a simile.

1. The huge *earthmovers were orange beetles* crawling up and down the hill.
2. For 1,000 miles the jet *plane was a magic carpet.*
3. The *stars were silver pepper* sprinkled on a *velvet sky.*
4. *Adolescence is* the *sunrise of life,* but *dark clouds* sometimes *hide it.*

In these metaphors the machines were beetles, the plane was a carpet, and not just any carpet, but a "magic" carpet. The third and fourth sentences each contain two metaphors: the stars *were* pepper and sky *was* velvet; adolescence *is* sunrise but clouds *hide* it. Metaphor gives vividness to general and abstract ideas like *adolescence.*

Just as you should stay away from clichés and platitudes, you should also stay away from worn-out similes and metaphors, like, "He is as pale as a ghost," and "She is as light as a feather." Saying nothing at all is better than using these.

Personification

When you want your reader to sense the animation or to feel the warmth of life in your subject, you may use *personification:* a comparison between a person or animal and an inanimate object. It is a way by which the writer, so to speak, breathes life into a lifeless thing. Since the readers sense and live life, they feel and are better able to identify with something which has life than with something which does not.

1. Rome seems to flirt and tease and beg everyone to stay another day.
2. Pig-snouted darkness grunted and rooted in the ghettos.
3. The angry sea stalked her prey.
4. "You would like to take me, but you never will," he shouted to the gale.
5. "Come, night, and help me forget."

In the following paragraph notice how the writer made the abstract idea (the inevitability of man's succumbing to the power of nature) more vivid by concrete details and figures of speech.

The beach sand, dented by the heels and toes of swimmers, sloped gently to the water. A kingfisher, poking at a strand of seaweed, hopped back and forth to avoid the foamy edge. At regular intervals the sea took a deep breath. Its bosom swelled and, as if tucking in its multilayered skirt, it let out a tremendous crescendo. The consequent wave that thundered towards the beach savagely swept it clean.

Ann Curran

Imagery and Tone

The two passages which follow, both on the same subject, provide a striking example of how diction, and particularly concrete details and figures of speech, produce the tone of a piece of writing. The first, without many of these devices, is rather formal.

During the earthquake, there were frequent vibrations in the ground which disturbed the air in such a way as to produce sounds within the range of the human ear's receiving band. These were earthquake sounds on the low booming side of the scale. Very near the source of the earthquake, the sound sometimes included sharp snaps which suggested the tearing apart of great blocks of rock. The beginning of the sound was accompanied by the greatest shaking, and the end of the sound coincided with the end of the shaking. The confused impressions which resulted were so mingled that subsequent attempts to classify them were uncertain.[2]

Here the language is relatively impersonal and objective; literal, not figurative. Notice the difference in the following on the same subject, which uses similes, metaphors, personification, concrete detail, and also addresses the reader in the second person. The result is a semiformal rather than a formal tone.

The huge temblor, like a clapper in a bell, set the earth — all six billion trillion tons of rock — ringing. For earthquake waves behave in many respects like sound waves; they echo, bend and "sing" at different pitches. But instead of air it is rock vibrating. And so our planet sang a hundred different "tunes" heard not by human ears but by seismographs.

If you had viewed the whole globe at that time, from space, you would have seen it jiggle like a spoonful of jelly. It took an hour for one shape, or mode, to form; others appeared and disappeared in minutes. In one mode, the world looked like a football, in another it developed girlish dimples. Instruments picked at least eighty different modes of vibrations. Of course, you would have needed super sight to see these changes of shape. For the earth actually moved up and down less than an inch at any regular spot, although the movement spread like a gentle ripple over hundreds.[3]

If clothes make the man and the woman, they make the idea too. For the clothing of an idea is the language in which it is expressed. Skill in the use of language is one of the most important qualities a writer can develop. More than any other quality, language creates personality on paper.

[2] Earl Ubell, "When the Earth Rang like a Bell," *The Reader's Digest,* August, 1965. Condensed from *The New York Herald Tribune.* Reprinted with permission.

[3] Earl Ubell, "When the Earth Rang like a Bell," *The Reader's Digest,* August, 1965. Condensed from *The New York Herald Tribune.* Reprinted with permission.

PRACTICE in Achieving This Chapter's Objectives

Practice in identifying, selecting, and developing consistently the appropriate formal, semiformal, or informal tone.

	Applications
1. Identifying tone by diction.	1, 2, 3, 5
2. Selecting and writing diction appropriate to the intended tone.	4
3. Distinguishing between general and specific words.	6
4. Using concrete details to produce tone.	7
5. Identifying and writing figures of speech.	8, 9, 10
6. Writing a full-length composition for tone.	10
7. You Be the Judge	

APPLICATION 15-1

In the blanks, indicate the tone in which each of the following passages is written. Then underline the words and ideas which create the tone.

_____ 1. I like good discussion as well as the next person. But over the years I have come to recognize that the premise of even the simplest oral exchange can get lost in a tangle of side issues and individual interpretations. On such occasions I am reminded of the time I went to church as a child, and we sang that hymn entitled "Gladly the Cross I'd Bear." While the elders in the congregation were picturing the long road to Calvary, I, like many another child before me, was visualizing a big furry animal with a strange name and an unfortunate ocular problem—Gladly, the cross-eyed bear.

_____ 2. With our great affection for brightly colored, souped-up, racing-slick equipped, four-on-the-floor, competition striped, horses on wheels, our freeways and roads are fast becoming a real drag strip for people going to and from work. Our streets have become a jungle of metal, rubber, glass, and plastic. Driving on them takes nerves of steel and plenty of guts. All in all, the result is tie-ups in traffic, "fender-bending" mishaps and blood-splattering smashups.

Geraldine Nichol

_____ 3. The best lookin' part of ol' Rocky was them hands o' his! They was a reg'lar work of one of them artists. His fingers was long, and thin, but went together perfect. They was real smooth and clean as a hospital's sheets. Looked like they directed the ol' veins and vessels to where they was gonna go. Looked like they was whittled out o' some fancy wood, they did. Didn't have no hair on his hand like you n' me. I always wondered how he kept 'em so pretty, never weared gloves 'til he died and was laid out in the saloon.

G. Benoit

_____ 4. Before moving to our new trilevel home in the suburb of Plano, Texas, my parents worried that they would become social outcasts, that is, they would not be taken in by their new affluent neighbors. Well, they have been taken in: now, they are trying to figure a way to be taken out. At first they were flattered to be invited for cocktails every evening. But after these solicitous neighbors made sure to include them in their bridge clubs, book clubs, poker clubs, and dinner clubs, they began to feel clubbed to death. Now they want to be included in the group that wants to be excluded.

J. Fatool

311

APPLICATION 15-2

Print an F before those sentences which are formal in tone, an S before those which are semiformal, and an I before those which are informal.

_____ 1. Us Southern folks'll stand pat on this issue.

_____ 2. Dick tried to tell about the story that he's read in the book.

_____ 3. "When I get on home," said the minister, "I ain't gonna hang around waiting for all the kids to get growed up."

_____ 4. The professor's exhortations were unheeded by her students.

_____ 5. When I bomb out of here I'll blast home for some grub; then I'll scoot back.

_____ 6. I received a profusion of felicitations upon my graduation.

_____ 7. Dick shot the bull about the jazz in the book.

Identify the following words in the above manner.

_____ 1. modicum   _____ 9. small amount

_____ 2. see eye to eye   _____ 10. agree

_____ 3. husband   _____ 11. spouse

_____ 4. a dab   _____ 12. tummy

_____ 5. abdomen   _____ 13. exterminate

_____ 6. concur   _____ 14. blot out

_____ 7. spouse   _____ 15. fiduciary

_____ 8. stomach

APPLICATION 15-3

In which tone would a writer be most likely to use each of the following words? Indicate by printing F, S, or I in the blanks.

_____ 1. ameliorate   _____ 6. dude

_____ 2. disentangle   _____ 7. ordinary

_____ 3. domicile   _____ 8. a buck (a dollar)

_____ 4. improve   _____ 9. mediocre (average)

_____ 5. extricate   _____ 10. approbation

APPLICATION 15-4

The words in the list below are appropriate for use in formal writing. Using a large dictionary or a thesaurus, write opposite each word a different word or phrase that would be suitable for semiformal writing and another suitable for informal writing.

	Semiformal	Informal
magnificent	_____	_____
turbulent	_____	_____
asceticism	_____	_____
sumptuous	_____	_____
clairvoyance	_____	_____
ludicrous	_____	_____
proximity	_____	_____
vigilant	_____	_____

APPLICATION 15-5

In the blanks, indicate whether the following passages are personal or impersonal in tone. Then underline those words and ideas which support your conclusion.

_____ 1. The clean white of winter has changed the view from our window wall across the back of our house. The slopes of the yard, tops of bird houses, barbeque, and picnic tables are covered with fresh snow. Bushes, trees, and fences provide contrast in shades of brown and gray. The channel at the edge of the lawn adds a swiftly moving line of steel blue water. In the expanse of the lake to our left, two mounds of white indicate the presence of our twin islands.

Harold Lecht

_____ 2. Water power is derived from the energy of flowing water by velocity, weight, or pressure. These processes are utilized by water descending from one level to a considerably lower level. The earliest use of water power dates back to ancient times when the water wheel was first devised. About the middle of the nineteenth century, all types of water wheels gave way to the invention of the turbine, which used both pressure and velocity of the water. Presently, mechanical energy seems to have taken more effect in industry, although water power is still used widely all over the world.

Glen Soleair

APPLICATION 15-6

In the blank beside each pair of words, print G or S to indicate whether the *first* word is more general or more specific than the second.

_____ 1. bakery—shop
_____ 2. reflection—image
_____ 3. smell—fragrance
_____ 4. earth—planet
_____ 5. gem—diamond
_____ 6. omelet—egg
_____ 7. text—book
_____ 8. cavern—cavity
_____ 9. Homo sapiens—mammal
_____ 10. sparkle—shimmer
_____ 11. walk—trudge
_____ 12. shatter—break
_____ 13. sit—slouch
_____ 14. scrape—grate
_____ 15. laugh—snicker

APPLICATION 15-7

The following composition, intended to inform, is not effective because it lacks specific details. Rewrite it below, adding specific details in a tone consistent with the first part.

Some species of birds do not fly. The largest of these are found in Africa and the Near East. The arctic regions have their own kinds of birds that do not fly. The most primitive flightless bird is found in New Zealand.

_____

_____

_____

_____

_____

_____

_____

_____

_____

_____

_____

APPLICATION 15-8

In your favorite magazine, find two examples of each of the following:

A. Simile	C. Personification
B. Metaphor	D. Connotation

Be prepared to discuss these in class.

APPLICATION 15-9

Using the key above, identify the following:

_____ 1. Oh life, protect me from death's darkness.

_____ 2. The clammy California climate causes one to catch the common cold.

_____ 3. The pool was a sheet of silver in the moonlight.

_____ 4. The cross he carried was his golden crown.

_____ 5. The winter air was cold and crackling.

_____ 6. Ford Motor Company is 600 horses and a wild little pony.

_____ 7. Their faces, cured by the sun and wind, were like smoked bacon.

_____ 8. Fate had pleasant thoughts and dreams in her loom for the pair.

_____ 9. We heard the clanging of the bells.

_____ 10. The enemy planes dived out of the sky like vultures.

_____ 11. The summer breeze whispered softly to the fields of corn.

_____ 12. The windows of the building looked with blank eyes out on the street.

_____ 13. The rookie was as brave as a war veteran when he faced the pitcher.

_____ 14. The river shuddered under the impact of the waterfalls.

_____ 15. "Not yet, please, death; I am not ready," she cried.

_____ 16. The bench was merciful in her judgment and sentence.

APPLICATION 15-10

Write a full-length composition intended to convey an impression. It should be about 600 words long and consist of a title; an opener if you wish, either separate or incorporated into the main paragraph; a main paragraph, including a subject sentence and several explanatory sentences; at least two paragraphs helping to develop a dominant impression; and a concluding paragraph.

Beneath the statement of your dominant general purpose, indicate whether you intended to use a formal, semiformal, or informal tone. Underline any of the following devices of diction which you intentionally used to introduce, develop, or maintain the tone or to increase vividness: (1) connotation, (2) substandard diction, (3) vivid concrete detail, and (4) figurative language. Use these numbers to identify these devices. Here are some suggested ideas:

1. The atmosphere at a sports event
2. A certain location
3. The impression made by a new acquaintance
4. A class reunion
5. A wedding, graduation, funeral, or some other ceremony.

YOU BE THE JUDGE

Evaluator's Initials ☐☐☐

Date _____

Section _____

Grade _____

Writer's Name _____

Date _____ Section _____

Title of paper _____

Chapter _____ Application No. _____

General Instructions on the You Be the Judge Applications, and specific instructions for Parts I and III, are printed inside the back cover of this book. Read those instructions carefully, then do Part I.

In the lines below, and on another sheet of paper, answer the questions in Part II. Then enter a grade for the paper in the space above left, and write your evaluation for Part III. Reread the composition to see how well the writer understands and applies the principles studied in this chapter. As you read the composition write any helpful suggestions that occur to you in the margins.

PART II

1. How effective are the title, opener if any, main paragraph and conclusion? Comment on any special features they show. _____

   _____

   _____

   _____

   _____

2. What is the intended tone of the composition? _____

   _____

   _____

   _____

   _____

3. How well does the writer carry out this tone _____

   (a) by the use of details _____

   _____

   _____

   _____

(b) by diction _____

_____

_____

_____

_____

4. Comment on the writer's use of figurative language. Suggest any additional figures you think might have been used that would have improved the composition. _____

_____

_____

_____

_____

_____

_____

5. How well does the writer's tone carry out the purpose? Comment specifically. _____

_____

_____

_____

_____

_____

_____

PART III   Grade and Explanation:

_____

_____

_____

_____

_____

_____

_____

CHAPTER 16

EMPHASIS: SOME DEVICES OF STYLE

After studying this chapter and completing the applications that follow it, you should be able to do the following:
1. To identify and differentiate some additional devices of style by which the emphasis placed on ideas and other details can be increased or decreased, depending upon the importance of their relationship to the predetermined elements.
2. To use for appropriate and effective emphasis: *repetition; parallel construction; position of words in sentences; coordination and subordination; concrete details*—to make abstract ideas more vivid, and to avoid *thinness; deletion of unrelated or marginally related detail.*
3. To apply these devices of style in a full-length composition.

THE WRITER puts more stress on main ideas and less on minor ones in order to emphasize the intended purpose. Any piece of writing is more interesting to a reader if there is extra stress on important things and less stress on less important ones. If every sentence in an essay or even in a paragraph received exactly the same stress the reader would find it hard to stay awake.

NONVERBAL DEVICES

There are many ways of creating variety in emphasis. One is by purely mechanical devices, such as CAPITAL LETTERS, Capitals and Lower Case, *italic* and **boldface** type in print and underlining in handwriting and typescript, the use of (1) numbers or (a) letters in enumerations, headings in books and articles, such as those used throughout this book, and various indentations from the standard margin, which also are very frequent in this book. In fact, punctuation marks, including the period at the end of a sentence and the capital letter at the beginning, are nonverbal devices for gaining emphasis. They separate units and show pauses and breaks of varying intensity. Thus they provide variety and emphasis as well as help in clarifying meaning. Even the form of an outline, with its main heads, subheads, and sub-subheads, is a device for showing emphasis by distinguishing the most important points from those of middle and least importance.

REPETITION OF WORDS

One of the most effective ways of gaining emphasis is by purposeful repetition of words. (See the discussion of repetition as a device of coherence in Chapter 10.) Repetition of a word is also an important device for gaining emphasis, as in these lines from a famous poem:

Water, water, everywhere,
And all the boards did shrink;
Water, water, everywhere,
Nor any drop to drink.

Here the repeated element is not just a single word, but a whole line, creating the effect of unbearable drought and parching thirst on a ship surrounded by water but with no drinking water aboard.

In the following sentence the repetition of one phrase creates a slightly comic, slightly ridiculous image of a man, one which brings a smile or a chuckle rather than an open laugh:

Ms. Whipple was wearing a dull gray suit. It was the same dull gray suit she was described as wearing at the convention in Chicago. Undoubtedly it was the same dull gray suit she wore at last year's convention in Los Angles.

A very famous speech in which repetition helped to create an atmosphere of high seriousness was Lincoln's "Gettysburg Address." The address was delivered while the Civil War was still raging, at a ceremony that dedicated a portion of a battlefield as a memorial to the dead. So like themes in music, the words *dedicate* and *nation* weave in and out, but there are many other repetitions too. The address is one of the great pieces of American prose and well worth careful rereading, even if you read it when you studied Chapter 5.

Four score and seven years ago our fathers brought forth on this continent, a new nation, conceived in liberty, and dedicated to the proposition that all men are created equal.

Now we are engaged in a great civil war, testing whether that nation, or any nation so conceived and so dedicated, can long endure. We are met on a great battle-field of that war. We have come to dedicate a portion of that field, as a final resting place for those who here gave their lives that that nation might live. It is altogether fitting and proper that we should do this.

But, in a larger sense, we cannot dedicate — we cannot consecrate — we cannot hallow — this ground. The brave men, living and dead, who struggled here, have consecrated it, far above our poor power to add or detract. The world will little note, nor long remember what we say here, but it can never forget what they did here. It is for us the living, rather, to be dedicated here to the unfinished work which they who fought here have thus far so nobly advanced. It is rather for us to be here dedicated to the great task remaining before us — that from these honored dead we take increased devotion to that cause for which they gave the last full measure of devotion — that we here highly resolve that these dead shall not have died in vain — that this nation, under God, shall have a new birth of freedom — and that government of the people, by the people, for the people, shall not perish from the earth.

Repetition is much used in public speeches for its ability to arouse emotion. One of the great speeches of World War II was the "Speech on Dunkirk," delivered in the House of Commons by Prime Minister Winston Churchill when British forces were fleeing in rout across the Channel, literally forced off the continent. It stirs up stubborn determination by its blunt repetitions:

We shall go on to the end, we shall fight in France, we shall fight on the seas and ocean, we shall fight with growing confidence and growing strength in the air, we shall defend our Island, whatever the cost may be, we shall fight on the beaches, we shall fight on the landing grounds, we shall fight in the fields and in the streets, we shall fight in the hills; we shall never surrender. . . .

**PARALLEL
CONSTRUCTION**

Parallel construction, the repetition of grammatical patterns within a sentence or a series of sentences, is closely allied to repetition of words and phrases as a means of emphasis. Indeed, the two devices are so closely associated that it is rare to find one without the other. The two are found together in each of the four examples of repetition we have just examined: The line "Water, water, everywhere" is used twice, a fairly simple kind of parallelism, though a clear example of repetition.

a dull gray suit. . . . It was the same dull gray suit . . . . Undoubtedly it was the same dull gray suit. . . .

Winston Churchill begins ten parallel clauses in the quoted sentence with "we shall," and thus not only uses verbal repetition but also introduces ten successive clauses all in the same construction.

But the master of parallelism was Lincoln. To show how intricate his patterns are, and how parallelism and repetition interweave, we diagram two of his sentences:

```
But                        we cannot dedicate
                           we cannot consecrate        this ground.
in a larger sense          we cannot hallow
```
. . . that from these honored dead we take increased devotion
that we here highly resolve . . .
that this nation . . . shall have a new birth of freedom —
and
```
        that government
                    of the people
                    by the people
                    for the people
                                    shall not perish from the earth.
```

The repetition of these words and structures creates a rhythm and a sound pattern almost like that of music. For its purpose, it is hard to find writing better than this.

EMPHASIS THROUGH POSITION

Emphasis on the important element in a sentence is often gained or lost by its position. In stress, the most important position in a sentence is the end, the next most important is the beginning, and the least important is the middle. It follows that putting a major sentence element in a minor position tends to reduce the emphasis on it, and putting a minor element in a major position, particularly at the end of the sentence, gives an effect of weakness which is often anticlimactic and unintentionally comic. Consider the following:

1. The crippled acrobat came home finally.
2. The crippled acrobat finally came home.
3. Finally the crippled acrobat came home.
4. The acrobat finally came home, crippled.

The first version limps badly because "finally" at the end is anticlimactic. The word simply isn't important enough for that position, though in the second version where it is tucked in the middle, the stress falls properly on "came home," which is important enough for the final position. The third sentence also is good, though the stress is different, somewhat more on his hesitation than in the second version. And in the last version the stress is wholly on the fact that he was crippled; the delay is played down.

The English sentence has a "natural order": subject, verb, complement.

Marge plays chess.

The modifiers of these various elements are normally placed near the things they modify. However, when there are a number of modifiers, usually the beginning and end of the sentence are convenient places to dispose of some of them:

Almost every evening, Marge, who detests it, plays *a quick game of chess with her brother, for whom it is the high point of the day.*

Notice how the modifiers are distributed around the subject, verb and complement. A large part of the skill needed to write a sentence like this is the ability to put each modifier where it will clearly relate to the right word and cause no confusion. Note also that the final clause quite appropriately gets the main emphasis, since it expresses an important thought and rounds out the whole.

Consider the following, in which the separate elements are marked off by slashes:

1. He taught Spanish/for a teacher/who had a broken leg/for four weeks.

It is possible that this teacher had a broken leg for four weeks, but more likely the time phrase belongs with *taught:*

2. *For four weeks*/he taught Spanish/*for a teacher/who had a broken leg.*

The placing of elements in sentences, whether in positions of emphasis or otherwise, can make all the difference. In order to place them well, one must first be able to identify and separate them.

EMPHASIS AND THE KEY

To be sure that every sentence in a paragraph has the right emphasis, you should keep the controlling sentence and the key within its main idea clearly in mind while writing the paragraph. It will then be easy to know which element in the sentence deserves top emphasis, which next, and so on down the line.

We have already seen that just as stages, movies, and television screens have prominent places in which the most important action takes place, written expression also has its prominent and emphatic positions. To keep the emphasis steady throughout, every sentence should be considered in relation to the writer's purpose. For example, here are three versions of the same sentence, each with a different emphasis. Any one of them could have the right emphasis, depending on the purpose:

1. My Aunt Ruth is a professor, and she likes cowboy stories.
2. My Aunt Ruth, who is a professor, likes cowboy stories.
3. My Aunt Ruth, who likes cowboy stories, is a professor.

If the controlling sentence reads, "My Aunt Ruth is a highly educated person," the right emphasis will be that of No. 3, which stresses "professor." But if the control is "My Aunt Ruth is a person of broad interests," No. 2 will give the best emphasis, though No. 1 will be possible.

EMPHASIS THROUGH COORDINATION AND SUBORDINATION

Of the three sentences about Aunt Ruth, No. 1 contains two *coordinate* or *independent* clauses joined by the conjunction *and,* while No. 2 and No. 3 each contain one *independent* clause and one *subordinate* or *dependent* clause, in each case an *adjective* or *relative* clause introduced by the *relative* pronoun *who.* That is why No. 1 puts equal emphasis on both ideas, while No. 2 and No. 3 put different emphasis on each, with the main emphasis each time going to the independent clause.
Note: These sentences illustrate coordination and one main type of subordination. If you understand the terminology we have just used, and the structures referred to, you will probably understand other types of subordination by adverbial clauses and by various types of phrases. If you do not, review pages 385–389 in the Handbook of Correct and Effective Usage. You cannot possibly put the emphasis where you want it in your sentences unless you can always tell a coordinating from a subordinating structure and recognize the principal clue words—prepositions and conjunctions of which the *and* and *who* in the sentences above are only two examples.

We are now ready to go on with our discussion of emphasis through coordination and subordination. Here is another example of emphasizing the main idea and its key by putting it in the main structure of the sentence. In this case let us assume that the controlling sentence is:

The Supreme Court plays an *important* part in the state government.

And the key idea in this sentence is the italicized phrase.

The sentence which follows this one can then take any of the three following forms:

1. It holds its hearings in the state capital, *and* it passes on cases involving interpretation of the state's laws.
2. It holds its hearings in the state capital *because* it passes on cases involving an interpretation of the state's laws.
3. *In hearings* in the state capital, it passes on cases involving an interpretation of the state's laws.

No. 1 coordinates the two clauses with "and," a structure which pays no attention to the key, "important." No. 2 plays down the idea in the second clause, which contains the important part, by making it a subordinate clause introduced by "because." No. 3 stresses the second clause by subordinating the first, taking away its subject and verb and making it a phrase. So No. 3 is the only one that gives the right emphasis by stressing the key. Every sentence in a paragraph should show its relation to the key in the controlling idea by its structure. After some practice, a writer does this almost automatically while writing and more deliberately while revising.

In almost any sentence, secondary ideas can be expressed in many different kinds of subordinating structures:

Verbal phrase:	*Feeling blue,* he cooked himself a fancy dinner.
Prepositional phrase:	On the town for the evening, he then took in a foreign film.
Adverbial phrase:	*Because he had been up for twenty-four hours,* he felt desperately sleepy.
Adjective phrase:	And so he closed his eyes, *which felt as though they had sand in them.*

One word of caution: sometimes the relationship between parts of a sentence is quite clear without obvious structural clues, and elaborate subordination can seem awkward and artificial, as in the following:

1. *Barking,* the dog dashed to the car.
2. *On a hot night,* we went bowling.
3. *Because it was dirty,* we washed the car.

These sentences are quite clear and much more natural if more simply constructed:

1. The dog barked and dashed to the car.
2. It was a hot night and we went bowling.
3. The car was dirty so we washed it.

EMPHASIS THROUGH CONCRETE DETAIL

One of the most effective ways to emphasize an important idea, anecdote, character, or experience is by concrete detail that tells how the subject looked, felt, tasted, sounded, and what an experience was like. Contrast the amount of concrete detail in the following pairs of sentences:

1. The children smiled as they showed the first apples they had picked.
   With gleeful grins, the children struggled to raise the heavy basket, their giant trophy, the first apples they had ever picked.

2. Again the man was missed by the bull's horns.
   Time and again the matador eluded death from the flashing horns as they grazed the gold braid on his jacket and he twisted his body away.

3. Not finding the toy, the child began to cry.
   After a prolonged but vain search, the little child began to whimper in frustration.,

4. The candles were lighted.
   The candles flickered in the mild breeze, trails of smoke curling upward and the wax dripping from their unevenly-burning tops.

5. We smelled the roses.
   We knelt in the grass, savoring the fragrance of the year's first rose.

6. She played to win.
   With every muscle tense, she awaited every shot, and fired it back across the net as if she might die before the next one.

   In each of these pairs, the second sentence uses details of sight, sound, smell, taste, touch, and emotion to make the bare idea expressed in the first version more vivid and emphatic. Thus the readers get more enjoyment out of what they read and will remember it better.

Making Abstract Ideas Vivid

Abstract ideas represent a high level of thought; without them, homo sapiens would not have got very far on the road to civilization. Although they express some of the greatest ideas and ideals ever achieved, they are not colorful in themselves and thus not particularly emphatic— understanding them often demands much greater mental effort on the part of a reader than grasping a concrete image or a specific statement. It is often important for a writer to give concrete applications to the abstractions used if readers are to understand and appreciate them.

   The following paragraph starts with the abstract thought that the pressure of the times affects people in all walks of life.

The pressures of the times have the whole world in high gear. *Cars* move at high speeds, traveling long distances across the continent in a few hours. *Countries* are racing to get to the moon and to conquer space. *Workers* are under constant pressure in their daily jobs. They also fight traffic to and from work. Then they return home to face the pressures of community living and to assume the responsibilities of the civic-minded suburban dweller. *Children* are rushed from one lesson to another. They attend school during the day where all the activities of the outside world are drummed into their heads. At the end of the school day, they begin the next segment of their education. They run from swimming lessons to piano lessons then to scout lessons, horseback riding lessons, and elocution lessons. *Parents* run a jitney service from one lesson to another. They also attend PTA meetings, telephone to remind people to vote, then run to attend various civic meetings. *Even the dogs* find a retreat when the house is full of people milling about, or the noise of several children at play becomes too much.

Hope Lang

The abstraction which is the controlling idea of this paragraph is developed by a series of concrete examples—about cars, countries, workers, children, parents, and even dogs.

Avoiding Thinness

One of the most common faults in student writing is *thinness,* an anemic, underdeveloped, colorless quality in writing that never gets beyond the bare bones of abstract statement and is not fleshed out with the details and examples which give color and life. In the following pair of contrasting paragraphs, the writer's purpose is to inform the reader by the use of factual details. Notice how thin and unemphatic the first version is:

The evidence of the cycle of regional water erosion in an arid land is not always easy to detect. Although water is the primary erosive agent in some arid regions, sand dunes and other wind deposits often obscure its erosive effects.

In contrast, the following paragraph is fully and richly developed, and is much more interesting and certainly more emphatic.

The evidence of the cycle of regional water erosion in an arid land is not always easy to detect. Even though rainfall is scarce in a dry climate, it is a devastating erosive agent when it does occur; consequently, running water often is a primary cause of erosion in these areas. Because a lack of rainfall allows only a minimum amount of vegetation to grow to hold the soil in place, a much freer and more forceful movement of water results when it does rain. This lack of plant life also allows the wind to blow the sand about, changing the land topography so that the evidence of water erosion is obscured. Therefore, although water is a primary erosive agent even in some arid regions, sand dunes and other wind deposits often obscure its erosive effects.

Can you spot the principal difference between these two paragraphs? The first consists of only two sentences; the first and last sentences of the second version. These constitute only the control and conclusion; the factual explanation of *why* erosion is not always easy to detect is given in full in the second version, but does not appear at all in the first. The second is therefore a much clearer and a more emphatic explanation.

Emphasis through Sharp Focus

Finally, it sometimes happens that a piece of writing loses emphasis because part of it strays from the point and talks about marginal things not closely related to the writer's purpose. The following paragraph gets off the track. Can you tell where?

One day, wanting to do something different because there was a touch of spring in the air, I turned off the busy street and went into the park. I wanted to get away from the busy street on which the bus line runs. The very tall trees were magnificent, so big that I felt small walking under them on the gravel path. The first berries were bursting out on the hedges, because spring was on its way. Also they got moisture from a pond over on my left about a hundred yards. I had had a date the night before, which was a Thursday, and wondered why it had gone wrong but figured that it wouldn't be worth worrying about. She had left my apartment very early, and I wondered whether she had gone home to forget our relationship. Was she, instead, concerned about remedying the differences that we have about how much time to spend at whose apartment, among other things? While I was wondering these things, the mud felt warm. I had taken off my shoes and socks so the air felt cool on my insteps. Maybe spring has finally arrived.

The following version, in which the irrelevant parts have been cut out, is more sharply focused and therefore more emphatic.

Just like that, I took off for the park one day. I wanted to be alone. The trees were magnificant, and they made me feel small in their presence. The first berries of spring were bursting out on the hedges, nurtured by the moisture from a nearby pond. I sat down for a moment, took off my shoes, and pressed my heels into the nonporous mud on the banks of the water. I wondered what went wrong with my date last night, but figured that it wouldn't be worth worrying about. I wonder why she left my apartment so early. Did she go home to forget our relationship? Or is she concerned about remedying the differences that we have? The mud feels warm; but I can feel the cool sky touch my insteps where the sky meets the earth. Maybe spring has finally arrived.

Emphasis in writing can be achieved in a variety of ways. It can be created by nonverbal devices such as headings, variations in type, indentations, and so forth. On the verbal level, emphasis is achieved by the repetition of strong and important words and phrases and is often combined with parallel construction, a kind of repetition in its own right. In sentences, the most emphatic positions are the beginning and the end, and the emphasis within the sentences of a paragraph should be in harmony with the emphasis suggested by the controlling sentence and the key idea within it. Other devices for emphasis are coordination and subordination, development by the use of concrete detail, and fullness vs. thinness in the extent of development.

PRACTICE in Achieving This Chapter's Objectives

Practice in identifying, differentiating, and applying some additional devices of style by which to control and use emphasis correctly and effectively.

	Applications
1. Identifying and using abstract and concrete details.	1, 2, 5, 7
2. Placing details in appropriately emphatic sentence positions.	3
3. Writing effective coordination and subordination.	4, 6
4. Gaining appropriate emphasis by adequate development.	5, 8, 9
5. Writing a full-length composition for emphatic development.	10
6. You Be the Judge	

APPLICATION 16-1

Place an A before abstract words and a C before concrete ones.

_____ grace	_____ lemon	_____ clown
_____ agreement	_____ intelligence	_____ frequence
_____ wood	_____ intermission	_____ prejudice
_____ hope	_____ kite	_____ river
_____ smoke	_____ steak	_____ sin

APPLICATION 16-2

Underline the concrete words in the following paragraph.

The valve in the steam engine had obviously been opened too wide. The soft chuf-chuf was slowly giving way to a restrained, muffled bark while the shattering piston rod began to vibrate with motion. The flywheel spokes had long since disappeared and an ominous shuddering could be felt in the floor. Just as the whole assembly seemed ready to rattle itself to pieces, the operator came and cranked down a squeaky valve, and the machine slowly rumbled forward at its regular slow pace.

Joan Treff

APPLICATION 16-3

Improve the emphasis in the following sentences by moving the italicized elements to more emphatic positions.

1. He lay *in a state of shock* on the living room floor.

   _____

   _____

2. She consulted the professor, *in the laboratory*, about physics.

   _____

   _____

3. The student *may never become a doctor* if not taught thoroughly.

   _____

   _____

4. Dogs, *if you do not train them properly*, can become a public menace.

_____

_____

5. Amelia Earhart, *after flying across the Atlantic*, became famous.

_____

_____

APPLICATION 16-4

Rewrite the following sentences in order to put the most important ideas in independent clauses and less important ideas in subordinate constructions. Assume that the italicized element represents the main idea in each sentence. (If necessary, refer to the Handbook of Correct and Effective Usage, pages 389–390.)

1. As *he smiled,* he turned in his examination.

_____

_____

2. *Skidding and crashing into the fence,* the lead car went into the hairpin turn.

_____

_____

3. The freshman did not study, thus *failing the course.*

_____

_____

4. She wanted fame and fortune, so *she worked hard.*

_____

_____

5. It was snowing all afternoon, and *I was sitting by the fire reading.*

_____

_____

APPLICATION 16-5

Rewrite the following sentences to make them more vivid by using dramatic or figurative detail.

Example:　The candles were lit.

The candles were flickering with their slight trails of smoke slowly curling upwards about the room.

1. She lighted the fire.

_____

_____

_____

2. The lioness stood waiting for her prey.

_____

_____

_____

3. He fell and hurt himself.

_____

_____

_____

APPLICATION 16-6

Following are two thought units; the subordinate idea of each is italicized. Referring if necessary to the Handbook of Correct and Effective Usage, combine each pair into a single sentence in each of the five ways indicated by the instructions below.

The daffodils were like a yellow carpet. They covered the field.

The sun's rays descended like a veil. They gave the mountains a crimson hue.

1. Write a compound sentence with the subordinate idea in an independent clause.
2. Write a complex sentence with the subordinate idea reduced to a subordinate clause.
3. Write a simple sentence with the subordinate idea reduced to a phrase.
4. Write a simple sentence with the subordinate idea reduced to an appositive.
5. Write a simple sentence with the subordinate idea reduced to a predicate verb.

APPLICATION 16-7

In the first line beneath the following passage, identify the abstract thought expressed more meaningfully by the concrete details in it. Next, on the lines following the name of each of the five senses, list as many of the details related to each as you can. Also, underline as many of the words conveying figures of speech as you can.

Last night, the soft-moccasin footsteps of autumn silently crossed over the threshold of summer. Punctually, this autumnal equinox signaled the prompt beginning of the sequence of natural changes inherent in all life.

This morning, the first rustlings of fall leaves, the rallying calls of the Canadian geese, the flickers, and other migrants began to blend with the adagio orchestrated by the diminishing rasp of crickets. Later in the day and in the early evening, bluejays will irately scream while reclaiming their favorite haunts in the woods and surrounding orchards. Sensing the forebodings of death in these early changes, the katydids will alter their beat to the somber, half-step tempo of a funeral procession, and the black crows high overhead will raucously ridicule their apprehensions.

During the subsequent days, the recessional changes from the high pitch of summer will continue methodically. The asters will deepen their purple, the maples will splash the woods with blotches of crimson and gold, the hickory will change to toast, and the birch trees will lemon.

In late October, the frosty air will carry the aromas of ripe fruits throughout the valley and over the surrounding hills. The smell of ripe pumpkins, nested in icy dew, the cider-sweet aroma of winesap apples, heavy with juice, and the scent of plump, wine-ready fox grapes will permeate the brisk air.

Finally, like the beauty of summer, the vivacity of autumn will suddenly recede into memory. Sheets of cold snow will maintain the intermission until the vernal equinox signals the beginning again of the same cycle of changes.

Helen Kirk

Abstract thought _____

_____

Sight _____

_____

_____

Sound _____

_____

_____

Smell _____

_____

_____

Touch _____

_____

_____

Taste _____

_____

_____

APPLICATION 16-8

The following thought is intended to actuate the administrators of a school system. It does not succeed because it is not adequately developed to enable the intended reader to visualize the rewards and to understand the advantages to be derived from doing what the writer urges. Below, rewrite the composition, using one or more paragraphs, so that it will be more effective in achieving the writer's objective.

The plight of the American Indian demands immediate attention. Poverty, ignorance, and despair are common afflictions of Americans who still live on Indian reservations.

APPLICATION 16-9

The following composition—intended to convey an impression—lacks adequate concrete details. Rewrite it below, adding the needed concrete details to arouse the intended reader response.

As I walked into the lobby of the South Pacific Resort, I knew it was not what the brochure claimed. After checking the name and address, I regretfully resigned myself to the fact that I had indeed arrived at what was advertised as "the in place for swinging singles." It didn't take me long to conclude that it was just a run-down hotel. I picked up my bags and left without paying my bill.

APPLICATION 16-10

Write a full-length composition containing as many of the stylistic devices studied in this chapter as you can. The composition should be about 600 words long and should have a title; an opener, if you wish, either separate from the main paragraph or within it; a main paragraph, including a subject sentence and several explanatory sentences; at least two supporting paragraphs; and a concluding paragraph. Be sure to indicate your purpose.

In your paper, underline any uses of the following devices of style, and number them in the margin according to the following key: (1) repetition, (2) concrete detail, (3) position of word or phrase in its sentence, (4) parallel construction, (5) coordination, (6) subordination. Here are some suggested topics:

1. The atmosphere in a dance hall
2. Human behavior at a social event you attended
3. A frolicsome activity in which you participated
4. A peculiar phobia or apprehension afflicting someone
5. The irritations of TV commercials

YOU BE THE JUDGE

CHAPTER 16

Writer's Name _____

Date _____ Section _____

Title of paper _____

Chapter _____ Application No. _____

General instructions on the You Be the Judge Applications, and specific instructions for Parts I and III, are printed inside the back cover of this book. Read those instructions carefully; then do Part I.

In the lines below, and on another sheet of paper, answer the questions in Part II. Then enter a grade for the paper in the space above left, and write your evaluation for Part III. Reread the composition to see how well the writer understands and applies the principles studied in this chapter. As you read the composition write any helpful suggestions that occur to you in the margins.

PART II

1. Discuss the writer's use of emphasis in relation to

   a. the title _____

   _____

   _____

   b. the opener _____

   _____

   _____

   c. the main paragraph _____

   _____

   _____

2. Are the controlling sentences in the developing paragraphs sufficiently stressed to stand out clearly? _____

   _____

   _____

   _____

3. Do the paragraphs end emphatically? _____

   _____

   _____

   _____

4. Discuss the writer's handling of emphasis in relation to the following elements, noting any places where you think he or she went wrong.

a. Repetition _____

_____

_____

_____

b. Parallel construction _____

_____

_____

_____

c. Order within sentences _____

_____

_____

_____

d. Coordination and subordination _____

_____

_____

_____

e. Concrete details _____

_____

_____

_____

5. Is there any irrelevant material which damages or distorts emphasis?

_____

_____

_____

PART III   Grade and Explanation:

_____

_____

CHAPTER 17

DEVICES OF PERSUASION

After studying this chapter and completing the applications that follow it, you should be able to do the following:
1. To define and identify some common devices of persuasion: bandwagon appeal; testimonials—celebrity, just plain folks, and authority; appeal to popular sentiment; slanting—by playing up or down, by selection and suppression, and by stacked statistics; red herring—threat, and name-calling.
2. To use these devices to persuade or to actuate.
3. To apply these principles deliberately in a full-length composition of persuasion.

W HAT DO you mean when you say you want to *persuade* people? You mean one of two things: that you want to make them think or believe in a certain way, or that you want to make them act in a certain way. The word usually carries the suggestion that you are going to have to change their minds, or make them feel much more strongly about something than they did before—strongly enough, perhaps, to do something. Persuasion, then, has two purposes; to change somebody's mind, or to make somebody take action—and sometimes both.

In Chapter 4 we discussed the possible dominant general purposes a writer might have and said there were five: to entertain, to convey an impression, to inform, to persuade, and to actuate. Of these the fourth and fifth are persuasion, for "actuating" ones readers is simply another word for arousing them by persuasion to the point where they take action. Now, before continuing to read this chapter, you should review the material on persuasion in Chapter 4; that discussion makes certain theoretical statements about the *methods* and *purposes* of persuading that we need not repeat here. This chapter will be devoted to certain *techniques* and *devices* of persuasion. Certain others were discussed under the heading of fallacies in Chapter 2; some types of faulty thinking, called fallacies when a writer falls into them through error, can be used quite consciously with the intent to persuade. Thus fallacies and devices of persuasion overlap, but they can't all be neatly classified or separated. The principal distinction is one of intent: if a writer uses faulty logic by accident it is a fallacy; if intentionally, it is probably done to persuade.

Most persuasion is done by a combination of emotional appeals and reasoning. The quantities of each may vary from almost 100 percent to almost zero, though emotional appeal tends to be dominant. In fact, some people distinguish between persuasion and argument on just this basis, describing persuasion as dominantly emotional and argument as dominantly logical.

Devices of persuasion, whether emotional or logical, may be used to promote selfish and harmful ends as well as good and constructive ones. All great preachers have been skilled persuaders, for they have been remarkably successful in changing beliefs and exhorting people to action. Almost every successful political figure uses some mixture of persuasion and argument, since persons in politics must get action if they are to accomplish their goals; how much they use logical and how much emotional appeals is a matter which often varies with the issue, the occasion, and the audience. Through persuasion we have at our command great powers of good and ill; it is of utmost importance to human welfare that we use them with care and an ever-vigilant sense of responsibility.

THE USE OF LANGUAGE IN PERSUASION

The greatest single device of persuasion is language itself. We saw in Chapter 15 that tone in writing is created by language — words have connotations or suggestions which call up emotions and help to create attitudes and opinions for or against a person or a subject. There is no more powerful source of persuasion than feeling, and few things arouse feeling more consistently than carefully chosen words. Listen to these:

This powerful new collection of poems speaks, like all her work, to our most passionate yearnings for love and our deepest fears of evil and death.

More than any logical device, the connotations of the words you choose will make or break your attempts at persuasion. The wrong word can weaken the tone and the mood and destroy the effect. There is nothing worse than making a reader laugh at the wrong time. As soon as you do, you've lost him, at least for a while — and this is more likely to be true in persuasive writing than in any other kind. Consider this:

Its uncompromising honesty and vividness confirm her stature as one of the most compelling voices of our time. Put on your specs and discover this important poet for yourself.

What happens to you when you read the word *specs?* The bubble breaks, the spell is gone, and you may even find that you're laughing at yourself for being taken in, as well as at the ad for stubbing its toe. (The original, of course, didn't stub its toe. We put in the last sentence just to make a point.)

Is professor X a *pendant* or a *scholar?* Is somebody a *hustler* or a *billards buff?* Is a person *naive* or *dumb, frugal* or *penurious, cautious* or *cowardly, reticent* or *secretive?* Nothing can create an opinion or an attitude more quickly than the choice of a word with strong connotations. Keep this always in mind as you read the rest of this chapter.

OTHER DEVICES OF PERSUASION

The types of thinking discussed in Chapter 2 as logical fallacies are also devices of persuasion when they are used intentionally for this purpose: *rationalizing,* or making up reasons to justify something a person didn't really believe he ought to do; *wishful thinking,* or arguing that something would or would not happen because a person wanted or did not want it to; *hidden assumptions,* or unspoken beliefs and convictions that were a person's real motives although he tried to make others think they weren't; *sweeping generalizations,* broad statements without enough evidence to back them up; *circular reasoning,* or using a statement as proof of itself; *black-or-white reasoning,* or oversimplification of the either-or variety; arguing that *one more won't hurt anybody;* and *false cause,* or asserting that because one thing comes before another it is the cause of the other.

In the rest of this chapter we shall consider a number of other widely used devices of persuasion. Bear in mind that in every one of these the language used and the connotations or associations called up are at least as important as the logic. The ultimate effect of persuasion is far more psychological than logical.

The Bandwagon Appeal

One common device of persuasion is called the bandwagon appeal in reference to the days when one wagon in a parade often carried a band and boys loved to jump on the wagon to be where the glamor and action were. This is the appeal to think or do something because everybody else does. Most people derive a sense of comfort out of belonging, doing the approved thing, being members of an in-group. The appeal to this common urge often also implies that not belonging indicates that one is un-cooperative, stupid, or at the very least, peculiar. And there are a great many people who are not strong enough to act independently without the comfort of numbers. A great deal of advertising appeals to this urge to conform: more and more people are using Plum Soap, nearly everybody reads the Daily Bugle, and so on and so on. Fashion is perhaps an even more striking indicator of the human need to conform. Short hair or long hair, narrow trousers or floppy trousers, short skirts or long, high heels or low, and so forth. It's a brave soul who can swim against the current. The skillful persuader (including the vast majority of advertisers) knows this and gears his appeals accordingly.

The bandwagon appeal is particularly common during elections and political campaigns. Many public demonstrations also carry it as a hidden threat—a large number of demonstrators for something implies that it may be dangerous to be against it. A great deal of advertising on TV, radio, and in newspapers and magazines uses the bandwagon appeal. This appeal is often skillfully combined with others. Many of the cultural and social pressures of which we are most sharply aware have a strong element of the bandwagon effect in them. How many marriages are made because people want to be like everybody else? Many people choose mates who have traits approved by the community. Everybody wants to belong, to be accepted by a large group, particularly one they admire — to be on the social even more than the political bandwagon.

Testimonials

Testimonials are emotional appeals in the form of statements by some person whom the readers admire or respect and whose words they will accept and even cling to, regardless of this person's qualifications on the subject under discussion. Three common types are testimonials by celebrities, just plain folks, and authorities. The three types of appeal are obviously different in tone and in the feeling evoked, but the psychological factors involved are the same.

Celebrity Testimonials

Celebrity testimonials are statements made by persons possessing charisma or charm who have achieved great popularity or even fame in some field, often sports or motion pictures. The field in which the celebrity performs is often totally unrelated to the product or issue endorsed. Sports stars and heroes, male and female, will have strong appeal among large segments of the general populace and will be very effective in testimonials for certain widely used products such as cosmetics, toilet articles, automobiles, and sporting goods and sports clothes. Testimonials by such persons would, however, carry little weight with highly selected groups such as atomic scientists, particularly on products such as books and computers. So advertisers are careful in pairing celebrities with products, though the connection by no means has to be a rational one.

Just-Plain-Folks Testimonials

Aimed at persons who are suspicious or skeptical of statements attributed to celebrities, just-plain-folks testimonials are appeals to almost the opposite type of personality. Many people who mistrust celebrities have unlimited and uncritical faith in what they think of as unassuming, natural people like themselves. Often of course these two types of testimonials will appeal to the same people, depending on how skillfully they are handled. Many automobile, soap, cereal, beer, and patent medicine commercials make this kind of appeal. For example:

Eben's sausages are made from porkers raised right here on the farm. These hogs are fed golden corn raised in Eben's own fields by Eben and his kids. Eben knows his sausages are fit for a hungry stomach — he makes them, and he eats them himself. You'll like 'em too.

The plain folks type of advertising appeals to the virtues of motherhood, thrift, and wisdom. These are virtues inherited from our Puritan ancestors — or so we have been told — and they have had a powerful force in shaping our culture. Most Americans associate virtue with the kind of worthwhile simplicity implied by such advertisements as these, and such appeals seldom misfire unless they are grossly misapplied.

Testimonials by Authorities

Testimonials by authorities are generally beamed to the same people addressed in the endorsements signed by athletes, movie stars, and just plain folks, but on weightier topics, such as headache, acid indigestion, and aching back. By far the most usual authority is the doctor, and for years advertisements of patent medicines and pharmaceuticals were filled with white jackets, stethoscopes, and earnest medical faces surmounted by circular reflecting mirrors. Television provides an easy chance for before-and-after shots, so we now more commonly see the exhausted and haggard sufferer in one shot refreshed and smiling in the next.

The Red Herring Device

The metaphor of the red herring as a device in persuasion refers to the old practice of dragging a fish across a warm trail to divert hounds from the scent. Such appeals are deliberately used to distract someone from the real issue in a discussion or a line of questioning and to substitute irrelevant or emotional considerations for the real question at issue. The "red herring" is a diversionary tactic, and is probably more effective in movies, comic strips, and TV stories than in life.

Two common variations of the red herring device are what logicians call the *argumentum ad baculum* (argument of the club) and the *argumentum ad hominem* (argument against that person). Here we will call these *the threat* and *name-calling,* respectively.

The Threat

As its name implies, the threat substitutes a threat of force for a logical argument. It is an appeal to the emotions, usually to fear; it is used when writers have run out of logical reasons, haven't bothered to think any up, or so emotionally aroused themselves that they have no use for logic and can't get off an emotional plane. For example, a student is told not to park in the faculty parking lot, and when he or she asks why, is told "because your car will be towed away if you park there again." In this situation the real reason is that if the student parks in the faculty lot the car will be taking up one of a limited number of spaces which have been allotted for faculty use, whereas presumably other spaces, located elsewhere, have been allotted for student use. But this reason is not given, only the threat of what will happen if the rule is disobeyed.

Abusive Argument

Technically known as *argumentum ad hominem* or *argument against that person,* and similar to the device of dragging an irrelevant issue across the trail of a real one is the trick of dodging the argument by slandering the person who raises or supports it. This is done either by actually calling the person an abusive name, or by attacking that person's character. This kind of abuse is one of the most common of all the emotional devices used in speech and writing. A classic comment on this kind of argument was the philosopher Bertrand Russell's conjugation of a verb as: "I am firm, you are stubborn, he is pig-headed." What is a "devout Buddhist" to one person may be a "religious fanatic" to another.

Not all abusive language is potently effective; sometimes it is little more than feeble retaliation caused by personal annoyance, so transparent that it is best called *sour grapes*. Listen carefully to the conversations you hear about you every day and you will be surprised how often remarks critical of someone else show no realization that the speaker himself might have been in the wrong.

To be effective as a device in persuasion, personal comment must have enough possible truth in it, and be credible enough, to make the reader at least pause and consider. The principle behind it is diversion of interest from the real issue. In this way, the persuader creates false issues and sidetracks real ones.

Appeals to Popular Sentiment

Another device for shifting the attention away from real issues and arousing emotion for or against a person or a course of action is to appeal to popular sentiments easily aroused. Everybody is against crime, and for God, country, and the flag. Appeals to pity are often melodramatic in their attempt to arouse a more sympathetic reaction than the occasion justifies. For example:

Members of the jury, I say to you once more, this child should be acquitted of the murder of his parents. Be merciful. Remember his tender years. And remember above all that by this brutal murder he has been made an orphan, alone in a cruel world with no parents to protect him.

The real issue, of course, is whether or not the child committed the crime of which he had been accused. Again:

How can you believe that this woman — nay, this lady — is guilty of shoplifting? Look at her gray hair, her delicate hands, her patrician features. Can you, perceiving these qualities, believe that she could steal?

Once more the emotions deliberately aroused have nothing to do with the real question, but it is probable that whether or not they get the woman off completely, they will at least help to reduce her sentence.

Another common emotional appeal is to "the good old days," as in the following:

For fifty years we have been making cheese in the same way that your grandparents made it. Your grandparents bought our cheese, and so did your parents. Now it is your turn to pass this great American tradition on to your children.

The real issue, of course, is not that the old tradition be passed on, but whether the old way of making cheese was better than the new way.

In many political campaigns the names of Jefferson, Lincoln, Roosevelt, Eisenhower, and Kennedy are heard almost as often as the names of the candidates. This is done to arouse the widespread sentiment of reverence for these national figures and to have as much as possible of it associated with the present candidates, whether there is any real connection or not. Innocence by association and nobility by association are just as frequent in persuasion as guilt by association. The revered or hated name is an emotional trigger, and a certain amount of the good or bad feeling it releases rubs off onto whoever else happens to be mentioned in the same breath.

Slanting   Slanting is emphasis. It is playing something up or playing it down, in order to influence opinion and behavior. Newspapers do it most obviously by reporting a speech by a favored candidate on the front page and one by the opposition on an inside page. *Emphasis,* then, is one method of slanting, and it can be practiced as well on radio and television as in newspapers.

Another trick of slanting is to select only those points the writer wants to have known and to suppress others. No auto manufacturers are going to tell us that their cars get only eight miles to the gallon, but they will describe luxury features in great detail. A real estate advertisement will tell you a house has a fireplace, five bedrooms, a new roof, and a modern kitchen, but it will never mention that it is on a noisy street and just down the block from a factory.

Still a third method of slanting is the use of statistics or other facts stacked in favor of the persuader. One could argue, for example, that air travel should be restricted or prohibited by presenting only those statistics which show the number of fatal accidents. Or one could argue the opposite by the ratio between number of miles traveled by airplane and by automobile, and pointing out that there are fewer accidents per mile by air than by car. Again, an insurance company, accused of charging excessively high premiums, could present statistics which showed that the company paid out $10 million more in 1972 than it collected in premiums. It could explain in addition that damage claims, legal fees, and sales commissions all skyrocketed that year because of inflation. At the same time the company could neglect to mention that in 1972 it earned $28 million from its holdings in real estate, stocks, and interest from the Federal Insurance Commission on its cash reserves held to assure payment of claims.

There is nothing wrong with pointing out the good features of anything. But when an important issue is involved, and especially when the welfare of the reader is or could be involved, both sides of the issue should be fairly represented. The slanted argument is usually only half the story.

PRACTICE in Achieving This Chapter's Objectives

Practice in identifying, differentiating, and applying some common devices of persuasion.

	Applications
1. Identifying and explaining the use of devices of persuasion in someone else's writing.	1, 2, 3
2. Writing persuasion.	4, 5
3. Writing a full-length composition, using devices of persuasion studied in this chapter.	6
4. You Be the Judge	

APPLICATION 17-1

Bring to class an advertisement from a magazine, an editorial from a newspaper, and a news story from a newspaper on the same subject as the editorial. In each, underline the words used for their connotative appeal in persuasion. Explain whether each such word is used mainly to create an emotion, to induce belief, or to incite action. Compare and contrast the diction of the three pieces of writing in any other ways you find relevant to their effectiveness as pieces of persuasion.

APPLICATION 17-2

Find two different newspapers published on the same day (if possible both morning or both evening papers) and find in each a news story and an editorial on the same topic. Compare and contrast the two news stories and the two editorials for emphasis (placement, space, headline, and so forth), diction, attitude or interpretation, point of view, and any other devices you find which have a bearing on the persuasive devices reflecting the editorial opinions of the two papers.

APPLICATION 17-3

In the blank opposite each of the following, insert the letter from the list below that best identifies the type of device of persuasion each is.

         A. bandwagon appeal   E. red herring—threat
         B. celebrity testimonial   F. red herring—name-calling
         C. just plain folks testimonial   G. appeal to popular sentiment
         D. authority testimonial   H. slanting

_____ 1. True, the students stole the car, but remember that these students are orphans. They never had a family who owned a car. Can you blame them for wanting to try driving? They should be acquitted.

_____ 2. Fifty million people use Peppery Mouthwash; you should too.

_____ 3. If you had any brains, you wouldn't say that we should attack Cuba.

_____ 4. The greatest authority on the structure of the atom says that narrow lapels on suit coats are best.

_____ 5. Bette Davis, the movie star, supports this candidate.

_____ 6. A loan company specializing in consolidation of family debts, emphasizes the statistics showing how small the monthly payments will be.

_____ 7. This contemptible old scoundrel has the audacity to contend that the accused is innocent.

_____ 8. Vote for Bev Brown, a woman of the people. She is a farmer, like her folks before her. She is the salt of the earth, the workers' mayor.

_____ 9. The instructor shouted, "If you students don't stop arguing with me, I will send you to the Dean."

_____ 10. Maltese beer is a favorite refreshment for the tenors of the Metropolitan Opera Company. That's why it's for people of taste.

_____ 11. Earl Ham was born in a farm house, and as a boy, he plowed the cornfields, fed the pigs, and walked to and from school. He is modest, a man like you and me; he'll tell it like it is. There's nothing hoity-toity or high-hat about him. Let him negotiate for this union.

_____ 12. In a recent survey, 60 percent of the dentists interviewed recommended Bleach Teeth toothpaste.

_____ 13. If you don't send us the enclosed card so that we can tell you what to do, you just might lose the scholarship for your daughter.

_____ 14. Don't hire that English professor; she's been married three times.

APPLICATION 17-4

Find and write in brief form one example of each of the following devices of persuasion.
1. Bandwagon appeal

_____

_____

_____

2. Testimonials

   a. Celebrity

_____

_____

_____

   b. Just plain folks

_____

_____

_____

   c. Authority

_____

_____

_____

3. Red herring

   a. Threat

   _____

   _____

   _____

   b. Name-calling

   _____

   _____

   _____

4. Appeal to popular sentiment

   _____

   _____

   _____

5. Slanting

   a. By playing up or down

   _____

   _____

   _____

   b. By selection and suppression

   _____

   _____

   _____

   c. By stacked statistics

   _____

   _____

   _____

APPLICATION 17-5

On the lines below, write a supporting paragraph intended to convince the reader by persuasion. Be sure to use at least two of the devices studied in this chapter. Underline each of these devices, and in the left margin, identify the kind you intended. Here are some suggested topics:

1. At least four weeks vacation should be mandatory for everyone
2. Women (or men) are better lawyers, doctors, teachers, and so forth than members of the opposite sex
3. American hot dogs aren't so hot

_____

_____

_____

_____

_____

_____

_____

_____

_____

_____

_____

_____

_____

_____

APPLICATION 17-6

Write a full-length composition intended to convince your reader to change his convictions about an issue which he defends or attacks emotionally, and induce him to agree with your conclusions about it. Be sure to express your ideas in the appropriate tone by consistently maintaining it through the use of some of the language devices studied in Chapter 15. Be sure to use some of the devices of persuasion studied in this chapter. Here are some suggested general topics:

1. Abortion
2. Pornography
3. Women's lib
4. Transportation
5. Compulsory military training for men and women

CHAPTER 17

YOU BE THE JUDGE

Writer's Name _____

Date _____ Section _____

Title of paper _____

Chapter _____ Application No. _____

General instructions on the You Be the Judge Applications, and specific instructions for Parts I and III, are printed inside the back cover of this book. Read those instructions carefully; then do Part I.

In the lines below, and on another sheet of paper, answer the questions in Part II. Then enter a grade for the paper in the space above left, and write your evaluation for Part III. Reread the composition to see how well the writer understands and applies the principles studied in this chapter. As you read the composition write any helpful suggestions that occur to you in the margins.

PART II

1. Comment of the persuasiveness of the title, inducer, purpose statement and main paragraph. _____

_____

_____

_____

_____

_____

_____

_____

2. Comment on the interest-arousing qualities of the items mentioned in the previous question and on the relation of interest to persuasion.

_____

_____

_____

_____

_____

_____

_____

3. What is the main strategy of this writer's campaign to persuade you as a reader? _____

_____

_____

_____

_____

_____

4. Name and identify any specific devices of persuasion the writer uses.

_____

_____

_____

_____

_____

_____

5. How effective is this persuasive campaign? That is, how fully are you persuaded? Any flaws? _____

_____

_____

_____

_____

_____

PART III

Grade and Explanation:

_____

_____

_____

CHAPTER 18

THE RESEARCH PAPER

After studying this chapter and completing the applications that follow it, you should be able to do the following:

1. To apply the procedures of research to any report, academic or industrial.
2. To recognize and select theses appropriate for research writing.
3. To apply writing principles studied in previous chapters to the research paper.
4. To distinguish between kinds of research papers:
   informative—*status report, historical report,* and *process or procedural report;*
   interpretive—*causal investigative paper,* and *persuasive or argumentative paper.*
5. To read effectively for a research paper by: knowing the resources of your library, doing preliminary reading, and preparing and using bibliography cards.
6. To take efficient notes.
7. To plan your paper carefully by: organizing notes into clusters by topic, and organizing the paper according to the type of paper you are writing.
8. To write an effective paper by: using your own words in incorporating notes into written discussion, recognizing the need for and using footnotes, and using the proper form for footnotes and bibliography.

BECAUSE many of the papers you write in college will be based on reading and research in special topics, a common assignment in the composition course is the *research paper,* also called the *investigative* or *library paper.* Such a paper also gives valuable training in the kind of practical reporting required by many jobs in business and industry. No matter what the subject matter is, the procedures for gathering, summarizing, evaluating, and presenting information are basically the same for the business report and the research paper, as is the need for backing up your statements. These are the procedures of research, whatever the subject, the need, or the occasion. In addition to books and other printed sources, research is done through telephone calls, interviews, and opinion surveys. Usually the results of laboratory experiments are not called research papers but reports.

It follows from the definition above that some kinds of subjects are not appropriate for a research or investigative paper. Subjects which draw wholly on personal experience, for example, or those which rely heavily on personal opinion—such as which is the loveliest season of the year—require no special investigation and are not research topics. Moreover, topics on which all the necessary reading can be done in a single source provide no scope for research; it has all been done. Such topics as the climate of Guadalajara, Mexico, or the fundamentals of bookbinding are poor choices because they can be covered by reading a single source, such as an article in an encyclopedia, an atlas, or a general book on Mexico or on printing and book manufacture. Any research worth doing requires putting material together from a variety of sources to get a new compilation of information or a new interpretation.

While investigating, you should keep a careful record of the sources used and of the facts and inferences you discover and plan to use. When writing up your results, the sources of the materials used are carefully indicated so that readers can check if they want to. There are special techniques for all these processes, and these we shall discuss later in this chapter, under the headings of bibliography cards, note cards, footnotes, and final bibliography.

Finally, the research paper is longer than other papers you will write in this course, and thus requires more planning and organization. Because the subject is one the writer learns about only gradually as he reads, the preplanning cannot be done all at once ahead of time but piecemeal, as the subject opens up. Yet all we have said earlier about prethinking and prewriting applies. And it is just as important to distinguish between facts, inferences, and opinions, to recognize reliable sources, and to avoid fallacies, as in any other kind of writing. Because you are working on a larger scale, it is even more important to plan out a precise purpose statement or thesis, a good opener, a clear main paragraph, and accurate controlling sentences throughout.

KINDS OF RESEARCH PAPERS

The two general classes of research papers are to convey information or to interpret evidence and explain its significance. Thus each will be either informative or interpretive. Research papers are not written to entertain or to create an impression, though an evaluative paper tries to convince and may also attempt to stimulate the reader to take a specific desired action, that is, to actuate.

The Informative Paper

An informative paper is largely factual in content. It may be concerned with describing the status of the subject, its history, how it is constructed, how it works, or how it is used. Such a paper has one main function: to give information in a way that enables the reader to understand something he did not already know. Typical titles of informative papers are "The Building of the Hoover Dam," "The Origins of the Bolshoi Ballet Company," "The Uses of Astronomy in the Building of Tombs in Ancient Egypt," "Women's Changing Roles," and "Design of the Clipper Ship."

The Status Report

The simplest kind of informative research paper is the factual one mainly concerned with describing or defining a person (for example Thomas Jefferson), a place (Pompeii), an object (the newest gas-saving carburetor), an organization (the World Bank), or an idea (Marxism) by telling what it is, what it looks like, or what state of development it is in.

The Historical Report

In a slightly more complex form, this kind of paper may trace the origin, development, and history of its topic, usually though not necessarily in chronological order. The time factor adds complications to the treatment. The writer must be aware of improvements and deteriorations over time, and these introduce an element of analysis and judgment into the discussion — even if no more than deciding whether changes have been good or bad.

The Process or Procedural Report

Papers on such topics as solar heating, the generation of power by atomic energy, how a digital computer works or how it is programmed, will almost certainly lead you into a discussion of the steps in a process (how something works) or the steps in a procedure (how to do something). Whether such a paper will be more or less technical depends not only on the subject, but on at least one other of your predetermined elements, the reader-writer relationship. For some readers, your discussion can be fairly general, describing in broad terms the main stages in the process, the significance of each, and who and what is involved. For other more technically-oriented readers, a process description may be very specific about ingredients, materials, tools, apparatus, and operations performed at each stage in the process. Throughout your planning, reading, note-taking, and outlining, what you do will be almost totally controlled by the basic decisions you make about kind of paper, degree of detail, and nature of audience.

The Interpretive Paper

The interpretive paper goes one important step beyond the informative, for it presents not only information which you have gathered, but interpretations, inferences, and judgments which you yourself have developed from your study of the basic material. The interpretive paper thus has a second and higher level of interest: in the interaction of your mind with your information, and in the ideas and conclusions you have developed yourself. This second level of mental activity is reflected in the following interpretive variations on the possible factual titles we cited before: "The Hoover Dam and the Dangers of Erosion," "The Bolshoi Ballet and Socialist Attitudes," "Egyptian Astronomy: Science or Magic?" "Women's Changing Roles and a Changing Morality," and "The Clipper Ship and the China Trade." In each of these modifications a question, a problem, or an element of controversy has been added. It is this which gives scope to the second level of mental activity we mentioned above.

The Causal Investigative Paper

While some historical papers, and many process papers, require more than straight reporting of facts, few make such demands on your thinking processes as do even the simpler investigative papers. These not only tell *what* happened, but *how* and *why* it happened, and so require not only facts but a firm grasp of causes and effects and sure control of the techniques of argument. The interpretive paper rests not on a simple *subject sentence but on a thesis* that states the conclusion you have reached after examining a problem to which there may be several answers. For example, you may conclude that the chief cause of high meat prices is the shortage of feed grain—not poor transportation, larger population, or general increase in costs everywhere. Because there is evidence for each of these answers, you must be sure your evidence is stronger, and you must not exaggerate your claims. This means that while you present facts, you use them not for their own sake but to support your judgments and inferences, your conclusion, after you have examined the evidence fairly.

The Persuasive or Argumentative Paper

The persuasive or argumentative paper is designed to prove a contention or support a point of view; it is directed at a recognized adversary, one who disagrees. Therefore it is more argumentative than the causal analysis paper and openly designed to win support rather than merely to analyze causes and effects. You are therefore at pains to establish the reliability and qualifications of your sources and to win over the reader. This is accomplished by finding common grounds of agreement before the differences between opposing views are pointed out and before the evidence for your conclusions and against those of your opponents is presented. Depending on how objective or how personal you wish to be, you may use objective or emotionally colored and loaded language: you may call your opponent a *statesman,* a *politician,* or a *ward-healer.* You will, if you are honest, believe the views you support, but the degree of objectivity or subjectivity with which you support them may vary greatly.

MAKING A START

Choosing a General Subject

As with any other paper, the first step is to pick out a *general subject.* Because this will probably be the longest paper you write in the course, and will carry the greatest weight, this choice should be made with extreme care; it is wise to consult your instructor before making it final. He or she should be able to tell you whether the subject is one properly adaptable to research in the time and space available and should be of help in guiding you to a specific topic within the broad area of your general subject, though you will not usually be able to pin down your specific topic until you have done a moderate amount of reading and research. Limiting the subject goes hand in hand with reading about it, and a specific topic should not be considered absolutely final until you have read enough to be quite sure that your topic is adaptable to the research procedure as we defined it above, that there is enough material available to you, and that you can cover it all and write your paper in the allotted time. To summarize: select and limit your topic as you do your preliminary reading, and you should not consider these processes finished until you are sure you can find enough material to carry out your specific purpose.

Knowing Your Library

The first essential to efficient reading for a research paper is knowing your library. You may have had orientation lectures about it or a preliminary trip to your college library. If not, there may be an instruction booklet in the lobby, and librarians will always answer sincere questions and requests for assistance. The two most important things to learn about in any library are the *card catalog* and the *main reference room.* Usually the first of these is located in the second. The *microfilm* or *microfiche file* is another source of research materials which is appearing in more libraries and with which you should also familiarize yourself.

The Main Reference Room

The main reference room is a large room lined with bookshelves containing reference books of all kinds: dictionaries, atlases, encyclopedias, annuals, and books listing newspaper and magazine articles—shortcuts to condensed information on all subjects. If this is your first visit, spend a half hour or so just finding out what's there. In particular, find out the location of the following reference books. There are thousands of others, but these will be good ones to begin with for a very wide range of subjects.

American Heritage Dictionary. This dictionary uses clear, understandable definitions, authoritative word histories, and many illustrations. New words and terms from the rapidly expanding fields of business, science, and technology are included.

Reader's Guide to Periodical Literature. This is the most widely used guide to magazine articles on general subject. The opening pages of the *Guide* tell you how to use it.

The New York Times Index. This lists important news stories and articles in the largest newspaper in the country, and is useful (by referring to dates) in leading you to articles in other newspapers you may want to examine.

Webster's Third New International Dictionary of the English Language. This is the largest United States dictionary and a good place to start for an inclusive definition of almost any word you might wish to look up. A dictionary also has a vast quantity of general information.

Encyclopaedia Britannica and *Encyclopedia Americana.* These are the two biggest and best general encyclopedias in English, and they will give you an excellent introductory article on almost any subject you may write about except very recent subjects.

Dictionary of American Biography. A large set with articles on important Americans not living.

Dictionary of National Biography. The British equivalent of the above.

Notable American Women: 1607–1950. A three-volume dictionary with articles on important American women not living.

Winchell's Guide to Reference Books. This is the most useful general list of reference books. If nothing else, you should look into it to get some idea how many reference books there are, and what broad fields they cover.

The Card Catalog

The card catalog consists of a number of large cases containing drawers filled with 3″ x 5″ cards. These cards list every *book* the library contains—they do not list magazines or newspapers, for which you should check the reference books listed above. The cards in the catalog are listed alphabetically, and for every book there will be at least three cards, one listing the book by the last name of its *author,* one by the first important word in its *title,* and one or more others by *subjects* with which the book deals.

Typical catalog cards look like this:

QE365.H85
H965   **Hurlbut, Cornelius Searle,** 1906-
            Minerals and man, by Cornelius S. Hurlbut, Jr. Photos. by

---

QE365.H85   Minerals and man.
H965   **Hurlbut, Cornelius Searle,** 1906-
            Minerals and man, by Cornelius S. Hurlbut, Jr. Photos. by
            Studio Hartmann ₍and others₎   New York, Random House
            ₍1968₎

QE365.H85   Mineralogy.
H965   **Hurlbut, Cornelius Searle,** 1906-
            Minerals and man, by Cornelius S. Hurlbut, Jr. Photos. by
            Studio Hartmann ₍and others₎   New York, Random House
            ₍1968₎

            304 p.   illus. (part col.)   29 cm. $15.00

            "A Chanticleer Press edition."

            1. Mineralogy.   I. Title.

            QE365.H85   549   **68-28329**
                                                                    MARC

            Library of Congress

The three cards shown above are actually three copies of the same card, printed by the Library of Congress and distributed to libraries throughout the country. The first card is the basic author card. The second has the title typed above the first line, and the third has the subject "Mineralogy" typed in. All three have the library call number typed in the upper left corner. This is the Library of Congress number used by many libraries and printed (except for the final unit) at the bottom of the card. That line also contains two other numbers used in the identification of the book. The three cards will be filed alphabetically, so that you will have three chances of finding the book—by author, by title, or by subject. Some books have subject cards filed under three or four different headings.

Microform Materials

Recent technology has enabled libraries to store vast amounts of written material, such as several years of daily newspapers, by reducing it photographically onto strips called microfilm or cards called microfiche. There are indexes of materials which are reproduced in this form, and if your library does have microfilm or microfiche files you will probably find the indexes near the reference books.

Microform materials are often stored in a separate room that will usually contain readers as well as the files. Readers are machines which enlarge the film and light it from the rear. It is possible to scan the film to locate the particular page you need, and then focus the screen until the type is a size you can read easily.

The most common materials in microform are newspapers, such as the *New York Times,* and journal articles from specific academic areas, such as education's ERIC files.

Preliminary Reading

Once you have a general subject, you are ready to begin your preliminary reading. With most general subjects it is wise to start with a few survey articles in reference books such as encyclopedias which will give you a broad overview and may lead you to a specific topic. Thus the *Britannica* has a fifteen-page article on the general subject of petroleum, with sections on the more specific topics of exploration, production, offshore drilling, natural gas, transportation by pipeline and tanker, storage, refining, supply and demand, and the history of the petroleum industry. In addition to reference books, your preliminary exploration should also take you to the card catalog for books on the general subject which can lead you to a specific topic of your liking.

In this first search, don't read everything word for word; scan the material with just one purpose in mind: *to find a specific topic.* At this point don't take notes; they would be so general that you could never use them and you would be simply wasting time. Don't take notes until you have firmly decided on your specific topic and begin to discover specific facts and inferences you will want to use in your paper.

Bibliography Cards

Since your finished paper will include a bibliography—a list of books and articles you actually use—you should begin making out bibliography cards for books and articles as soon as you discover useful ones. Using ink or typewriter (not pencil) on 3″ x 5″ cards, record the author, title, facts of publication, and library call number, being sure that you have for each item all the information you will need when you compile the bibliography you will turn in with your paper (see pages 372–373). Following are some specimens.

For a typical single-author book:

```
Hurlbut, Cornelius S.              QE 365.
                                   H85
Minerals and Man                   H965
New York:  Random House, 1968


Good section on petroleum
```

For a book which is a compilation and has an editor rather than an author:

```
de Santillana, Giorgio, ed.

The Age of Adventure:  The Renaissance
Philosophers Selected, with Introduction and
Interpretive Commentary

Vol. II of six in The Great Ages of Western
Philosophy
Boston:  Houghton Mifflin, 1957.
```

For an article in a magazine or a journal:

```
Wagner, Vern, ''The Offense of Poetry,''
College English 35 (May, 1973), 045-1059.
```

For an article from a newspaper:

```
Reston, James, ''Don't Count Nixon Out,''
The New York Times, Wednesday, January 23,
1974, p. 33, col. 1.
```

Note that authors names are given last name first for alphabetizing. Titles of articles are in quotation marks; titles of books, journals, newspapers, and other separate publications are underlined to represent italic type. Enough is given about volume, number, date and page of items in periodicals to make them easy to find.

NOTE-TAKING

Don't start taking notes too soon. The first books and articles you read will probably be so general that they will give only the broad outlines of your subject. In general, you should take few if any notes until you have firmed up your specific topic.

Take your notes on cards, preferably 3″ x 5″, and keep them separate from your bibliography cards but key the two types of cards together by putting the author's name and the page number on each note card. A note should be a logical unit, made up of fact, opinion, or inference, which you will use *in one place* in your paper. Never take a note so long, or covering so much, that it spreads over several points in your outline and so may have to be split up between different places in your paper. Each note should cover just one item which you credit to one source. Items which are common information to a half dozen or more sources will probably become so well known to you that you won't need a note on them, nor will they have to be credited to any particular source in a foot-note (pages 370–372).

Your notes should be of three kinds (1) statements of fact *in your own words;* (2) summaries *in your own words* of chains of reasoning or lines or argument; (3) quotations of striking phrases or statements *in the exact words of the source.* The following is a factual note of the first type:

Source
Topic

Factual Note — Student's
Words, No Quotation
Marks

```
Engel, 114
DNA molecule—nature and size

Most substances have mol. of fixed size &
comp.: X atoms of this, Y atoms of that.
DNA only one known that varies in size &
specific comp., tho not genl. nature. Very
large: 1 virus has DNA with known molec. wt.
130,000,000 (hydrogen atom=1). Whole chromosome
could be 1 DNA mol.
```

The following is a summary note of the second type:

```
Source
Topic




Summary Note—
Student's Words, No
Quotation Marks
```

```
Lindsey, 95–98
Resources, North & South

North's 22 states had 22 mil. pop., South's
11 had 9 mil, or 2½ to 1. Out of 9, South had
3.5 mil Negroes, used as auxiliaries but not
soldiers. Most trained Army officers went to
South, tho Navy loyal to North. North ultimately
used 2 mil. men; South 900,000, hit peak late 63,
& thereafter declined with heavy casualties. North
had major industries, twice as much RR track &
equipment, most shipping. North's size, wealth, &
power gradually weakened South's military skill
& fighting power.
```

The information given in this note covered four pages in the source and is here reduced to a single 3″ x 5″ card. In the paper, the writer will "de-condense" this material, and may combine it with other material about the strength and resources of the North and the South obtained from other sources. Notice that the note covers one topic only: size and resources. It says nothing about the fighting of the war, the home front, morale, or any of a dozen or more other topics that might be covered in the paper. The note is a *unit,* even though it does condense material covering four pages in the original source.

The following is a quotation in a note of the third type:

```
Source
Topic




Quotation—Author's
Exact Words, in
Quotation Marks
```

```
Laird, 263
Noah Webster
   ''In Webster, America produced what might have been
expected from the New World, the preeminent cracker-[sic]
barrel lexicographer, who knew all the annwers. More
a hack of all intellectual trades than a scholar, he
was passably schooled but not learned, not even in the
subject for which he is now best known. . . . Ignorance
never dampened his fire, nor did a sense of humor temper
his finality.''
```

This note copies the author's words exactly and puts them in quotation marks. The two notes above are in the student's words, not the author's; hence they do not use quotation marks.

Photocopying

If you find a particularly long passage that you want to quote, wholly or in part, it is often possible to have it reproduced by one of the many photocopying processes in order to save yourself the time of copying it in longhand. The time-saving feature of photocopying is an advantage, but overuse of photocopying can leave you with a stack of undigested material that lacks the interpretation and phrasing of your own notetaking and therefore only increases the time it takes you to shape it to your own needs.

PLANNING THE PAPER Using Your Notes

We said earlier that because the material for a research paper does not come out of your experience but is gathered slowly by reading, planning can progress only as material comes to light. After choosing a specific subject, the next important decision is whether the paper will be informative or interpretive, and of which particular kind.

To help you make these decisions and to help you organize your material, read your notes frequently and organize them as your work progresses. You will soon see that your notes begin to form groups on particular topics, that on some topics you will develop a good deal of information quite quickly, and that others will remain sparse and thin. These groups will begin to suggest major and minor topics, will help you direct your reading toward filling the gaps, and will show you that certain gaps simply cannot be filled.

As your notes pile up and groups develop, begin to make tentative outlines, and keep working notes and outlines against each other. There is no better way to develop an outline than to let it grow naturally out of the material you have discovered.

At some point you will find that you are turning up little that you haven't read before, and that you have an outline and a clear thesis or subject sentence for a paper you feel confident that you can write. When you reach this point it is time to stop reading and start writing, although you may later find gaps you hadn't foreseen and be forced back to the library to fill these in.

Working Out Your Pattern

Because the research paper is longer than other papers you have written, it will help in your final planning if you make full use of things you have learned about organization and structure. Begin by reviewing the section on the types of research papers on pages 354–356 in this chapter, with particular reference to the kind of paper you are writing, informative or interpretive, and of which variety. Then part by part, decide what your paper is to contain and how it is to be developed. The following scheme will be helpful.

The Title

The title (pages 145–148) should suggest the factual and objective to indicate that this is a research paper. It should also suggest something of the tone and the degree of objectivity you intend. Thus a factual, objective paper on pesticides could be titled "DDT and Other Chemical Synthetic Pesticides," whereas the most famous book against pesticides bore the emotional and even literary title, *Silent Spring,* in reference to the danger that pesticides may kill off all the birds.

The Opener

Like other kinds of papers, the research paper may have a special opener (pages 149–152), or it may simply start with the main paragraph. In an informative paper the opener may attempt to engage the reader because of the importance or interest of the subject. In an interpretive paper, it may point out the dangers and advantages of different beliefs and courses of action to the reader and for the general welfare. In either case an opener will establish reader contact and induce him to read.

The Main Paragraph

Many research papers, especially informative ones, start right out with the main paragraph (pages 161–168), quickly announce the general subject and the specific topic, indicate whether the paper is informative or interpretive, and move quickly to the subject or thesis sentence. This sentence in turn should suggest the pattern for the developing or supporting section — the body of the paper. Thus in a status report it will touch on the characteristics of a person, the elements in an organization, the parts of a machine. In a process report it will give steps in a procedure, and perhaps tools, materials, parts, and techniques. In a causal investigation it will suggest that the paper will discover, enumerate, and assess causes and results, perhaps in order of occurrence or importance. And in a persuasive paper it may foreshadow arguments for both sides or for one side only. Whatever the form and content of the developing section, the purpose or thesis sentence should suggest it.

Additional Explanation

The opening section may give other information. It may clarify terms and concepts, explain the purpose more fully, or define terms. In an argumentative paper it may state the common ground — points agreed on — before discussing those at issue. In a paper on life on an American Indian reservation, it may be useful to explain historical vs. cultural anthropology, and to explain why cultural anthopologists place such stress on the languages of the peoples they study. Historical background may be needed in other papers, such as early stages in the development of the submarine, or canal building in America before the railroad age.

The Developing and Supporting Section

The body of the paper, this section presents the bulk of your research. In a primarily factual paper, it will give the main account of the subject, the main description of its appearance, parts, function, uses, development, or history. A factual paper can benefit particularly from charts, graphs, tables, drawings, and photographs. For a process or procedure paper the main parts of this section will be the steps or stages, together with any historical or other background, the explanation of any principles or laws involved, and any tools, instruments, ingredients, or supplies. In an investigative or persuasive paper any or all of the above kinds of materials may appear, but the main section will be organized around the problem, the possible solutions, and finally the chosen solution. In the course of doing this, you will present evidence, evaluate sources, discuss alternative answers, support your views and refute others, and lead finally to the solution you believe to be the correct one.

In an informative paper the structure of the main section will generally reflect that of the *subject:* a machine part by part; a process step by step; a historical event chronologically, and so on. In an interpretive or persuasive paper, the main section will generally reflect the structure of *your thought:* the points in your analysis such as reasons why the South lost the Civil War; the arguments for alternative solutions to a problem, ending with your own; sources of information or testimony, beginning perhaps with the least reliable and ending with the most.

The Concluding Section

The concluding section of an informative paper is likely to be largely summary in tone and intent. It may restate the main facts of the subject, the main developments in a chronological account or steps in a process or procedure. It will usually introduce no new material or new ideas, though it may end with an anecdote or other application to give a pleasant or surprise twist at the end.

In contrast, the concluding section of an analytical or a persuasive paper will frequently contain some element of climax rather than restatement. It may restate the thesis in a striking way, it may point out the future benefits from taking the right course of action or the evils of taking a wrong course. It may urge the readers to action or give them dire warnings. It will usually end on a higher key than the conclusion of a factual paper.

WRITING THE PAPER Transforming Notes into Your Own Discussion

When you have made final decisions about your predetermined elements, organized your notes, and constructed an outline, you are ready to begin the first draft. You must now learn the difference between the right and the wrong way to write a research paper.

The *wrong* way is simply to string your notes together, copying out or paraphrasing one after another without adding anything of your own. The *right* way is to write a discussion of your own, divided into sections and paragraphs that grow out of your outline with *your* opener, main paragraph, thesis and controlling sentences, and with material from *your* notes worked into your writing as support for *your* controlling material (see Chapter 7). The better you know your material, the more you have the content of your notes firmly in mind, the easier this is to do. If you aren't really on top of your material, if you don't have your outline and notes clearly in mind, you will almost certainly slip into the wrong way.

And there is nothing duller, to write or to read, than a research paper which is merely a tissue of other people's material taken over bodily.

Using the three specimen notes on pages 362–364 we will illustrate how this process works. The following passage weaves material from the factual note on the DNA molecule into an original discussion.

As Engel points out, one striking difference between the DNA molecule and that of every other known substance is that DNA does not have a fixed composition,* but varies immensely in detail. Contrast, for instance, the effect of the genes in an elephant with those in a flea. And yet the basic materials of DNA are always the same. The difference is in the number of units and the way they are put together.

* Leonard Engel, *The New Genetics*, p. 114.

This paragraph is expressed in the writer's own words and acknowledges the source of the information in a *footnote* even though he does not quote the author directly. The example of the elephant and the flea is the student writer's contribution, and the information from the source, which is clearly acknowledged, is expressed in the writer's own words.

The following uses material from the summary note on the Civil War.

The struggle was uneven from the start, and could hardly have ended differently, short of a miracle. The North had over twice the population, and of the South's 9 million, 3.5 million were blacks—scarcely dependable as soldiers in such a conflict. Thus the North was able to put 2 million men into the field in the four years of the war, while the South could muster less than a million. While the South attracted most trained Army officers, a quick advantage especially at the beginning, the Navy stuck with the North. In industry and transportation, the same overwhelming odds prevailed.*

* David Lindsey, *Americans in Conflict: The Civil War and Reconstruction*, pp. 95–98.

Again, the writer has used the material in his own way and in his own words. He starts with his own controlling sentence, and rewords details of the summary note in order to use them as support. And he acknowledges the source of his information in a footnote even though he does not quote the author's exact words.

Finally, the following embeds the quotation about Noah Webster in a discussion of the writer's own, so that the quotation becomes support

The American folk hero (or heroine) is very different in fact and in legend. George Washington never chopped down a cherry tree; Annie Oakley was graceful and soft-spoken and did needlework between performances; and Noah Webster, long known as the father of American dictionaries, was a pretty small potato, according to Professor Charlton Laird: "In Webster, America produced what might have been expected from the New World, the preeminent crackerbarrel lexicographer, who knew all the answers. More a hack of all intellectual trades than a scholar, he was passably schooled but not learned, not even in the subject for which he is now best known."*

Language in America, p. 263.

Note here that the writer copied the quotation exactly, with quotation marks, but chose not to use the final sentence. Therefore he omitted the three periods that showed an omission but kept the one that marked the end of the sentence. Note also that he used the quotation to support his own controlling sentence about American folk heroes. The quotation is not simply thrown in; it is carefully prepared for.

Another example of incorporating material from notes into a research paper is provided on pages 370–371. Two note cards and the bibliography cards for the two sources from which the notes were taken are shown, as well as the page from the student's paper in which the material from these notes was used. This page also contains footnotes citing the sources.

Plagiarism

This is as good a place as any to mention the practice known as **plagiarism** (from a Latin word meaning kidnapping): presenting the product of other people's work and thought as if it were one's own. In the light of what we have just said about the technique of citing sources both in your own writing and in footnotes, it is easy to see that much of what might look like plagiarism, or theft, is actually just the product of poor writing —not citing sources carefully enough, thus unintentionally presenting other people's ideas and conclusions as if they were your own. Once you get the hang of citing sources properly, it is easy to avoid any suspicion of this kind of unacknowledged borrowing. Moreover, citing sources carefully has some very practical advantages: material goes farther when it is handled properly, and your writing is more interesting to read, so that you are likely to earn a substantially higher grade for the same amount of reading and note-taking.

Examples of two types of note cards prepared by a student for the writing of a research paper appear on page 370. The contents of these cards were used in a paper dealing with the adverse effects immature children suffer when admitted into kindergarten before they are ready. Opposite these cards is the page in which they were incorporated. One bibliography card was used by the writer to prepare his footnotes by using the code word "Tussing," the last name of the author. The bibliography cards also are shown.

Revision

Because a research paper is long and requires unfamiliar techniques, the first draft may need unusually careful revision. If possible, put it aside for a day or two so you can come back to it with a fresh eye. Then read it carefully, checking it against your outline and against the section on working out your pattern in this chapter. Compare each use of borrowed material with the note it came from and be sure you make it clear by the wording of your text and by the use of footnotes when you have used borrowed material. Check quotations for accuracy, and factual and summary notes for emphasis and coverage. Be sure all controlling sentences are clear and that there are transitions between points in your outline, particularly wherever there is any chance of misunderstanding. Check all footnotes against your bibliography cards and be sure they are numbered serially throughout your paper. Specimen footnote forms are given on pages 371–372. Follow these carefully.

As a final step in revision, read through the entire paper *as a piece of writing,* aloud if possible, to see how it sounds.

Preparing the Final Draft

Your instructor may ask you to follow certain specified forms in preparing the final draft of your paper. If so, be sure to follow the instructions carefully. If possible, use a typewriter. The final paper may contain any or all of the following items:

1. *A title page or cover sheet.* This may contain the title of your paper, your name, section number, and the date.
2. *Your outline.* This is usually presented on a separate sheet, with the subject or thesis sentence at the top, and the major heads and subheads marked and indented according to the following scheme:

   I.
     A.
       1.
         a.

   Few outlines for student research papers will require more than three levels of heading. Topics should be in parallel form, all sentences or all phrases.
3. *The paper.* Pages should be numbered in the top right hand corner, and footnotes at the bottoms of the pages. For each page, estimate as well as you can the number of lines you will need for footnotes, and put a tiny pencil mark at the left edge of the sheet where you think the last line of text will come, leave one blank line, then put in your footnotes—single spaced if you typewrite. (See specimen page 371.)
4. *The bibliography.* This begins on a new sheet at the end of the paper, and is a single alphabetical listing of all books and articles you have used. For specimen bibliography see page 372.

SPECIMEN FOOTNOTE AND BIBLIOGRAPHICAL FORMS

Both your footnotes and the bibliographical entries at the end of your paper will be based on information you have recorded on the bibliography cards you made out early in your reading.[1] You should have a biblio-

[1] Both the footnote and the bibliographical entries which follow are based on those of *The MLA Style Sheet,* 2d ed., 1970.

Tussing, 111. Right attitude toward   20
                  problem solving   Effect on
       ''A child is able to progress in mathematics,   learning
reading, or spelling to the extent
he has successfully handled similar problems
previously.''

Tussing, 116. Cycle of skill mastery   21
                                             Effect on
                                             learning

Success in learning math, etc. increases
drive to learn a subject, leading to more success.
The opposite is also true. Failure increases
discouragement and decreases desire to learn
a subject, leading to more failure.

Note cards

Tussing, Lyle, <u>Psychology</u> <u>for</u> <u>Better</u> <u>Living.</u>[11]
   New York: John Wiley and Sons, 1959.

English, Spurgeon O., and Gerald Pearson.[10]
   <u>Emotional</u> <u>Problems</u> <u>of</u> <u>Living.</u> New York:
   W. W. Norton and Co., 1967.

Bibliog-
raphy
cards

It may be years before pleasure in reading overcomes the pain of failure. The child may always be a poor reader or not read any more than is necessary. Prevention is the best course as the cure may require abandonment of reading and starting all over again later to build a success-pleasure pattern.

Another psychological fact can be summarized thus: if a slight error (handicap, lack of preparation, and so forth) is added to a slight error, is added to another, the final error can be too great for adjustment.

See card 20 on page 370

Tussing points out that ''a child is able to progress in mathematics, reading, or spelling to the extent that he has successfully handled similar problems previously.''[1] His development of emotional and intellectual maturity is based on a background of successful problem solving.

Tussing goes on to say that success and failure also play an important role in social adjustments. Parents themselves, driving and ambitious, become disappointed in the child when he fails or is slow. This makes him feel inferior. He thinks less of himself and more unsure of his ability to enjoy the acceptance of others.[2] Even if he later adjusts and regains ambition, he has a history of failure and doubt. This gives him a poor self-image which can cause discouragement, defeat, and hopelessness.[3]

See card 21 on page 370

[1] Lyle Tussing, _Psychology for Better Living,_ p. 111.
[2] Tussing, p. 116.
[3] Spurgeon O. English and Gerald Pearson, _Emotional Problems of Living,_ p. 139.

graphical entry for each source you cite and for each footnote (and perhaps for other sources of general use as well). Since footnotes and bibliography are keyed together, certain facts of publication which appear in the bibliography need not also appear in the footnotes. In the following lists, study together the items that refer to the same sources.

Footnote Forms

Standard reference to a book:

1. Cornelius S. Hurlbut, *Minerals and Man,* p. 31. (Place and publisher's name are not given since they appear in the bibliography.)

Subsequent references:

2. Hurlbut, p. 42. (Sufficient unless the two notes are some distance apart.)
3. Hurlbut, *Minerals and Man,* p. 42. (Repeat or give short form of title if second reference is some distance from first.)

Standard reference to a book with two or more authors:

4. Spurgeon O. English and Gerald Pearson, *Emotional Problems of Living,* p. 116.

Reference to a book compiled by an editor:

5. Giorgio de Santillana, ed., "Copernicus," in *The Age of Adventure,* p. 157. (See bibliographical entry for additional facts of publication.)

Standard reference to an article from a magazine or journal:

6. Vern Wagner, "The Offense of Poetry," *College English,* 35 (May 1973), 1046.

Subsequent references:

7. Wagner, "The Offense of Poetry," p. 1058.
8. Wagner, p. 1059.

Standard reference to a newspaper article:

9. James Reston, "Don't Count Nixon Out," *The New York Times,* Wednesday, January 23, 1974, p. 33, col. 1.

Standard reference to an encyclopedia or other reference book alphabetically arranged:

10. "Daniel Boone," *Dictionary of American Biography.* (Page and volume numbers not necessary since arrangement is alphabetical.)

Two Latin abbreviations, once used extensively, are now used infrequently. *Ibid.,* for *ibidem,* "the same," used by itself meant that the reference was to the same work, same page, as the reference immediately preceding. When used with a page number it referred to a different place in the same work. *Op. cit.,* for *opere citato,* "in the work cited," was used with the author's name and a new page number in references to works cited earlier than the immediately preceding footnote. There is little reason for using either abbreviation.

Bibliographical Forms

The bibliography lists all the books and articles used in the preparation of the paper in alphabetical order (hence the first author is given last name first). The bibliography also contains essential facts of publication, which are therefore omitted from footnotes. Carefully compare the following with the corresponding footnote forms above.

"Daniel Boone," *Dictionary of American Biography.* (Daniel Boone is subject, not author. In this work, articles are anonymous.)

English, Spurgeon O., and Gerald Pearson. *Emotional Problems of Living.* New York: W. W. Norton, 1967. (First author only is given last name first for alphabetizing.)

Hurlbut, Cornelius S., Jr. *Minerals and Man.* New York: Random House, 1968.

Reston, James. "Don't Count Nixon Out," *The New York Times,* Wednesday, January 23, 1974, p. 33, col. 1.

de Santillana, Giorgio, ed. *The Age of Adventure: The Renaissance Philosophers.* Vol. II in *The Great Ages of Western Philosophy.* Boston: Houghton Mifflin, 1957. (Note subtitle not given in footnote; also that this is a volume in a series).

Wagner, Vern, "The Offense of Poetry," *College English,* 34, 4 (May 1973), 1045–59.

PRACTICE in Achieving This Chapter's Objectives

Practice in investigative procedures in preparing to write a research paper, in writing a research paper according to a suggested pattern of development, and correctly inserting into the final draft the necessary footnotes and bibliography.

	Application
1. Writing bibliography entries correctly.	1, 3
2. Writing footnote entries correctly.	3, 5
3. Taking notes on note cards efficiently.	3
4. Writing a paraphrase effectively.	4, 5
5. Writing a summary.	6
6. Applying the principles studied in this text, expecially those in this chapter, in the writing of a full length research paper.	7
7. You Be the Judge	

APPLICATION 18-1

In your library find at least two sources written by different authors on any three of the following subjects. Prepare a bibliography card for each in the manner discussed in this chapter.

1. An account of recent research with dolphins.
2. The World War II battle at Anzio, Italy.
3. The life of Virginia Woodhull, candidate for President.
4. Capital punishment.
5. Consumer awareness.
6. The chief exports of Lebanon.
7. The life and works of St. Augustine.

APPLICATION 18-2

On the lines below, enter a footnote for each of the following exactly as you would enter all of them on the same page of the final draft. Be sure to number them correctly.

1. The first reference to a book.

_____

_____

2. A subsequent reference to the same page of the preceding book.

_____

_____

3. A first reference to a book with more than three authors.

_____

_____

4. A subsequent reference to another page in No. 1 above.

_____

_____

5. A first reference to a book with both an author and an editor.

_____

_____

6. A signed article in an encyclopedia.

_____

_____

7. An unsigned magazine article.

8. A first reference to a poem in an anthology of poetry with one editor.

APPLICATION 18-3

For each of the following items, prepare one bibliography card and one note card as if you had looked up the information in the library to use in a research paper. Be sure to use 3 x 5" or 4 x 6" cards only. Write clearly in ink.

1. On pages 60 and 61 the authors say that a typical ten-year-old likes to read, to tell stories, to memorize poems and to take dictation. His handwriting is described as "loose and sloppy." This is from a book titled Youth: The Years from Ten to Sixteen. It was published by Harper and Brothers in New York. The copyright date is 1956. The authors are Arnold Gesell, Frances L. Ilg, and Louise B. Ames. The general subject of your paper will be teaching composition to fifth graders.

2. You plan to write a paper on prominent living jazz personalities. Time Magazine describes jazz pianist Tommy Flanagan as "the most retiring man since Li'l Abner." This is from the January 11, 1963, issue, Volume LXXXI, No. 2. The article is unsigned and headed "Modesty's Rewards." It is entirely on page 49.

3. You wish to quote a line, "The seal's wide, spindrift gaze toward paradise," from a poem by Hart Crane titled "Voyages II," which you found in a volume of his collected poems, *The Collected Poems of Hart Crane,* edited by Waldo Frank, Liveright Publishing Corporation, New York, 1946. You take it down as an example of a sea image for a paper on recurrent images in modern poetry. It appears on page 103.

4. In *Meeting With Japan,* Fosco Maraini says that there are five characteristics of the Japanese that help explain their success in the modern world. These are (1) "Their sense of communion with nature," (2) their "extraordinary manual skill," (3) "the traditional specialization of the classes," (4) "their frugal and Spartan habits," and (5) "the docility of groups to their leader." You are writing a paper on the post-war economic boom in Japan. This information occurs on pages 71–73. The book was published by the Viking Press, Inc., New York, in 1960.

5. "The skin varies in thickness from .02 inch, on the eyelids, to .17 inch or more, on the palms of the hands and soles of the feet." This quotation came from an unsigned article on "Skin" in *The Universal Standard Encyclopedia,* p. 7791, Vol. 21. This is from the 1957 edition. You are writing a paper on techniques of skin grafting.

6. The Outdoor Recreation Review Commission of the Rockefeller Foundation's "Report to Congress, 1962" declares, "Highest priority should be given to acquisition of areas located closest to major population centers and other areas that are immediately threatened. The need is critical . . . ." This is quoted in an article by William Peeples in the *Atlantic,* February 1963, Vol. 211. The article is "The Indiana Dunes and Pressure Politics," from page 84 to 88. You are writing a paper on the need for more national parks. This is on page 88.

7. In the article cited in the previous question, Peeples says that at one time the Indiana dunes stretched along Lake Michigan for twenty-five miles between East Chicago and Michigan City, but that now only about seven miles are unspoiled. This information is on page 85.

8. You are writing a paper on the new explorations into the phenomenon of memory. In a library file copy of *The Ann Arbor News* for February 11, 1963, on page 17, you see an article headed "Cram a Pill Down? Someday Perhaps It'll Help You to Learn More Easily." You want to use information from this article about a psychology experiment in which flatworms are conditioned to expect a shock whenever they see a red light. The learning seems to be retained if the worm is cut in half, and each half grows a new worm. Untrained worms learn faster if they are fed on trained worms.

APPLICATION 18-4

Select a brief editorial from a local newspaper, and on the lines provided, write a paraphrase of it. Cut the editorial out of the paper and attach it to the page.

_____

_____

_____

_____

_____

_____

_____

_____

_____

_____

_____

_____

_____

_____

_____

_____

APPLICATION 18-5

Using the card catalog in your library, find a copy of the poem entitled "The Silken Tent" by Robert Frost. On the lines immediately following, write a footnote giving the source in which you found the poem.

_____

_____

Below write a paraphrase of the poem:

_____

_____

_____

_____

_____

APPLICATION 18-6

Cut out a news story from a local newspaper, and attach it to this page. At the right, write a factual note based on it.

_____
_____
_____
_____
_____
_____
_____
_____
_____
_____
_____
_____
_____
_____
_____
_____

APPLICATION 18-7

Write a research paper according to the instructions given by your instructor. Be sure to indicate your dominant general purpose and the kind of research paper you intend yours to be.

YOU BE THE JUDGE

Evaluator's Initials ☐☐☐

Date _____

Section _____

Grade _____

Writer's Name _____

Date _____ Section _____

Title of paper _____

Chapter _____ Application No. _____

General Instructions on the You Be the Judge Applications, and specific instructions for Parts I and III, are printed inside the back cover of this book. Read those instructions carefully; then do Part I.

In the lines below, and on another sheet of paper, answer the questions in Part II. Then enter a grade for the paper in the space above left, and write your evaluation for Part III. Reread the composition to see how well the writer understands and applies the principles studied in this chapter. As you read the composition write any helpful suggestions that occur to you in the margins.

PART II

1. Does the title effectively suggest the tone and the degree of objectivity required in a research paper? If not, what changes would you suggest?

   _____

   _____

   _____

   _____

2. Does the thesis sentence indicate the dominant general purpose? _____

   _____

3. Is the thesis sentence effective in establishing both the scope of the paper and the pattern of development? How? _____

   _____

   _____

   _____

4. Does the writer have a worthwhile thesis (main idea) suitable for the intended kind of research paper? Explain _____

   _____

   _____

5. Does the writer provide any additional explanation to clarify the thesis sentence? What kinds of information are provided? _____

_____

_____

_____

_____

6. Does the writer develop material according to the type of paper he or she is writing? If it is an informative paper does he or she develop subject? How? _____

_____

_____

_____

If it is an interpretive paper, are his or her own ideas developed? How?

_____

_____

_____

7. How effective is the writer's conclusion? Is it consistent with the material developed? If not, what does it need? _____

_____

_____

8. Does the writer document the material with footnotes? Are the footnotes accurate, complete, and in proper form? _____

_____

_____

9. Is the bibliography in correct form? _____

_____

_____

PART III

Grade and Evaluation:

_____

_____

_____

_____

HANDBOOK OF CORRECT AND EFFECTIVE USAGE

NINE-TENTHS of the grammar we ever need to know we learn automatically through our daily speech. But that other one-tenth bothers some people all their lives because there are a few basic things they never master. You'd be in a good deal of trouble if you never learned to tell a red light from a green one, or left from right. Many people are in trouble because they never learned to tell a part of a sentence from a whole one. If you still have trouble sometimes—and your instructor can tell you after your very first paper—this Handbook will help you. You probably won't need to study all of it; you may be weak on just a few things. The following pages are arranged to make selective study as easy as possible.

WRITING WHOLE SENTENCES

In writing whole sentences instead of parts of sentences or *fragments,* it is as in all learning; theory comes first, and then practice. You have to know what you're supposed to do before you can do it. This means (1) knowing some terms and concepts, (2) recognizing their application in other people's writing, and finally, (3) learning to apply them in your own writing. In this Handbook the stress is on practice, but the concepts and definitions of terms come first because they constitute the theory.

To write whole sentences consistently, there are three kinds of things you have to know: parts of speech, parts of sentences, and a few things about punctuation.

PARTS OF SPEECH

We classify words in two different but related ways, as parts of speech (verb, noun, and so forth) and as parts of sentences (predicate verb, subject, and so forth). You have to know both classifications before you can tell whether you have written a whole sentence or a fragment. We start with the eight parts of speech, beginning with the most important one, the verb.

Verb

A verb expresses action, condition, or equivalence. Every sentence has to have at least one verb.

> Jones *dropped* back, *pivoted,* and *passed.* (action)
> He *counted* his money and *saved* his breath. (action)
> The day *was* perfect; the weather *was* delightful. (condition)
> Betsy *was elected.* (action, passive voice)
> At last she *was* president. (equivalence)

Principal Parts

Every verb has three principal parts, on which all its various forms are based.

Present tense	talk	live	do	swim	rise	fly
Past tense	talked	lived	did	swam	rose	flew
Past participle	talked	lived	done	swum	risen	flown

**Principal Parts of
Some Commonly Used
Irregular Verbs**

Present Tense	Past Tense	Past Participle
awake	awoke	awaked
begin	began	begun
bring	brought	brought
burst	burst	burst
choose	chose	chosen
come	came	come
creep	crept	crept
deal	dealt	dealt
dive	dived (or dove)	dived
do	did	done
draw	drew	drawn
drink	drank	drunk
eat	ate	eaten
fall	fell	fallen
fly	flew	flown
forget	forgot	forgotten (or forgot)
freeze	froze	frozen
get	got	got
go	went	gone
grow	grew	grown
know	knew	known
lie	lay	lain
prove	proved	proved
ride	rode	ridden
ring	rang	rung
rise	rose	risen
run	ran	run
see	saw	seen
set	set	set
shake	shook	shaken
sing	sang	sung
sink	sank	sunk
sit	sat	sat
slide	slid	slid
speak	spoke	spoken
spring	sprang	sprung
steal	stole	stolen
sweep	swept	swept
swim	swam	swum
swing	swung	swung
take	took	taken
tear	tore	torn
throw	threw	thrown
wear	wore	worn
write	wrote	written

Verbals

Verbs like *talk* and *live,* which simply add *ed,* are called *regular.* Fortunately most verbs are like these. The others, which change all through, are called *irregular.* These must simply be learned. The present and past tense forms can stand by themselves as verbs in sentences. The uses of the third principal part will be considered in the discussion of participles.

A verbal is a special form based on a verb and used as a noun, an adjective, an adverb, or part of a verb, but not a whole verb by itself. There are three kinds of verbals.

1. The infinitive: the present tense form usually preceded by *to* and serving as a noun, an adjective, or an adverb.

   To skate was her main ambition.   (noun, subject)
   She always wanted *to skate.*   (noun, object)
   She skated *to keep* in training.   (adverb, modifies verb)
   She had a real ambition *to skate.*   (adjective, modifies noun)

2. The gerund: ends in *-ing* and serves as a noun. Has the same form as the present participle (see below) but is different in function.

   The *singing* was worse than usual.   (subject)
   He loved *singing.*   (object of verb)
   He thanked them for *coming.*   (object of preposition)

3. The participles: there are two, the *present participle,* which is the present tense form + *-ing;* and the *past participle,* which is the third principal part mentioned on page 384. Participles serve as adjectives and as parts of verbs with auxiliary or helping verbs, but never as whole verbs by themselves.

   laughing boy   *seeing*-eye dog   (present participle as adjective)
   dyed cloth   *dealt cards*   (past participle as adjective)
   is *smoking*   was *running*   will be *going*   (present participle with helping verb = predicate verb)
   had *smoked*   had *run*   will have *talked*   (past participle with helping verb = predicate verb)

The following groups of words, even though they are written with a capital letter and a period, are not whole sentences but fragments. They contain verbals, but not subject-verb combinations.

   Seeing him fall.
   Smoking too much.
   To run a race.
   Found the place.

The next group of words still contain the verbals, but have added subject-verb combinations to complete the sentences.

   Finding the party was easy.

The doctor warned them about smoking too much.
Her dream was to run a race in the Olympics.
We found the place.

Noun A noun names a person, place, idea, or thing. With the verb, it is one of the two most important parts of speech, because it helps to make the statement which is the heart of the sentence (see Predicate Verb).

> *Jones* hit the puck into the goal.
> Two *scientists* were discussing *relativity*.

Pronoun A pronoun stands for a noun.

> *I* gave *it* to *him*, smiling at *them* the whole time.
> *Whoever* said *that* surely believes *it*.
> *No one who* knew *her* could vote for *another*.

Adjective An adjective modifies (limits or describes) a noun or a pronoun.

That boy	*this* time	*each* one	*every* other	(limiting)
fat boy	*rough* time	*quiet* day	*beautiful* week	(describing)

Adverb An adverb can modify a verb, an adjective, another adverb, even a preposition.

(Modifying a verb)

> We sang *beautifully*.
> They walked *fast*.
> We returned *early*.

(Modifying an adjective)

> He was *exceedingly* polite.
> A *quite* fast drive
> An *extremely* early return

(Modifying another adverb)

> He ran *quite* rapidly.
> He arrived *too* soon.
> She spoke *most* convincingly.

(Modifying a preposition)

> She pushed her chair *partially* under the table.
> They were expected *shortly* before noon.

Preposition A preposition relates a following noun or pronoun to another word in the sentence.

> Keep this *under* your hat.
> (*under* relates *hat* to *keep*)

> The race was *in* the bag.
> (*in* relates *bag* to *was*)

The house *on* the hill belonged *to* my uncle.
(*on* relates *hill* to *house*; *to* relates *uncle* to *belonged*)

The cat crouched *by* my chair and snarled *at* the dog.
(*by* relates *chair* to *crouched*; *at* relates *dog* to *snarled*)

Conjunction

A conjunction connects words, phrases, and clauses.

*Coordinating
Conjunction*

Coordinating conjunctions connect elements of equal structure:
and, but, or, for, so, yet, either . . . or, neither . . . nor.

(Connecting equal words)	Mary *and* I Mary *or* I Not peace *but* a sword
(Connecting equal phrases)	She raced out of the house *and* into the car. It's not under the porch *but* down in the cellar.
(Connecting equal clauses)	I believed, *for* I wanted to. Either you leave now or you stay until the speech is over.

*Subordinating
Conjunction*

Subordinating conjunctions introduce subordinating or dependent clauses, and are of three types, adjective, adverb, and noun.

1. Adjective: *who, which, what, that, whoever,* and so forth. (relative pronouns)

    the woman *who* would be queen   (*who* is used of persons)
    the house *which* burned   (*which* is used of things)
    the horse *that* won   (*that* is used of persons, animals, and things)

2. Adverb: *because, although, while, since, as, so, until, when, then, before,* and so forth.

    They went swimming *because* the weather was hot.
    Before she arrives we should light the fire.

3. Noun: *that, what, whether*

    We believe *that* life is precious.   (object of verb *believe*)
    That life is precious is easy to believe.   (subject of verb *is*)
    I cannot decide *whether* I should keep it.   (object)

Interjection

An interjection expresses feeling or strong emotion.

Wow! is he strong.
Oh, if I only knew she was coming.
Yes, I can see him.
Well, I don't know whether I can do that.

PARTS OF A SENTENCE

A sentence has two main parts, subject and predicate. The predicate makes a statement about the subject. The predicate always contains a predicate verb, a word or group of words that expresses the action in the statement. It often also has a complement or completer. All these elements can have modifiers, words or groups of words that point out, limit, or describe them.

Predicate Verb

The verb and the subject are the two most important parts of the sentence, for together they make the heart of the statement.

> The preacher *spoke.* His voice *rang* out. (active voice: subject acts)
> He *was heard* by every person in the congregation. (passive voice: subject receives the action)

Subject

The subject, generally a noun or a pronoun, usually precedes its verb. As shown above, it may act or receive the action expressed by the verb.

> The preacher spoke. His *voice* rang out. His *words* reassured the
>
> congregation. *I* heard him. *What he said* was moving.

Complement

A complement is a noun, pronoun, or group of words which completes the meaning expressed by the subject and verb. Complements are of several kinds. Not all verbs need complements.

> Birds *fly.* (action complete without complement)

Direct Object

> John *threw* . . . (action not complete; John threw *what?*)
> John threw the *ball.* John threw a *party.* John threw a *fit.*

Indirect Object

Preceding a direct object, the person to or for whom an action is taken.

> Maria threw *him* the ball. Give *her* the gun. Give *Murphy* your vote.

Predicate Noun or Adjective

Completes the meaning of the subject after a verb expressing condition or equivalence.

> He was *charming.* I shall be *delighted.* They were the *leaders.*

Do not use an adverb in place of a predicate adjective. When you can substitute the word *is, was, were,* or *been* for a verb of the senses like *look, feel, sound, taste,* or *smell,* the verb is a linking verb and takes a predicate adjective, not an adverb, to complete it. Use an adverb to tell how the action was performed, an adjective to describe the subject.

Incorrect:	I feel *miserably* about it.
	(*Am* can be substituted for *feel.*)
Correct:	I feel *miserable* about it.
Incorrect:	The flowers smelled *sweetly.*

Correct:	The flowers smelled *sweet.*
	(*Are* can be substituted for *smelled.*)
Describing action:	Frank tasted the hot soup *carefully.*
Describing subject:	The hot soup tasted *delicious* to Frank.

Modifier

A modifier is a word or group of words which points out, limits, or describes another element in a sentence. The two main types of modifiers are *adjectival,* modifying nouns or pronouns; and *adverbial,* modifying verbs primarily, but also adjectives, other adverbs, and prepositions. (For word modifiers, see Adjective and Adverb. For modifiers composed of groups of words, see Phrase and Clause.

Phrase

A phrase is a group of words without a subject-verb combination and acting as a *part* of a sentence.

Verb Phrase

A verb phrase is a predicate verb more than one word long, that is, made up of a participle and a helping verb (see Verbal).

He *had been* a Marine.　(verb phrase, predicate verb; expresses equivalence: he = Marine)
He *was killed* after peace *was declared.*　(passive voice, auxiliary + past participle)

Verbal Phrase

A phrase containing an infinitive, a participle, or a gerund.

Climbing the heights, we had the city before us.
(participle *climbing* modifies *we* – adjective)

We signed the petition, *believing* him innocent.
(participle *believing* modifies *we* – adjective)

John ran *to call* the police.
(infinitive *to call* modifies *ran* – adverb)

Helen plans *to drive* home.
(infinitive *to drive* object of *plans* – noun)

Telling the news was not easy.
(gerund *telling* subject of *was* – noun)

I hated *going* to school.
(gerund *going* object of *hated* – noun)

Prepositional Phrase

A prepositional phrase expresses a relationship between the noun or pronoun following the preposition (its object) and another word in the sentence (see Preposition). It is usually a modifier.

A bird *in hand*
(*in* links *hand* to *bird*)

room *at the top*
(*at* links *top* to *room* – tells where)

At my appearance, he flew *off the handle.*
(both modify *flew;* the first tells why, the second where)

Clauses

A clause is a group of words with a subject and a predicate. Clauses can be independent or dependent.

Independent Clause

An independent clause can stand by itself as a sentence. Independent clauses also may be joined by a coordinating conjunction into longer sentences (see Coordinating Conjunction).

I had watched her for a long time. I knew just how she would react.
I had watched her for a long time, *and/so* I knew just how she would react.
I knew just how she would react, *for* I had watched her for a long time.

Dependent Clause

A dependent or subordinate clause contains a word which signals its dependency on some element in another clause and therefore cannot stand alone as a sentence. This word usually introduces the clause. Many fragments (see Fragment) are dependent clauses written and punctuated as if they were independent clauses or sentences.

1. Adjective clause: An adjective clause is introduced by a relative pronoun (*who, which, what, that,* see page 387) and modifies a noun or a pronoun in another clause.

    One *who would conquer* must not pity.
    (relative *who* modifies *one,* subject of main clause; *who* signals dependency)

    This is the house *that Jack built.*
    (relative *that* modifies *house* and signals dependency)

2. Adverbial clause: An adverbial clause is introduced by one of a large number of adverbial conjunctions (see page 387).

    Although it was late, they sat up a while longer.
    (introductory clause modifies *sat up*)

    They sat up late *because* they were afraid.
    (modifies *sat up*)

    Whenever they sat up late, they were sleepy next day.
    (modifies *were sleepy*)

3. Noun clause: A noun clause is usually a subject, object, or complement, and is thus not usually a modifier but a part of the main clause in its sentence.

    Whatever is is right.
    (*Whatever is,* subject of verb *is* in the main clause)

    They believe *whatever they hear.*
    (*whatever they hear,* object of verb *believe* in main clause)

To avoid fragments and to write only whole sentences, it is essential that you recognize phrases and dependent clauses and not write them as if they were sentences.

WRITING SENTENCES

Three related errors in writing whole sentences all show that the writer who is guilty of them doesn't know a sentence when he sees one. The most common of these is writing a part of a sentence or a *fragment* as if it were a whole sentence. The second is writing two sentences with only a comma between them, and the third is running two sentences together with no mark of separation at all. To avoid these errors, and to write whole sentences consistently, you have to know and recognize the parts of speech, the parts of a sentence, and certain very simple rules for punctuating sentences. We consider the punctuation first; punctuation inside the sentence is considered later.

Sentence Punctuation

A sentence begins with a capital letter and ends with a period, a question mark, or an exclamation point.

> Rosa walked all the way home.   (statement—period)
> Did Rosa walk all the way home?   (question—question mark)
> What, Rosa walked all the way home!   (exclamation—exclamation point)

Fragment

A fragment is a part of a sentence written and punctuated as a whole sentence. It often shows that the writer doesn't know a whole sentence from a part of one.

Phrases

The following fragments are *phrases wrongly separated* from the independent clauses they belong with:

1. Verbal:

> Al studied hard all winter. *Trying to earn good grades.*

2. Prepositional:

> Students are expected to study in the dorms. *With people coming and going and phones ringing.*

Both these phrases should be joined to their clauses, punctuated only by an introductory comma.

Correct:

1. Al studied hard all winter, trying to earn good grades.
2. Students are expected to study in the dorms, with people coming and going and phones ringing.

Clauses

Some fragments are subordinate clauses punctuated as whole sentences.

1. Adjective:

This is a boy. *Who stole my boat.*
The boy who stole my boat. He drowned.

2. Adverb:

John could never decide. *When he should dribble and when he should pass.*

3. Noun:

Whether I should try out for golf or shoot for honors in English. It took me a long time to make up my mind.

Like the phrase fragments above, these should simply be joined to their main clauses:

Correct:

1. This is the boy who stole my boat.
2. John could never decide when he should dribble and when he should
   pass.
3. It took me a long time to make up my mind whether I should try out for
   golf or shoot for honors in English.

Parts Missing

Other fragments are free-floating sentence parts without an independent clause to hook on to. These should be rephrased and absorbed into other sentences, or made into separate whole sentences in their own right.

Three letters, two bills to pay, and only one stamp.
Fill in: *I had* three letters *to mail,* two bills to pay, and only one stamp.
(subject-verb combination supplied; *to mail* balances *to pay*)

My birthday, no money to get my car fixed and nowhere to go.
Fill in: *Here it was* my birthday, *and I had* no money to get my car fixed and nowhere to go.
(two subject-verb combinations supplied)

A hole in my sweater as big as a baseball.
Fill in: *Here I was all ready to go out and at the last minute discovered* a hole in my sweater as big as a baseball. In this last sentence a whole new element of thought is added. Many times this is the best cure, for often fragments suggest a kind of mental lockjaw.

Fragments, then, are of two main kinds: (1) Dependent elements—usually phrases or clauses—detached from the independent clause to which they belong; and (2) potential whole sentences with gaps in them—that is, with main parts missing. Only by knowing a whole sentence when you see it can you learn to avoid fragments.

Comma Splice

The comma splice, or comma fault, is the writing of two sentences (two independent clauses) as if they were one, with only a comma between them. Not quite as great a giveaway of one's ignorance as a fragment, it still shows poor grasp of sentence mechanics.

It was morning, I threw up the shades.
Ted carefully tightened the nut with his pliers, with one last pull he snapped the bolt.
The gymnasts tried harder, their coaches were excited.
We left him at the airport, he waited for the plane.

Fused Sentences

The comma splice is confusing because the reader expects something more than a comma between independent clauses; therefore he temporarily misinterprets the sentence and has to refigure its meaning.

Even more confusing than the comma splice is a fused construction in which two sentences are run together without any separation, not even a comma.

It was morning I threw up the shades.
Ted carefully tightened the nut with his pliers with one last pull he snapped the bolt.
The gymnasts tried harder their coaches were excited.
We left him at the airport he waited for the plane.

Corrections

There are many ways of correcting comma splices and fused sentences, and in any given case one way may be better than most others. If the two clauses are really of equal importance they should be kept coordinate and linked by a semicolon; if the connection needs to be brought out, they should be linked by a coordinating conjunction in addition to the original comma.

It was morning; I threw up the shades.
It was morning, *so* I threw up the shades.   (or possibly *and* I . . .)

Ted carefully tightened the nut with his pliers, *but* with one last pull he snapped the bolt.   (or, . . . pliers; *then* with . . .)

The gymnasts tried harder *because* their coaches were excited.
(*because* makes second clause subordinate to first)
The gymnasts tried harder, *for* their coaches were excited.
(*for* keeps second clause independent; same connective idea)

We left him at the airport *where* he waited for the plane.
(*where* makes second clause subordinate to first)

In any given sentence the best correction of a comma splice or run-on depends on meaning. The connective and punctuation that most accurately expresses the intended relation between the two clauses is the one to choose.

**GRAMMAR INSIDE
THE SENTENCE**

So far we have considered the grammar of the sentence as a whole. There are also many grammatical conventions relating to parts within the sentence. Most of these you know and follow automatically, but a few cause trouble. These can be grouped under (1) the principle of congruence or agreement between sentence parts, (2) changes in the forms of words to

show their functions in a sentence, (3) some problems with modifiers, and
(4) punctuation and capitalization.

AGREEMENT

Certain sentence parts show their relationship to each other by "agree-
ing" with each other in form. Thus a verb agrees with its subject, a pronoun agrees with its antecedent, and a pronoun must refer clearly to the
correct antecedent.

Agreement of Subject and Verb

A verb agrees with its subject in person and number.

> I am.   (first person singular)
> You are.   (second person singular)
> He, she, it, John is.   (third person singular, all genders, nouns and
> pronouns)
> We, you, they, people are.   (all three persons, plural, nouns and
> pronouns)

Subjects joined by *and* take a plural verb.

> The truck *and* the automobile *are* loaded.
> The truck*s and* and automobile*s are* loaded.

With subjects joined by *or* or related words *(either . . . or, neither . . .
nor)*, the verb agrees with the nearer one.

> *Either* the minesweeper *or* the destroyers *were* lost.
> *Neither* the students *nor* the instructor *was* confused.

A collective noun (*crowd, flock, committee,* and so forth) take a singular
verb when considered as a unit, a plural verb when considered as separate
individuals.

> The *jury was* bewildered.
> The *committee are* investigating different aspects of the case.

With an indefinite pronoun subject *(each, every, somebody, no one,
either, neither)* the verb is singular.

> *Everyone was* in the right place.
> *Nobody believes* me.

A compound subject (with *and*) standing for a single thing takes a
singular verb.

> *Ham and eggs is* the great American dish.
> The *wear and tear* was figured in.

The verb after a relative pronoun subject agrees with the antecedent
of the pronoun.

Agreement of Pronoun and Antecedent

> *People* in our town *who are concerned* about ecology meet weekly.

A pronoun agrees with its antecedent in number.

Everybody must bring *his* (not *their*) lunch.
Neither of the cars had *its* (not *their*) brakes checked.

**Reference
of Pronouns**

Except for the indefinite pronouns (*some, any, either,* and so forth), a pronoun usually refers to a noun called its antecedent. A pronoun should not seem to refer to a wrong antecedent, and for most pronouns the antecedent should be clearly expressed.

Clear:	John put *his* hat on *his* head. *He* wore *it* jauntily.
Confusing:	Joe asked Tom to count his money.
	(whose money, Joe's or Tom's?)
Faulty antecedent:	I love *to skate* and did a lot of *it* in Canada.
	(*it* cannot refer to infinitive *to skate*.)
Clear:	I love *skating* and did a lot of *it* in Canada.
	(*It* can refer to gerund *skating*.)
Confusing:	This is the girl's bicycle *who* lives next door.
	(*Who* refers only to persons; here links to nearer noun *bicycle*, a thing. Wrong on two counts)
Clear:	This bicycle belongs to the *girl who* lives next door.
Acceptable:	They made such a fuss that *it* embarrassed me.
	(*It* can refer to noun *fuss*, though actually the reference is to the whole idea, that she made a fuss.)
Clearer:	They made such a fuss that I was embarrassed.
Not acceptable:	She hated *dancing, which* made the evening a bore.
	(*Which* links to noun *dancing*, but actually refers to idea that she hated dancing.)
Clear:	Because she hated dancing, the evening was a bore.

FORMS OF WORDS

Many kinds of words show changes in form in order to indicate their function in a sentence and their relation to other sentence parts. Thus nouns change to show number (singular and plural); pronouns to show person, number, and case; verbs change form to show tense, person, number, and voice; and adjectives and adverbs change to show whether they are being used in the positive, comparative, or superlative degree. These changes are an important part of grammar.

Case

Some pronouns change in form to show their use in a sentence. The various forms are called *cases,* which approximately means conditions — that is, a pronoun may be in the "condition" of a subject, an object, or a possessive. In earlier English, nouns also changed form to show case, but have retained only the possessive form.

Subjective	I	you	he	she	we	John
Possessive	my, mine	your, yours	his	her, hers	our, ours	John's
Objective	me	you	him	her	us	John

The main uses of the subjective case are (see page 395):

1. Subject of a predicate verb
2. Predicate nominative

The main uses of the objective case are (see page 395).

1. Direct or indirect object of the predicate verb
2. Object of a preposition

> Ike threw the ball to *him.*
> (not to *he; him* is the object of the preposition *to.*)

> Just between you and *me* (not *I*), this is true.
> (*Me* is the object of the preposition *between.*)

The main use of the possessive case is to show ownership. The possessive case is often used as a pronominal adjective modifying a noun or group of words acting as a noun. The words *my, your, his, her, our,* and *their* are usually adjectives, and the words *mine, yours, his, hers, ours,* and *theirs* are usually possessive pronouns.

Pronoun: *Mine* is torn.
                      His was sold.

Pronomial adjective: *My* shirt is torn. (modifying noun)
                      His guitar was sold. (modifying noun)
                      My typing disturbed my roommate. (modifying gerund)

Formation of Plurals

Plurals of most nouns are formed by adding *s*. But if the singular noun ends in an *s* sound spelled *s, sh, ch, x,* or *z, es* is added for easier pronunciation.

dog — dogs	fuss — fusses
room — rooms	box — boxes
sheet — sheets	church — churches
cracker — crackers	buzz — buzzes

A few nouns have the same form for the singular or plural: *deer — deer, sheep — sheep.* Some have irregular plurals: *zero — zeroes, melody — melodies, half — halves, ox — oxen, child — children.* When in doubt, always consult a dictionary.

Tenses of Verbs

Along with their other important functions, verbs are timing mechanisms within sentences. They indicate time relationships, telling when something exists or happens. To indicate time differences, the form of a main verb or its helping verb is changed. Using the incorrect tense form of a verb is a common writing problem.

The tense forms of a verb indicate time differences. Every English verb has six principal tenses.

Simple Tenses:

Present:	I *talk* to him every day.
Past:	I *talked* to him yesterday.
Future:	I *will talk* to him tomorrow.

The simple tense forms are not precise in the time they express. But the perfect tense forms usually state or imply a time before which something exists or occurs.

Perfect Tenses:

Present Perfect:	I *have (or he has) talked* to him already.
Past Perfect:	I *had talked* to him before lunch.
Future Perfect:	I *will have talked* to him by midnight.

In the progressive tense forms, the form of the main verb remains the same; the helping verb indicates the tense.

Simple Progressive Tenses:

Present:	I *am* talking
Past:	I *was* talking
Future:	I *will be* talking

Perfect Progressive Tenses:

Present Perfect:	I *have* (or he *has*) *been* talking until now.
Past Perfect:	I *had been talking* before you came.
Future Perfect:	I *will have been* talking for two hours by ten o'clock.

There are only two emphatic tense forms, present and past, with a form of the verb *do* acting as the helping verb.

Present:	I *do talk.*
Past:	I *did talk.*

In the emphatic as in the progressive form, the main verb remains the same; the helping verb indicates the tense.

Sequence of Tenses

When the tense of one verb depends on that of another, we speak of sequence of tenses. Linked tenses should reflect actual time relationships.

Wrong:	They *caught* the trout and *cook* them over the fire.
Right:	They *caught* the trout and *cooked* them over the fire.
Or:	They *catch* the trout and *cook* them . . .
Wrong:	When I *saw* Joe, he *has* a black eye.
Right:	When I *saw* Joe, he *had* a black eye.

Weak Passive Voice

A verb has two voices (see Predicate Verb), the active and passive. The active voice indicates that its subject performs the action, the passive voice that the subject is acted upon. The sign of the passive voice is a form of the helping verb *to be* followed by the past participle of the main verb. Tense changes are shown by the helping verb; the main verb remains the same.

Active voice: I *kicked* the ball.

Passive voice: The ball *was kicked* by me.

Active voice: The chart *illustrates* the increase in production last year.

Passive voice: The increase in production last year *is illustrated* by the chart.

Dangling Modifiers

Participles (see Verbals) in phrases which modify nouns or pronouns must refer clearly to the right noun or pronoun. If they do not, they are said to *dangle.*

Dangler: *Barking* and *growling,* I unleashed my dog at the intruder. (The two participles must link with the logical word, which is *dog.* As the sentence is written, the pronoun *I* gets in the way.)

Clearer: I unleashed my dog, which had been barking and growling, at the intruder.

Dangler: *Creaking* and *clanking,* I watched the train pull into the station.

Clearer: Creaking and clanking, the train pulled into the station.

Comparison of Adjectives and Adverbs

Adjectives and adverbs have three degrees of comparison: positive, comparative, and superlative. The positive degree is the simple form of the modifier when no comparison is made. The comparative degree is used when only two things are compared. The superlative degree is used when three or more things are compared.

Form the comparative degree by adding *-er* to the adjective or adverb or by using *more* when the word is hard to pronounce with *-er* added. Form the superlative degree either by adding *-est* to the adjective or adverb or by using *most* if the word is difficult to pronounce.

Forming the Comparative Degree

Positive Degree (no comparison)	Comparative Degree (comparing only two)	Superlative Degree (comparing more than two)
small	smaller	smallest
beautiful	more beautiful	most beautiful
rapidly	more rapidly	most rapidly

Incorrect: Doris Mink is the tall*est* of the two.
Correct: Doris Mink is the tall*er* of the two.

Avoid omitting the word *other* when it is needed in a comparison.

Incorrect: Los Angeles is larger than any city in California.
(Since Los Angeles *is* a city in California, the word *other* is necessary to make sense.)
Correct: Los Angeles is larger than *any other* city in California.

Position of Modifiers

Avoid putting a modifier in the wrong place. Place them as close to the words they modify as the exact meaning requires.

I *only* have worked there six months.
(This may erroneously mean that *only* I worked there.)
Better: I have worked there *only* six months.

When using an adverb to modify an infinitive, most careful writers avoid placing the adverb between *to* and the verb form. This separation is known as a *split infinitive.*

Split: The babysitter coaxed the child to *quietly* go to bed.
Not split: The babysitter coaxed the child to go to bed *quietly.*

PUNCTUATION

No really effective writing is possible without clear and helpful punctuation. Sloppy or misleading punctuation usually causes confusion or even misunderstanding. The whole effect of a piece of writing can depend on the skillful use of the nonverbal elements called punctuation marks.

Many of the nonverbal elements used in our speech — our voice intonations, facial expressions, and gestures with arms and hands — are reflected in writing by means of punctuation. The precise expression of ideas in writing depends heavily on the order in which words are arranged and on the correct use of punctuation.

The most important marks of punctuation, those used at the ends of sentences, were treated in Sentence Punctuation. The rest follow.

Apostrophe

The apostrophe is used for the following:
1. To form the possessive of nouns and indefinite pronouns *(John's, my brother's, the men's, the Joneses', one's)* but not personal pronouns *(its, whose, theirs).*
2. To form contractions or to indicate omissions.
can't-can not, *you're*-you are, *'74*-1974
3. To form plurals of numbers and letters.
Your *a's* and *c's* are hard to distinguish.
Avoid using too many *and's* and *so's* in your papers.

Comma

The main uses of the comma are to separate or set off, and to set off or enclose.

1. To separate introductory verbal phrases (see page 389).

To succeed in business, a person must be willing to invest.

2. To set off introductory prepositional phrases, unless they are very short (see page 389).

> During the early part of the war, I drove a Jeep.

3. To set off introductory adverbial clauses (see page 390).

> Because I was too tired to work, I went home.

4. To separate independent clauses joined by a coordinating conjunction such as *and, but, or, for,* or *nor;* but not before adverbial conjunctions such as *therefore, however, moreover, nevertheless, still,* and *yet* (see page 390).

> I spent two hours writing my paper, *but* the instructor gave it only a *C.*
> I spent two hours writing my paper; *however,* the instructor gave it only a *C.*

5. To separate items in a series of three or more words, phrases, or clauses, though many people now omit the comma before *and.*

> The classroom was cold, dreary, and uninviting.
> Helen ran into the house, into the kitchen, and out the front door again.
> The fund-raising committee decided to have a concert, Bill found a couple of groups to play, and Sally organized the publicity.

6. To separate two or more coordinate adjectives. To tell whether adjectives are equal or coordinate, try inserting the word *and* between them. If *and* does not fit between them smoothly, the comma should not be used.

> I have never been to a more quiet, peaceful place.
> (The words *quiet* and *peaceful* modify *place* in the same way. *Quiet and peaceful* is a smooth phrase; therefore, the comma should be used.

> A *white-haired little old couple* sat by the fire.
> (Commas are not needed because the adjectives are cumulative, not coordinating; you would not use *and* between them.)

Certain types of elements within a sentence are set off or enclosed by commas. These include nonrestrictive modifiers and appositives, parenthetical expressions, mild interjections or exclamations, persons addressed directly, and parts of dates and addresses.

1. Nonrestrictive modifiers: these are elements which describe or add information but do not restrict—that is, point out and tell "which one."

> Joel Greene, *who asked the question,* always defended the underdog.
> (Nonrestrictive: does not tell which Joel Greene, but adds information about him. Set off by commas.)
> The student *who asked the question* always defended the underdog.

(Restrictive—tells which student. So not set off by commas because necessary to the sentence.)

2. Nonrestrictive appositives: an appositive is a noun or noun substitute which explains or adds to the meaning of another noun or a pronoun.

Mr. John Hellman, *our instructor,* is a coin collector. (Nonrestrictive— adds information but does not tell which one. Set off by commas.) Our instructor Mr. John Hellman is a coin collector. (Restrictive— tells which instructor. So not set off by commas.)

3. Parenthetical expressions: these are words or groups of words which interrupt the main thought and are not structurally part of a sentence.

This student, *someone said,* had planted a bomb in the locker room.

4. Mild interjections or exclamations (see page 387).

Well, I might as well go with you.
Yes, the program was entertaining.

5. Words in direct address.

Tell me, *boys and girls,* just where you saw the ghost.
Madame Chairperson, members of the committee, greetings.

6. The name of the speaker in a direct quotation.

"The righteous," said Dr. Shiekh, "shall grow as straight as the Cedars of Lebanon."

7. Addresses, places, and dates.

On January 2, 1973, my home at 18234 Jamestown Circle, Sudbury, Massachusetts, was purchased.
(Especially notice the commas after 1973 and after Massachusetts.)

Semicolon

The main use of the semicolon is to separate independent clauses not joined by a coordinating conjunction *(and, but, or, nor,* or *for.)* It is also used before an adverbial conjunction (*therefore, however, furthermore, nevertheless, consequently, moreover,* and so forth) when it links independent clauses.

He hoped to win the election; his hope was not fulfilled.
To buy the car she had to have some cash; consequently, she borrowed some from the bank.

Colon

In prose, the colon has one main use: it follows an independent clause and marks a formal pause before a list, a quotation, or a complete sentence.

Bring the following to class: a red pencil, two sheets of paper, a dictionary, and a thesaurus.

Quotation Marks

Quotation marks have two main uses.

To identify the exact words of a direct quotation. Use single quotation marks to identify a quotation within a quotation.

"Everyone must submit this report on time," said the instructor.
John said, "I know what he meant when he said 'What will be, will be.'"

To identify the titles of short poems, articles, and stories. The titles of longer works are underlined to represent italic type.

The second chapter of *The Virginian* is entitled "When You Call Me That, Smile."
"The Raven" is Poe's most quoted poem.
The short story "Flowering Judas" is by Katherine Anne Porter.

Quotation marks always follow a period or comma and precede a semicolon. Question and exclamation marks precede if they are part of the quotation, and follow if they belong to the sentence as a whole.

Dash

Use the dash to show an abrupt change in the direction of the thought in a sentence:

Now, if hunger and poverty can be prevented — but let's talk about something more pleasant.

Dashes may also be used to set off something for special emphasis.

He gave them a gift before he left — a song he had written for them.

Parentheses

Parentheses are used to enclose interrupters or side comments sometimes enclosed between commas and sometimes set off between dashes. Parentheses are stronger than commas, and more formal than dashes.

The dissenters (and there were more of them than we expected) sat in a huddle at the back of the room.
Heroin (one of the hardest of the hard drugs) has recently been in short supply.

Square Brackets

Square brackets are usually used to enclose explanations interpolated by an editor, sometimes within a quotation, as to show that an error was in the original.

"For the cost of 10 sounds [sic] we were able to book passage across the channel."

Underlining

All italicized words in typewritten or handwritten material should be underlined. Underline the following:

1. Titles of books, magazines, plays, operas, long poems, motion pictures, and newspapers.

The Nile, Time, A Street Car Named Desire, Carmen, Beowulf, Gone with the Wind, The Detroit Free Press.

2. The names of ships and aircraft.

   Titanic (ship), Panama Clipper (aircraft)

3. Foreign words and phrases.

   est modus in rebus (temperance is a virtue—Horace)

4. To emphasize items of specific reference, such as a word or a letter used as such.

   There are too many and's in the sentence.
   Don't write your d's like your l's.

**CAPITAL LETTERS
Capitalization**

Occasionally there is some disagreement about the correct use of capital letters for nouns and the adjectives made from them. The following generally accepted principles will serve as a guide.

1. Capitalize the first word of every sentence and the first word of every direct quotation which is a complete sentence.

   The question John asked was, "Did Hitler cause World War II?"

2. Capitalize proper nouns, not common nouns. Common nouns name whole classes, but proper nouns name certain individual members of a class.

Janice Jones—woman	Sunday—day
Detroit—city	July—month
Tom Sawyer—novel	Fifth Avenue—street

   Do not capitalize the names of seasons: spring, summer, and so forth.

3. Capitalize the important words in titles of books, plays, poems, short stories, and so forth. Do not capitalize the less important words, such as articles (a, an, the), prepositions (of, in, to), and conjunctions unless they appear at the beginning or end of the title. If articles, prepositions, or conjunctions in titles consist of five or more letters, they are usually capitalized.

   The Making of the President
   The Town Beyond

4. Capitalize the names of countries, territories, and other geographic areas.

   Lebanon, Egypt, South America, New England

5. Capitalize certain religious names.

   God, Saviour, Heavenly Father. The pronouns referring to the Deity: Thy, Thine, His, Him, Catholic, Presbyterian, Jesuit, Bible, Koran.

6. Capitalize the names of family relationships when accompanying the

personal name or when they stand for the person. This also applies to professional titles.

> Her *father* and *Uncle John* visited *Mother* and her *sister.*
> The *doctor* told me to visit *Dr. Smith.*

7. Capitalize points of the compass when they refer to regions, but not when they refer to directions.

> The people *south* of Detroit live in the *North.*

8. School subjects are capitalized if they are languages and if accompanied by the number designating them in the catalog.

> I am taking chemistry, but not Chemistry 102, and my sister is majoring in French and sociology.

SPELLING PROBLEMS

Anything that causes a reader to lose respect for the writer short-circuits communication. One of the most common causes of disruption of the necessary relationship between a writer and his reader is a misspelled word. In addition to the writer-reader relationship, faith in the accuracy of the writer's statements is affected seriously by words incorrectly spelled. Some employers evaluate a person's ability to communicate solely on the accuracy of his spelling.

Following is a list of words commonly misspelled in the compositions of college students. The troublesome letters are underlined.

Commonly Misspelled Words

accept	beneficial	connoisseur	desirous
accidentally	benefit	conscientious	desperate
accommodate	benefited	conscious	despicable
acquaint	benefiting	consensus	develop
acquaintance	boundary	contemptible	diagonal
affect	business	controlled	diaphragm
all right	cabinet	convenience	difference
ally	certain	countenance	different
amateur	changeable	counterfeit	disappear
ancient	character	courtesy	disappoint
angle	chief	criticism	doesn't
apologize	coming	data	during
appearance	commit	decide	ecstasy
argument	committed	decision	elaborate
asylum	committee	definite	eliminate
athletic	committing	descend	embarrass
attorneys-at-law	complete	descendent	embarrassment
beginning	conceive	describe	environment
believe	conferred	description	equipment

equipped	imaginary	movable	questionnaire
escape	imagination	necessary	quiet
etiquette	imagine	necessity	receive
exaggerate	immediate	noticeable	recommend
excel	immediately	occasion	reconcilable
excellent	improvement	occasionally	referred
excite	incadescent	occur	resemblance
excited	indispensable	occurred	restaurant
excitement	ineligible	occurrence	resuscitate
exciting	inevitable	occurring	rhythm
exist	inflammation	omitting	ridiculous
existence	innocence	opinion	sacrilegious
experience	inoculate	opportunity	sandwiches
fallacy	intercede	panicky	scholastic
familiar	interest	parallel	schedule
fascinate	irrepressible	paralyze	seize
feudal	irresistible	parliament	sense
finally	irridescent	passers-by	separate
financier	its	percolator	separator
fluorescent	it's	performance	sergeant
forcible	jeopardize	perimeter	sieve
foreign	judgment	persistent	silhouette
foreigners	knowledge	personnel	similar
formulas	laboratory	perspiration	sophomore
forty	legible	picnicking	souvenir
friend	leisure	picturesque	sovereign
government	lieutenant	pleasant	spaghetti
grammar	lonely	pneumonia	speech
grievance	lose	possess	stop
grievous	losing	possessive	stopped
guarantee	lovable	prejudice	stopping
harass	management	principal	studied
heifer	marriage	principle	studios
hemorrhage	marry	privilege	study
hero	mayonnaise	probably	studying
heroes	meant	procedure	succeed
heroine	melon	proceed	success
hindrance	mercurochrome	professor	successful
hosiery	mileage	proficient	superintendent
humor	mimicking	propelling	supersede
humorous	miscellaneous	prophecy	surprise
hypocrisy	mischievous	prophesy	symmetry
image	misspelled	pursue	temperature

than	too	until	writer
their	tragedy	vacuum	writhe
then	tried	villain	writing
there	truly	weird	written
to	tyranny	where	your
together	umbrella	wholly	you're
tonnage	unnecessary	woman	

VOCABULARY
Words Commonly
Confused

Following is a list of words commonly confused in student writing. Some of these pairs are *homonyms*, that is, words that sound alike but have different spellings and different meanings. Others are words different in form but sometimes confused in meaning. Still others consist of one standard and one nonstandard formation. If any of these groupings cause you trouble, the best way to learn them is to look them up in a dictionary and then write a sentence using each word correctly.

accede—exceed	demur—demure
add—ad	disinterested—uninterested
affect—effect	eager—anxious
aggravate—irritate	farther—further
alibi—excuse	fewer—less
all together—altogether	fluorescent—fluorescent
allude—elude—refer	freeze—frieze
bear—bare	historic—historical
beside—besides	imply—infer
born—borne	liable—apt—likely
brake—break	loose—lose
canvas—canvass	practical—practicable
claim—maintain	prophesy—prophecy
complement—compliment	regardless—irregardless
continual—continuous	respectfully—respectively
corps—corpse	sight—site—cite
council—counsel	specie—species
credible—creditable	stationary—stationery
decent—descent—dissent	their—there—they're

Howlers

Following is a list of expressions which are illiterate and should never be used by college students either in speech or in writing unless on purpose to imitate substandard English. Memorize this list.

youse guys	him and me
I ain't	I and him
ain't got no	you and him
he don't	between you and I
could of	can't hardly
I been	irregardless

I seen	these kind
I come home	those kind
he done it	had ought
I ast him	

**Words Commonly
Misused**

The words in the following list are of two kinds. Some are colloquialisms which should not be used in formal writing unless there is a special reason for using them. Others are illiteracies which should never be used except for special effect.

Aggravate—to intensify or make worse
Irritate—to annoy
All right—not spelled alright, allright, or all-right.
All the—*all the farther, all the higher, all the faster* should not be used for *as far as,* and so forth.

Incorrect: That was *all the farther* we went.
Correct: That was *as far as* we went.

Alot—incorrect for *a lot,* meaning *many.*
Already, all ready—*already* means by this time. *All ready* means *completely ready.*

The hotel was *already* full.
They were *all ready.*

And etc.—never put *and* before *etc.*
Anxious—worried or uneasy in mind.
Balance—colloquial to mean *remainder,* except in *bank balance.*

Colloquial: One was Greek; the balance were Italian.
Preferred: One was Greek: the others were Italian.

Claim—assert right of ownership.

This problem claims our attention.

Maintain—to defend one's opinion or position.

I maintain that they are innocent.

Contemplate—should not be used with a preposition.

Incorrect: He contemplates *on* a trip to Florida.
Correct: He contemplated a trip to Alaska.

Data, Phenomena, strata—these are plural not singular. (However, data is sometimes used as a collective noun, and is therefore singular.)

Due to—an adjective and should not modify a verb. It is confused with *owing to, because of, on account of,* which are phrasal prepositions. Never use at the beginning of a sentence, where an adverbial phrase is always required.

Undesirable: The forces were divided, due to a misunderstanding.
Improved: The forces were divided because of a misunderstanding.

Eager—"wanting very much." Should not be used to mean anxious.

Farther, further—*farther* usually refers to distance which can be measured in inches, feet, pounds, and so forth. *Further* indicates degree, for example, a mile *farther, further* details, *further* disintegration.

Fewer, less—*fewer* is used to refer to number, things one can count. *Less* is used to refer to quantity.

There are fewer books but less space in this library.

Hardly, scarcely, only, but—should not be used with another negative. Avoid "not hardly," and so forth.

Imply, infer—*imply* means to suggest. *Infer* means to draw a conclusion.
   In his speech, he *implied* strong opposition to our candidate.
   From your comments, I *infer* that you do not approve of my plan.

It's, its—*it's* is the contraction for *it is; its* is the possessive case of the pronoun *it.*

Contraction: *It's* raining violently along the entire East coast.
Possessive Case: The storm focused *its* destruction on the area surrounding the harbor.

Leave, let—*leave* means to go away. *Let* means to allow or permit.

Incorrect: Leave him go.
Correct: Let him go. Let him leave when he wishes.

Liable, likely, apt—do not use interchangeably. *Liable* suggests danger or liability. *Liable to* often is equivalent to *subject to*. *Likely* means probably. *Apt* suggests a tendency, often resulting from habit or skill.

Correct: Being nervous, he is *liable* to insomnia.   (subject to)
           Being conscientious, he is *likely* to worry.   (will probably worry)
           A practiced skiier, she is *apt* at making turns.   (skillful)

Like—should not be used to introduce a clause. Use *as* or *as if*.

Incorrect: He acted like the rest did.
Correct: He acted as the rest did.

Nice—means keen and precise in discrimination or delicately made: "a nice judge of values, or "a nice distinction in meaning." It may also mean pleasant or agreeable, but in this sense it is overused.

Percent—use only after a numeral. Percent means by the hundred, therefore, should be used with a number. *Percentage* means part or proportion of a whole.

Inexact: A large percent were Italian.
Correct: A large percentage were Italian.
Correct: Ten percent were Italian.

Superior-inferior—should be followed by *to*, not *than*.

Incorrect: It was superior *than* the tool previously used.
Correct: It was superior *to* the tool previously used.

Try and—often used for try to; should be avoided in writing.

I must try *to* (not try *and*) find a job.

Transpire—means to breathe forth or to become known. It is stilted and pompous when used to mean happen or occur.

It soon transpired that the whole plan had fallen through.
The accident transpired at noon.

When—not used in definitions.

A rogue elephant is *one that* (not *when*) is vicious and separated from the herd.

Where—not used for *that*.

I read *that* (not *where*) the price of food is going up.

Which that, who—*which* should refer to things, *that* to things and people, and *who* to people only.

Whose—strictly the possessive form of *who*, it may be used of animals and things to avoid an awkward *of which*.

This is the dog *whose* paw I bandaged.
Not: This is the dog *of which* I bandaged the paw.

Would have—often incorrectly used in *if* clauses instead of *had*.

Incorrect: If he would have stood by us, we might have won.
Correct: If he had stood by us, we might have won.

Would of—used incorrectly instead of *would have*.

Incorrect: They *would of* come if they had known.
Correct: They *would have* come if they had known.

INDEX

Abusive argument, 343–344
Accuracy
  and definition, 325
  and purpose, 72
  and viewpoint, 94
Action, 77, 79, 339
  and narrative, 207
Active voice, 388, 397–398
Actuation as purpose, 70, 77–79, 89, 163, 164,
    184
  and persuasion, 339
  and tone, 296
Addresses, 400, 401
Adjectives, 10, 386
  adjectival modifier, 389
  clause, 390, 391–392
  comparison of, 398–399
  conjunction, 387
  coordinate, 400
Adverbs, 10, 386
  adverbial modifier, 389
  clause, 390, 392, 400
  comparison of, 398–399
  conjunction, 387
  use of, 388
Advertising, 73, 341, 342
Affiliations, 91
Age, 91
Agreement
  grammatical, 393, 394–395
  and persuasion, 77
American Heritage Dictionary, 357
Analogies, 34, 247, 255–257, 299
Analysis, 179, 186–189
  causal, 189
  functional, 189, 202–203
  structural, 189
Angle, in viewpoint, 277–279
Antecedent, 394, 395
Apostrophe, 399
Appositives, 400–401
Appropriateness, of purpose statement, 112
Argumentation, 231, 339, 355
Argumentative paper, 356
"Argument of the beard," 33
Argumentum ad baculum, 343
Argumentum ad hominem, 343
Articles, in title, 148
Attitude, writer's, 92–97
  objective, 106, 112, 356
  subjective, 106, 356. *See also* Viewpoint
Authorities, and testimonials, 343
Autobiography, 209

Bandwagon appeal, 341–342
Begging the question, 32

Beginning, 1
  paragraph, 130
  placement of subject sentence, 166
  section, 131, 133–134, 135, 145–152, 162,
    365
Beliefs, 27
Bibliography, 369, 371, 372–373
  cards for, 359–362, 368
Biography, 97, 209
Boldface type, and emphasis, 319
Business report, 353

Capitalization, 403–404
  and emphasis, 319
  in titles, 148
Card catalog, 357, 358–359
Case of pronouns, 395–396
Causal investigative paper, 355–356, 365–366
Causation, 28, 211, 221, 228–232
Causes and effects, 229, 232
  in causal investigative paper, 355–356
  and logical transitions, 280–281
Celebrities, testimonials by, 342
Class, 221–223
  and analogy, 255
  and contrast, 251
  in definition, 225, 228
Classification, 221–224, 227
Clauses, 390–392, 400
  transitional, 275
Clichés, 302, 308
Coherence, 271–286
Collective noun, 394
Colloquialisms, 303
Colon, 401
Comedy, 72
Comic strips, 343
Comma, 399–401
  splice, 392–393
Communication, 89
  structure of, 129–131
Comparative degree, 398–399
Comparisons, 34, 227, 247–251, 252, 254, 257,
    398–399
  alternating, 249, 251
  and analogy, 255
  block, 250
  implied, 250–251
  simultaneous, 248–249, 251
Compass points, capitalization of, 404
Complement in sentence, 322, 388, 390
Completer of sentence, 129, 388
Concluding section, 131, 134, 136, 162, 366
Conclusions, 3
  and circular reasoning, 30
  and false causes, 33

YOU BE
THE JUDGE

**GENERAL
EXPLANATION
AND
INSTRUCTIONS**

At the end of each chapter in this book is an activity called "You Be the Judge." Each student in the class will write a paper, as directed in the last numbered application of the chapter. Your instructor will then give each of you another student's paper to evaluate according to the general instructions for Parts I and III outlined below and the specific questions for Part II on each "You Be the Judge" sheet.

First print all three of your initials in the blanks in the upper left-hand corner. To keep your evaluation confidential, your instructor may choose to delete your initials after checking how well you evaluated and graded the assigned paper. Your instructor reserves the right to grade you on how well you do the judging.

PART I

After receiving the student's paper, read it first checking only for mechanical errors. Circle the errors and print above them (in red pencil or pen, if possible) the following symbols:

S   spelling error
C   capitalization error
P   punctuation error
G   grammatical error

Next to each error, or opposite it in the nearest margin, write in the needed correction. If you are not sure about something, check it in a dictionary or the "Handbook of Correct and Effective Usage" on pages 383–409.

PART II

Answer the questions for Part II on the individual "You Be the Judge" sheet.